COMMEMORATIVE LITERACIES AND LABORS OF JUSTICE

This book examines literacy practices of commemoration marking the 40th anniversary of the March 24, 1976 coup in Argentina. Drawing on research conducted across three distinct sites in Buenos Aires in March 2016—a public university, a Catholic church, and a former naval base and clandestine detention center transformed into a museum space for memory and justice—this book sheds light on the ways commemorative literacies at these locations work spatially to mobilize memory of the past to address and advance justice concerns in the present. These labors of justice manifest in three ways: as resistance, reconciliation, and recovery. Damico, Lybarger, and Brudney also demonstrate how these particular kinds of commemorative literacies resonate transnationally in ways that necessitate a commitment to commemorative ethics.

This book is ideal not only for researchers, graduate students, and scholars in literacy studies but also for all those working in related fields, including memory studies, religious studies, area studies, and Latin American studies, to address issues pertaining to memory, testimony, transitional justice, state repression, and human rights in Argentina, Latin America, or the Global South, more generally.

James S. Damico is Professor of Literacy, Culture, and Language Education at Indiana University, Bloomington, U.S.A.

Loren D. Lybarger is Professor of Classics and Religious Studies at Ohio University, Athens, U.S.A.

Edward Brudney is Assistant Professor of History at the University of Tennessee, Chattanooga, U.S.A.

COMMEMORATIVE LITERACIES AND LABORS OF JUSTICE

Resistance, Reconciliation, and Recovery in Buenos Aires and Beyond

James S. Damico, Loren D. Lybarger, and Edward Brudney

First published 2022
by Routledge
605 Third Avenue, New York, NY 10158

and by Routledge
2 Park Square, Milton Park, Abingdon, Oxon, OX14 4RN

Routledge is an imprint of the Taylor & Francis Group, an informa business

© 2022 James S. Damico, Loren D. Lybarger, and Edward Brudney

The right of James S. Damico, Loren D. Lybarger, and Edward Brudney to be identified as authors of this work has been asserted in accordance with sections 77 and 78 of the Copyright, Designs and Patents Act 1988.

All rights reserved. No part of this book may be reprinted or reproduced or utilised in any form or by any electronic, mechanical, or other means, now known or hereafter invented, including photocopying and recording, or in any information storage or retrieval system, without permission in writing from the publishers.

Trademark notice: Product or corporate names may be trademarks or registered trademarks, and are used only for identification and explanation without intent to infringe.

Library of Congress Cataloging-in-Publication Data
A catalog record for this title has been requested

ISBN: 978-1-032-02611-4 (hbk)
ISBN: 978-1-032-01197-4 (pbk)
ISBN: 978-1-003-18419-5 (ebk)

DOI: 10.4324/9781003184195

Typeset in Bembo
by SPi Technologies India Pvt Ltd (Straive)

This book is dedicated in memory of Father (Fr.) Francisco Murray, a Catholic priest at the Church of Santa Cruz in Buenos Aires during our travels to Argentina in March 2016. Sadly, Fr. Francisco died on June 24, 2020 as we were completing a full draft of this book manuscript. We had recently been in contact, receiving a message from him just two weeks before his passing. He knew of our intention to dedicate this book to him and expressed that this was "a great honor." We remain deeply grateful to Fr. Francisco for his generosity, kindness, and compassion.

CONTENTS

List of Figures viii
List of Key Abbreviations x
Author Biographies xi
Acknowledgments xiii

   Introduction 1

1 Setting the Stage: *¡Todos a la Plaza!* 11

2 Historical Background 35

3 Labors of Justice as Resistance across Two University Sites 61

4 Labors of Justice as Reconciliation at the Church of Santa Cruz 93

5 Labors of Justice as Recovery: Individual, Societal, and Spatial Modes of Meaning-Making 120

6 Commemorative Literacies and Labors of Justice in Buenos Aires and beyond 149

Epilogue 165
Index 168

LIST OF FIGURES

All photographs in the book were taken by James S. Damico or Loren D. Lybarger.

3.1	Critical of Macri government	68
3.2	To the streets to protest the government!	69
3.3	Women's rights	69
3.4	Critical of vultures, Obama, repressive protocols	70
3.5	March against Obama and impunity	71
3.6	Neither forget nor forgive	72
3.7	Mass produced poster against impunity	73
3.8	Neoliberalism counter-attack	76
3.9	Critical of pact with vulture funds	77
3.10	Critical of Obama	78
3.11	Vultures and the IMF	79
3.12	Vulture with the U.S. flag on a tree branch in South America	80
3.13	Linking Obama, Putin, and Assad to genocide	81
3.14	We are all refugees!	82
3.15	Palestina Libre	83
3.16	La lucha	85
3.17	Mural in support of Palestine	86
4.1	Nuestros Profetas	99
4.2	Angelelli poster at ex-ESMA	100
4.3	Nuestras hermanas	102
4.4	Madres de la Plaza	102
4.5	Familiares/Militantes	103
4.6	Banners above the pre-Vatican altar	106
4.7	Banner at the back of church near the main entrance	107

List of Figures **ix**

4.8	Esquivel painting	111
5.1	Grandparents and siblings	126
5.2	Parents by the sea; child on a swing	127
5.3	Father, child on step; mother, child; child on swing	128
5.4	Pregnant woman	129
6.1	Dr. Martin Luther King, Jr.	158
6.2	Vertical row of four religious icons	159
6.3	Plaque in floor paraphrasing Gospel of Matthew 5:12	160

LIST OF KEY ABBREVIATIONS

ABUELAS Abuelas de Plaza de Mayo (Grandmothers of the Plaza de Mayo)
CCD Centro clandestino de detención (clandestine detention center)
CONADEP Comisión Nacional sobre la Desaparición de Personas (National Commission on the Disappearance of Persons)
CS Ciencias Sociales or the Facultad de Ciencias Sociales
EMVYJ Encuentro Memoria Verdad y Justicia (Encounter for Memory, Truth, and Justice), coordinating body that brings together a range of human rights organizations, women's groups, student groups, labor unions, and other similarly aligned movements.
ESMA Escuela de Mecánica de la Armada (Navy Mechanics School)
EX-ESMA Former Navy Mechanics School, now a prominent site for justice-focused memory preservation efforts
FILO Facultad de Filosofía y Letras
FPV Frente para la Victoria (Front for Victory, Peronist party alliance)
H.I.J.O.S. Hijos por la identidad y la justicia contra el Olvido y el Silencio (Sons and Daughters for Identity and against Forgetting and Silence)
IMF International Monetary Fund
MADRES Madres de la Plaza de Mayo (Mothers of the Plaza de Mayo) refers to mothers of missing children
PRN Proceso de Reorganización Nacional (Process of National Reorganization) or the Proceso
UBA Universidad de Buenos Aires

AUTHOR BIOGRAPHIES

James S. Damico is Professor of Literacy, Culture, and Language Education at Indiana University where he is also an affiliate faculty member of the Center for Latin American and Caribbean Studies and the Integrated Program in the Environment. His scholarship and teaching emphasize critical literacies and inquiry-based approaches for working with digital media and complex topics, especially climate change. He is the author of many journal articles and book chapters and is co-author of the book, *Social Studies as New Literacies: Relational Cosmopolitanism in the Classroom* (Routledge, 2011). He is also completing a book about how to confront climate change denial, to be published by Teachers College Press.

Loren D. Lybarger is Professor of Religious Studies in the Department of Classics and Religious Studies at Ohio University. He has lived in Latin America (Colombia) and the Middle East (Palestine, Egypt). His peer-reviewed articles have appeared in the leading journals of diverse fields such as religious studies, history of religion, sociology of religion, Islamic studies, and Palestinian studies. He is also the author of two monographs: *Identity and Religion in Palestine: The Struggle between Islamism and Secularism in the Occupied Territories* (Princeton University Press 2007) and *Palestinian Chicago: Identity in Exile* (University of California Press 2020).

Edward Brudney is Assistant Professor in the Department of History at the University of Tennessee, Chattanooga. He completed his Ph.D. in Latin American history at Indiana University in 2019. Edward's research focuses on the intersections of legal and labor history in Argentina in the 1970s and 1980s. His current book project, titled *Changing the "Rules of the Game": Labor, Law, and Citizenship* *in Argentina, 1973–1981*, challenges commonly accepted readings of Argentina's most recent dictatorship by highlighting ideological and practical continuities across different levels of labor relations. He has lived and worked in Buenos Aires on multiple occasions over more than 15 years. Edward's research on Argentina has been published in *Labor: Studies in Working-Class History* and *The Journal of Global South Studies*, and as part of an edited volume titled *Clase obrera y dictadura cívico-militar. Nuevos estudios sobre conflictividad y cambios estructurales*, forthcoming with A Contracorriente Editorial, distributed by UNC Press.

ACKNOWLEDGMENTS

We owe a significant debt of gratitude to the many people in Buenos Aires we had the privilege to talk to and get to know. All were generous with their time and gracious with providing us with their insights into memory and justice work in Argentina. We remain grateful and inspired by each of them, including Fr. Francisco Murray, Alejandra Oberti, Emilio Tenti Fanfani, Nico Arrué, Betina Arrué, Fortunato Mallimaci, María Rosa Neufeld, Jens Ariel Thisted, and Marcos Guillén. Special thanks to Adolfo Pérez Esquivel, the 1980 Nobel Peace laureate, who graciously granted his permission for us to include an image of his mural from the Church of Santa Cruz. We also extend our gratitude to Nico Arrué for his willingness to include our photographs of his art installation, "Presencias."

Back home in the United States, we have many people to thank for their contributions to this project. Professor Bradley Levinson at Indiana University (IU) deserves special thanks. In 2006, Bradley secured funding to bring a few junior scholars, including James, to Buenos Aires for the Ethnography in Education Conference held at the University of Buenos Aires. Bradley also played a key role in 2016, connecting us with his colleagues in Argentina, some of whom we were able to interview for this project. We are grateful for Bradley's generosity, thoughtfulness, and support. An IU team of graduate students also deserves special thanks. Alexandra (Alex) Panos, Suriati Abas, JesAlana Stewart, and Heriberto N. Rodriguez Vazquez all traveled to Buenos Aires in March 2016 to make their own singular contributions to this project. Two additional members of our team in Buenos Aires played indispensable roles. Paul Abowd, a journalist and documentary filmmaker, was there every step of the ten-day journey in March 2016. We benefited greatly from his insights and wise counsel. Paul also took the lead in creating a video to capture core elements of our experience. This video can be viewed at https://vimeo.com/285268494/d832f08f1b. Liliana Barro Zecker, an

Associate Professor of Language and Literacy at DePaul University in Chicago, who grew up in Buenos Aires, was a knowing guide, skillful interpreter, and thoughtful colleague. She introduced us to Francisco Murray and Nicolás Arrué, who became main participants in our project. Along the way, Liliana also became a trusted friend. This book would not exist without her.

After our return from Buenos Aires, Alex Panos and Anna Sera played an instrumental role assembling and organizing the massive data set containing hours of audio and video recordings. We are especially grateful to Anna, who created a comprehensive database for the project. We also thank David Parra, an IU undergraduate at the time, who helped transcribe and translate many interviews. David was an IU Cox Scholar, with James serving as his faculty mentor in this notable IU program. We also owe a debt to Iván A. Maceda Vela who also played a key role translating interviews. We thank Nicolás Sillitti, too, for offering nuanced perspectives about the University of Buenos Aires based on his experience as a student there. We extend our thanks, as well, to Rob Kunzman for reading an early draft of the manuscript and offering clarifying questions.

Institutional support is vital for a project like this and we acknowledge the IU Institute for Advanced Study (IAS) and the IU School of Education, Bloomington. Each provided essential funding that enabled us to travel to Buenos Aires and carry out this research. We are also grateful to Ohio University's College of Arts and Sciences, which provided indexing support through its Humanities Research Fund. We benefited, too, from the opportunity to present early findings of our work and receive critical feedback. We thank Alfio Saitta, who invited us to share our research at the IU Center for Latin American and Carribean Studies. We also acknowledge Ronald Simkins who published an earlier version of our work in the *Journal of Religion and Society*.

At Routledge, we thank Senior Editor Karen Adler for her consistent and enthusiastic support of this project and Editorial Assistant Emily Dombrovskaya for their expert attention to detail. We are also grateful to the anonymous reviewers, who offered their suggestions to improve the manuscript.

Finally, our families have been invaluable in sustaining us through the years of this project. For James, the steadfast love and support of Gabrièle Abowd Damico is a foundation for all creative work. With a background in arts education and folklore, her ways of being in the world remind James how story, memory, family, commemoration, and justice can be the centerpiece of our lives. Daniel Damico also offered his unwavering support, encouraging his dad every step of the way with much lighthearted, good-natured humor. The consistent support of Carol Damico and Thomas V. Abowd and Anne Marie Abowd, along with extended family members and friends, was greatly appreciated.

Similarly, for Loren, the love and encouragement of Mary Abowd has remained essential to his efforts to understand struggles for justice. A talented journalist and editor, Mary has inspired Loren through her clear and vivid writing and her ability to balance critical perspective with a principled commitment to achieving a better world. She has also been a loving parent to their daughters, Olivia and Rachel, bright, creative young women who will inherit responsibility for the world we leave them. Their questions about why the world is the way it is have deepened Loren's understanding of the importance of an honest and open intergenerational conversation about the past. With James, Loren also recognizes his extended families, including Loren's parents, Lee and Connie Lybarger.

For Edward, the process of writing this book has coincided with a period of tremendous change. Completing a dissertation, finishing graduate school, moving, and beginning a new job in the space of six months occasionally made his work on the book project more difficult. In addition to thanking James and Loren for their patience, Edward also thanks his colleagues, friends, and family members who provided support throughout. Mostly, Edward acknowledges the consistent presence and loving encouragement of Emma McDonell, who has shared both the new adventures and the hardships, and who was always willing to offer thoughts and suggestions, or to just listen to complaints and uncertainties. Edward's deepest gratitude—both in relation to this book project and more generally—is to her.

The three of us are also grateful to have had this opportunity to join forces on this project. Through many conversations over the past five years, we learned a great deal with and from each other about memory and justice, and we came to know a great deal about the value of a transdisciplinary inquiry like this. We are glad to get this book across the finish line and into the world, yet we will miss the many enriching conversations that brought us to this point.

Of course, the three of us also remain responsible for any errors or shortcomings in this book. We recognize it offers only one possible representation of rich, deeply multi-layered memory practices in Buenos Aires at a particular historical moment. We hope our effort makes a useful contribution to these critically important ongoing conversations about memory and justice.

INTRODUCTION

This book examines literacy practices of commemoration marking the 40th anniversary of the March 24, 1976 coup d'état in Argentina. In Argentina, March 24 has become a public holiday named the *Día de la Memoria por la Verdad y la Justicia* (Day of Remembrance for Truth and Justice). The 1976 coup inaugurated a military dictatorship which disappeared, tortured, and killed as many as 30,000 people between 1976 and 1983. Since the return of democracy in 1983, Argentines have grappled with this legacy and the narratives that have emerged from these struggles remain highly contested and deeply politicized. Some Argentines supported the military coup and the repressive policies that followed as a necessary step to save the nation from Marxism and secularism. Others, especially the families of the victims and groups committed to human rights and democracy, resisted the repression and have, since the return to democracy, fought to document the scale of the violence and commemorate the disappeared. The majority of Argentines, however, chose to avoid either open support of the dictatorship or open resistance to it. The actual March 24 holiday, as it came to be, reflected the aspirations of those seeking to find out about lost loved ones, hold the perpetrators accountable, and establish an account of the past that prioritizes the need to defend human rights.

Drawing on research conducted during a ten-day period in Buenos Aires in March 2016 across three distinct sites—a public university, a Catholic church, and a former naval base and clandestine detention center transformed into a museum space for memory and justice—this book introduces and advances the idea of *commemorative literacies* to shed light on how literacy practices at these locations work spatially to mobilize memory and advance varied forms of justice work. In doing so, this book aims to make several contributions. First, it demonstrates how particular kinds of commemorative literacies address historical injustices

DOI: 10.4324/9781003184195-1

by repurposing the past to address present-day political needs. This repurposing shifts in emphasis and concern across each of the three focal sites, demonstrating how specific narratives and texts within distinct spaces shape retrievals of the past in relationship to the national debates and political currents that defined Argentina in 2016.

In focusing on the repurposing of the past, this book brings literacy studies into much needed conversation with foundational scholarship in other fields, primarily history and religious studies, to address memory/testimony, transitional justice, state repression, and human rights in Argentina and the Global South, more generally. Toward the end, we integrate methods from across our backgrounds and respective fields, combining literacy studies (James), religious studies (Loren), and Latin American history and cultural studies (Edward) to build an interpretative framework that enables us to make sense of the commemorative literacies we observed or engaged in. For example, a fuller richness of meanings related to posters at a university (Chapter 3) emerges through a careful textual reading combined with a focused historical framing of the Argentine university system and of the particular university sites in this case study. Similarly, our discussion of texts and ritual practices at a Catholic church (Chapter 4) gains depth through a cogent review of Catholicism in Argentina and analysis specific to this case study site. And, our examination of the former detention and torture center (Chapter 5) demonstrates how tracing a longer history helps unpack additional meanings related to the recovery of this space as both a site of justice work and an object to be recovered in and of itself.

As a second, related contribution of this book, we provide grounded analyses that highlight overlapping and distinct labors of justice as *resistance, reconciliation,* and *recovery* across the three case-study sites in Buenos Aires. We draw from seminal scholarship that examines theories and mechanisms of transitional justice in Argentina, specifically, and the Global South, broadly (Lessa, 2013; Robben, 2018). Yet, rather than apply a justice lens to make sense of governmental, institutional, or other macro-level events and processes, such as trials, truth commissions, and reparations, we focus instead on varied commemorative literacies in specific places. This examination of how local justice-centered practices interact dynamically with past traumas anchors macro-level discussions of human rights work in the practices of actual communities. This emphasis on localized literacy practices also points to the considerable emotional, physical, and psychological labors involved in resistance, reconciliation, and recovery.

Finally, a third theme and contribution of this book shows how these particular kinds of *commemorative literacies* that seek to address historical injustices resonate transnationally. We consider some of these transnational resonances at each of the three focal sites: a university, a Catholic church, and a museum, formerly a detention and torture center. In the concluding chapter, we also explore possibilities of a transnational lens grounded in commemorative literacies and labors of justice.

Who We Are

This book project about our March 2016 experience in Argentina—what you now hold in your hands or view through an electronic screen of your choice—offers a distillation of what we have learned in Buenos Aires during and after the 40th anniversary commemorations. For James, the seeds of this project were planted ten years earlier in March 2006 when he had the opportunity to be in downtown Buenos Aires for a conference held at the University of Buenos Aires, Filosofía y Letras (Filo). The conference coincided with events leading up to the March 24, 2006 public holiday and march to La Plaza de Mayo to commemorate the 30-year anniversary of the beginning of the military-led dictatorship, the *Proceso de Reorganización Nacional* (Process of National Reorganization, also referred to as simply the *Proceso*, or the PRN). While there, James documented his experience, taking dozens of photographs of the signs, posters, and banners adorning what seemed to be every square foot of university hallway and classroom space. He also attended commemorative events in the community, including the march to the Plaza de Mayo on March 24, 2006.

Loren's involvement with this project began in September 2013 when James invited him to discuss the photographs he had taken of the commemoration events and activities in Buenos Aires in 2006. Loren was completing fieldwork on another project that addressed questions of memory, commemoration, and identity within the Palestinian immigrant community in Chicago (Lybarger, 2020). Working with James allowed him to explore these matters comparatively but also ethically as problems relating to our responsibilities as U.S. citizens and educators. Our subsequent article, "Commemoration, Testimony, and Protest in Argentina: An Exploration of Response and Responsibilities," became the basis for our research trip to Buenos Aires in 2016 and the beginning point for our reflections in this book (Damico & Lybarger, 2016).

Edward came to the project with almost a decade of experience conducting research in Argentina, focusing primarily on the history of labor legislation and labor relations during the country's most recent dictatorship (1976–1983). Since 2005, he has lived in Buenos Aires on multiple occasions totaling several years and has carried out fieldwork in the capital, at various sites in Greater Buenos Aires and in the interior provinces. Although not part of the 2016 research trip on the 40th anniversary of the coup, Edward joined the project later in 2016 as a research assistant while completing his doctoral work. He, along with Loren and James, published an analysis of, and reflection on, the concept of martyrological memory and the Church of Santa Cruz in 2018 (Lybarger et al., 2018). This would be the first published piece based on the research conducted in 2016 and in many ways laid the groundwork for this book.

We are also three White male scholars and citizens from the United States, and we recognize the long legacies of colonialism (Galeano, [1971] 2010) connected to patriarchy, racism, and imperialism, alongside continuing efforts by the U.S. government and U.S.-based corporations and financial institutions to advance their own social and economic interests and suppress pro-democracy, socialist-leaning movements throughout Latin America.[1] This project inevitably raises those ethical challenges endemic to ethnographic research around "speaking about" or "speaking for" participants, and ultimately the need to make the necessary "prepositional shift" to "speaking *with*" them (Partnoy, 2006). We also acknowledge a growing body of literacy scholarship from scholars in the Global South that promotes greater diversity in the ways literacies are studied and understood (Trigos-Carrillo & Rogers, 2017), contributing to what de Sousa Santos (2014) has called "epistemologies of the south" which need to be promoted as part of a broader global "cognitive justice" project.

Our subject positions necessarily limit our ability to grasp fully the nuanced complexities of on-the-ground meaning-making in Buenos Aires, and we recognize the potential hazards tied to our particular attempt to represent "the other." We understand the need to acknowledge and reckon with the inherent power imbalance between researcher and subject, particularly in ethnographic work. We have endeavored to address this concern through the expected practices of working closely on the ground with knowledgeable guides and receiving feedback about our interpretations. Returning to our third theme, about how particular kinds of *commemorative literacies* that seek to address historical injustices resonate transnationally, it is important to note how local and national perceptions of "the other" in Argentina further complicate this process. Racial, ethnic, and hemispheric identity affiliations (e.g., Global South) remain complex and often contradictory in Argentina (as in almost all local contexts). Ideas of race, for example, function differently in Argentina than in the United States, given a prevailing view in Argentina, and especially in the country's urban centers, of its history and continued existence as a predominately White nation of European descent (Alberto & Elena, 2016).[2] Thus, while those with ancestral connections to Argentina who live in the United States might identify as Latina/o or Latinx, in Buenos Aires they would be far more likely to identify as White. A Latinx identity in the United States is even more likely if the person speaks Spanish due to the ways language often maps onto race in the United States. As such, our own racial identity and phenotype was less an explicit marker of difference in Buenos Aires than it might have been in other parts of Latin America with larger non-White, non-European-descended populations.

Moreover, the common view of Argentina as part of the Global South again demonstrates the tensions between local/national identities and regional/global designations. Historically, many Argentines have viewed themselves as distinct from their national neighbors. Argentina's complex relationship with the Global South affects our subject position as authors from the Global North. U.S.-based scholars and writers often fall into the trap of depicting the "Global South" in one-dimensional terms, flattening differences and suggesting widespread solidarity across all countries and peoples of the Global South. This is obviously not the case, but the idea retains its appeal, especially among those whose personal political commitments lead them to imagine such solidarity in opposition to the forces of imperialism and colonialism. This book contributes to rethinking that assumption by recognizing the political diversity within Argentina—its cities, towns, and neighborhoods, for example—but also by situating these commemorative literacies in a transnational sociopolitical context.[3]

In this book, we document and interpret our experiences in Buenos Aires at a specific moment in time. We do not claim that this description captures the entirety of that moment—what occurred and what it meant in all of its complexity. We offer instead one particular viewpoint filtered through our interpretive commitments. These commitments relate to our methodologies and to understanding commemorative literacies as connected to broader justice issues and democratic movements. The following section unpacks some of those commitments.

Transdisciplinary Commitments

One of the challenges and joys of this project has been the opportunity to work across our academic fields and disciplines. All three of us locate ourselves as scholars working in the humanities, broadly conceived. For James, this is grounded in sociological framings of literacy as culturally and historically situated processes and practices as well as an engagement with complex, multifaceted topics like climate change in collaboration with colleagues in history and social studies education (e.g., Baildon & Damico, 2011; Damico et al., 2020). For Loren, whose work has focused primarily on religion and political identity among Palestinians in the Middle East and North America, it has meant an approach to religious studies that draws on methods in ethnography and interpretive sociology (Lybarger, 2005, 2007, 2020, in press); reflexive ethical and epistemological considerations in fieldwork methods (e.g., Lybarger, 2015); and, recently, examination of literacy practices in relation to the process of articulating perspectives, secular and religious, toward traumatic political memories (e.g., Damico & Lybarger, 2016; Lybarger et al., 2018). Edward's methods both reflect and extend beyond his disciplinary training as a historian. If the major questions behind his research agenda relate to labor and legal history in Latin America, he has approached these topics via deep engagement with archival material, collecting oral histories, and even transnational comparisons of similar geopolitical projects (e.g., Brudney, 2019a, 2019b, 2020).

Consistent across our work are commitments to qualitative inquiry with an epistemological stance rooted in the interpretivist tradition. It is in this sense that we think of our collaboration as transdisciplinary as opposed to interdisciplinary. Rather than maintaining distinctive and defined disciplinary lenses in different chapters or sections, we instead found ourselves writing each chapter together, often coming to a point in which we no longer were able to discern whose voice was foremost. The shared interpretivist background, we now realize, enabled us to engage in this deep collaborative writing.

By "interpretivist," specifically, we mean that in our respective research and teaching, we engage in sense-making processes related to the experiences of others as conveyed through a variety of "texts." Such texts include, for example, archival documents, posters, paintings, interview transcripts, video recordings, and field observations drawn from direct participation in events (e.g., protests, rituals, commemorations, and meetings). Interpretation of these materials entails close description and analysis in relation to broader theoretical concerns and categories. If done properly, this interpretive process maintains continuity with the internal, primary perspectives of the research participants and communities whose experiences and expressions we are engaging: our descriptions and analyses should make sense to participants even if our abstractions and systematizing of their perspectives—for example, through comparisons to discourses and performative expressions of other groups in other spaces—place their experiences within a new context of understanding (Riesebrodt, 1993, 2010).

It is also essential to note that while we endeavored to accurately and fairly represent the ideas and perspectives of the people we interviewed in Buenos Aires, these recorded conversations remained subordinate to our primary emphasis, which were the commemorative literacies we observed at our focal sites. Viewed through a spatial lens (Massey, 2005), these literacies, for example, related to signs and posters on university and church walls, vigils, and an art installation. As Chapter 1 explores, our analysis is guided by a spatial lens in such a way that we have come to view the three focal sites as our primary "research participants." The main goal for our interviews was to enrich and deepen our contextual understandings of each site.

Transnational Resonances

Alongside our transdisciplinary commitments, we also share a concern to acknowledge and grapple with the transnational connections we perceive, and that were apparent within the texts we encountered in Buenos Aires, with justice struggles in other parts of the world, especially in the United States. The years immediately leading to March 2016 were a potent time of civil and human rights struggles around the world. The growing prominence of social media platforms, such as YouTube, Twitter, and Facebook, led to greater access to the immediacy of social justice events as they unfolded, providing many windows, for example, into the Occupy movement in New York City's Zuccotti Park and in other locales, the Arab Spring uprisings in the Middle East, the disappearances in the State of Guerrero, Mexico, and police violence across a number of cities in the United States. We witnessed community, student, or worker unrest fueling calls for democratic accountability and systemic changes and observed these efforts achieving some success. For example, protests in Egypt toppled the authoritarian government and demonstrations in Mexico forced party leaders to resign while city police forces in Baltimore, Chicago, and Ferguson, Missouri, became targets for institutional change. Larger movement structures, such as Black Lives Matter and the Occupy Movement, also developed during this time.

As these events and issues continued to unfold and evolve, we traveled to Buenos Aires in March 2016 to observe, document, and participate in commemorative events tied to the 1976 coup. This is when a "commemorative literacies" lens began to take shape as we became even more attuned to the ways particular literacy practices framed these commemorative events on the ground in Buenos Aires. And the value of this lens became more evident after our return from Buenos Aires in 2016, when we witnessed or participated in demonstrations and marches for climate justice, indigenous rights, ending police brutality, and promoting racial and economic justice. Much like events in 2016 Buenos Aires, the spring 2020 demonstrations, for example, led by Black Lives Matter to challenge systemic anti-Black racism, included calls to commemorate—that is, to honor and mark as significant—the tragic loss of Black women and men to police brutality and lethal violence. Among the many lives commemorated were George Floyd, Breonna Taylor, and Ahmaud Arbery. Thus, the account in this book, while partial, reflects an ongoing, emergent process through which we have come to deepen and expand our engagement with practices of commemoration as they express and enact conceptions of justice across space and time.

Implied in this emergent process we are describing is the understanding that the knowledge we are creating is fundamentally intersubjective, constituted in our dialogic interactions with others "in the field" or in the archive. There is no sovereign, "objective" standpoint outside of and separate from the social world we share with individuals who participate in our research. Our interpretations are negotiated in the spaces between us and them in Buenos Aires and between us and you, the audience, who read this book. We incur a responsibility to one another in these interactions—certainly to get the details right but also to reflect on how the stories we tell implicate us in the histories and lives of the individuals with whom we enter into relationships. We bring our entire selves—our histories, experiences, and positionalities—to this encounter and in doing so must risk becoming vulnerable to the truths that others tell. What might the accounts of remembrance that we describe and analyze in this book open up emotionally, morally, and politically for all of us? What are the implications of the resonances we sense in our own lives and communities? What responsibilities do we incur when we perceive connections and implications? We do not presume to have definitive answers to these questions. But the questions are nevertheless important to acknowledge and grapple with, if only to gain critical self-perspective as well as an understanding of possible new ways of seeking justice alongside others, locally and transnationally.

Outline of Chapters

In this introduction, we have outlined key themes and contributions of the book and have considered our methodological commitments and subject positions in this project. Chapter 1 advances our main arguments with some treatment of the Argentine context as we provide sketches of our three focal sites and lay out the book's framework of *commemorative literacies* and *labors of justice*. Before we examine commemorative literacies at each of these three sites, a more comprehensive historical framing is necessary. This is the focus of Chapter 2, which offers a condensed yet substantive historical account of salient political and economic events across twentieth-century Argentina. As such, more than the other chapters, it highlights the hand of a historian at work, prioritizing the need to offer readers, especially those with less background knowledge, a sufficient foothold in Argentine history. Chapter 3 examines the commemorative literacies at the two UBA sites that work spatially to articulate justice as resistance. Chapter 4 considers how commemorative literacies at the Church of Santa Cruz work spatially toward justice work as reconciliation, while Chapter 5 analyzes how commemorative literacies at the ex-ESMA suggest justice work as recovery. Chapter 6 pulls together the main insights from the preceding chapters and points to the wider implications of this book project.

Finally, in a brief epilogue, we discuss the 2019 Argentine presidential elections, which saw the center-right President Macri lose power and Christina Fernández de Kirchner assume the position of vice president to President Alberto Fernández (no relation). The epilogue also serves as a reminder that commemorative literacies and labors of justice we examine in this book will continue into the future, whether or not they are a central plank of any specific government's platform.

Notes

1 This ongoing series of actions and policies is too broad to be adequately summarized here, but includes arming and training national security forces, as in Colombia and Mexico; leveraging unfavorable financial conditions to increase profits for U.S. corporations, as in the Dominican Republic and Puerto Rico; supporting right-wing authoritarian regimes, as in Paraguay and Honduras; and overtly interfering with sovereign governments, as in Venezuela.
2 That this popular opinion of Argentina as a "White" nation is uncritically accepted by many Argentines does not mean that it accurately represents the polity. Recent scholarship (Gordillo & Hirsch, 2003; Edwards, 2020) has shown that myths of Argentine uniformity and Whiteness are precisely that—myths. However, their continued prevalence makes them important for processes of meaning-making in contemporary Argentina.
3 Argentines hold ideological diverse perspectives. We acknowledge this diversity in this book but focus primarily on the positions aligned with human rights advocacy and the necessity to commemorate the 30,000 disappeared.

References

Alberto, P. & Elena, E. (2016). *Rethinking race in modern Argentina*. Cambridge University Press.

Baildon, M. & Damico, J.S. (2011). *Social studies as new literacies in a global society: Relational cosmopolitanism in the classroom*. Routledge/Taylor & Francis.

Brudney, E. (2019a). In defense of our livelihoods: Rethinking authoritarian legality and worker resistance during Argentina's Proceso de Reorganización Nacional. *Labor: Studies in Working-Class History of the Americas*, 16(4), 67–88.

Brudney, E. (2019b). Manifest destiny, the frontier, and 'El Indio' in Argentina's conquista del desierto. *Journal of Global South Studies*, 36(1), 116–144.

Brudney, E. (2020). (P)Reimagining the nation: Citizenship, labor, and the state in António Ribeiro Sanches's Cartas sobre a educação da mocidade. *Luso-Brazilian Review*, 57(1), 4–29.

Damico, J.S., Baildon, M., & Panos, A. (2020). Climate justice literacy: Stories-we-live-by, ecolinguistics, and classroom practice. *Journal of Adolescent & Adult Literacy*, 63(6), 683–691. https://doi.org/10.1002/jaal.1051

Damico, J.S. & Lybarger, L.D. (2016). Commemoration, testimony, and protest in Argentina: An exploration of response and responsibilities. *Ubiquity: The Journal of Literature, Literacy, and the Arts*, 3(1), 7–44.

de Sousa Santos, B. (2014). *Epistemologies of the South: Justice against epistemicide*. Routledge.

Edwards, E. (2020). *Hiding in plain sight: Black women, the law, and the making of a white Argentine republic*. University of Alabama Press.

Galeano, E. ([1971] 2010). *Las venas abiertas de América Latina*. Siglo XXI de España Editores, S.A.

Gordillo, G. & Hirsch, S. (2003). Indigenous struggles and contested identities in Argentina: Histories of invisibilization and reemergence. *The Journal of Latin American Anthropology*, 7(3), 4–30.

Lessa, F. (2013). *Memory and transitional justice in Argentina and Uruguay: Against impunity*. Palgrave Macmillan.

Lybarger, L.D. (2005). Palestinian political identities during the post-Oslo period: A case-study of generation effects in a West Bank refugee camp. *Social Compass*, 52(2), 143–156.

Lybarger, L.D. (2007). *Identity and religion in Palestine: The struggle between Islamism and secularism in the occupied territories*. Princeton University Press.

Lybarger, L.D. (2015). How far Is too far? Defining self and other in religious studies and Christian missiology. *Journal of the American Academy of Religion*, 84(1), 127–156.

Lybarger, L.D. (2020). *Palestinian Chicago: Identity in exile*. University of California Press.

Lybarger, L.D. (in press). Secularism and the religious shift in Palestinian Chicago: Implications for solidarity and activism. *Journal of Palestine Studies*.

Lybarger, L.D., Damico, J.S., & Brudney, E. (2018). Religion and the commemoration of the disappeared in Argentina 40 years after the dictatorship: A study of martyrological memory at the Church of Santa Cruz. *Journal of Religion and Society*, 20. https://dspace2.creighton.edu/xmlui/bitstream/handle/10504/116848/2018-15.pdf

Massey, D.B. (2005). *For space*. SAGE.

Partnoy, A. (2006). Cuando vienen matando: On prepositional shifts and the struggle of testimonial subjects for agency. *PMLA*, 121(5), 1665–1669.

Riesebrodt, M. (1993). *Pious passion: The emergence of modern fundamentalism in the United States and Iran*. Translated by Don Reneau. University of California Press.

Riesebrodt, M. (2010). *The promise of salvation: A theory of religion*. Translated by Steven Rendall. University of Chicago Press.
Robben, A.C.G.M. (2018). *Argentina betrayed: Memory, mourning, and accountability*. University of Pennsylvania Press.
Trigos-Carrillo, L. & Rogers, R. (2017). Latin American influences on multiliteracies: From epistemological diversity to cognitive justice. *Literacy Research: Theory, Method, and Practice, 66*(1), 373–388.

1
SETTING THE STAGE
¡Todos a la Plaza!

We are in downtown Buenos Aires on the morning of March 24, 2016. Tens of thousands of people are preparing to march to the Plaza de Mayo, the social and political hub of the city. In May 1810, the Argentine War of Independence began in this plaza, at that time called the Plaza de la Victoria, with the formation of the first revolutionary junta in the Americas. More than a hundred years later, the most significant political movement of the Argentine twentieth century was launched here when thousands of supporters of the incarcerated Juan Domingo Perón occupied the Plaza on October 17 and 18, 1945 to demand his release. These dates quickly became a near-mythical origin point for the populist, worker-centered platform and policies of Peronism. Just months after the protests, Perón would be elected president for the first time.

Through the years, the Plaza has remained a vibrant space for political expression and protest. During the past four decades, the Madres de la Plaza de Mayo have been among the most emblematic symbols of engaged resistance. The Madres formed during the early years of the most recent military dictatorship, the self-styled Proceso de Reorganización Nacional (Process of National Reorganization or PRN; 1976–1983), and used their status as women and as mothers to push back against a repressive regime where others could not. Starting in 1977, the Madres marched silently around the plaza every Thursday afternoon demanding to know what happened to their disappeared children. These demonstrations continued long after the dictatorship ended in 1983. In 2001, the Plaza also witnessed some of the fiercest protests during the economic collapse and debt default that plunged Argentina into political chaos.

To mark the 40th anniversary of the March 24, 1976 coup d'état, some of the Madres are here and we see countless posters and signs with the iconic image of their white handkerchiefs. We observe dozens of groups, organized under banners

DOI: 10.4324/9781003184195-2

representing different political and economic parties and programs, making their way down the Avenida de Mayo toward the Plaza. This public space is also undeniably intergenerational: young children sit atop the shoulders of parents; the elderly move slowly or with assistance from others.

Several people whom we have met and interviewed during the past week are also here. Scores of students from two University of Buenos Aires sites, Ciencias Sociales (CS) and Filosofía y Letras (Filo), are present. Parishioners from the Church of Santa Cruz and its head priest, Fr. Francisco, are also nearby, arms linked and singing. The artist, Nico Arrúe, is here, too, with his wife and children to commemorate the disappearance of his father, one story within a much larger national narrative.

This day, named the Day of Remembrance for Truth and Justice (Día de la Memoria por la Verdad y la Justicia), became an official public holiday in 2006. It memorializes the victims of government repression and violence during the most recent military-led dictatorship. Most human rights organizations estimate the total number of people murdered and/or disappeared by the regime at 30,000. Chants of "Nunca más!" (Never again!)[1] and "Presente, ahora y siempre!" (Present, now, and always!) echo in our ears. Over the past week, we have become increasingly aware of the tragic scope of the historical trauma—the scale of the repression and catastrophic loss of human life—and the varied, complex, and multivocal nature of commemorations across different sites in Buenos Aires. We are attuned to how these chants of "Nunca más!" link stories of the past to an ever-changing present and how memory is marshalled for personal, social, and political purposes in the here and now.

And it will take time to better comprehend our experience in Buenos Aires, to interpret and understand the spaces we were invited into. Returning to the name of the March 24 public holiday, what truth and justice work did we bear witness to? What accounts of our experience in Buenos Aires might we share?

Several years have passed since that moment in Buenos Aires. As we write this chapter, we turn to the words of Argentine sociologist Elizabeth Jelin:

> I hope that discussion of the issues… [can] open the way to a broader reflection on the human need to make sense of catastrophic events and suffering, on memorialization practices, on rituals of homage, and on political initiatives that advance the principle of 'never again' in reaction to all affronts on human dignity.
>
> (Jelin, 2003, p. x)

With her hope for discussions and ideas to advance the principle of "never again" in response to "all affronts on human dignity," Jelin's own work has made clear these advancements, or their potential, are bound up in memories and meanings of the past, in particular, the conflicts and struggles over slogans and discourse like *Nunca más!* (Never again!).

Argentina offers fertile ground for this type of inquiry. In the ensuing chapters, we locate our investigation at three specific sites in Buenos Aires, the nation's capital and largest city.[2] As we attempted to understand how Argentines constructed significance from the past, we began to perceive the multilayered quality of meaning-making processes and practices across these sites. This interpretive complexity deepened for us as we simultaneously grappled with our own sense-making of this Argentine past and our relationship to these events as citizens and educators from the United States. All of this work, as Jelin reminds us, "takes place in the present, which must simultaneously come close to and distance itself both from the pasts accumulated in the spaces of experience and from the futures included as horizons of expectations" (2003, p. 4).

While grounded in specific locales, with all their nuanced complexities, the three "spaces of experience" central to our study are not circumscribed by rigid geographical boundaries, restricted to the physical borders that define each of these sites. Rather, these spaces are dynamic, emergent, and shifting with catalytic potential for linkages across any number of contexts in Argentina, South America, and the world. In order to engage transnational links, however, we believe that it is essential to begin with a careful and thorough treatment of "the local"—or our site-specific focus in Buenos Aires. So that is where we start.

Contextualizing Commemoration in Buenos Aires, March 2016

Political agitation and upheaval are common in Argentina, but the early months of 2016 marked a time of particular uneasiness, especially for those politically left of center. In December 2015, businessman Mauricio Macri, leading a center-right coalition, won a fiercely contested presidential election, defeating the preferred candidate of the incumbent president Cristina Fernández de Kirchner in a run-off.[3] Macri's victory marked the end of a dozen years of Kirchner governance, from Néstor Kirchner's initial presidential victory in 2003 through his wife's two terms (2007–2011 and 2011–2015). During this period, the Kirchners consolidated their power by cobbling together a diverse alliance, the *Frente para la Victoria* (FpV), made up of centrists, leftists, trade union leadership, and human rights groups. The Kirchners aligned themselves closely with the Madres and took various concrete steps to push forward a political agenda with justice work at its center. They also invalidated existing amnesties and reopened tribunals for the military officials who had overseen torture, executions, and disappearances during the most recent civic-military dictatorship, the *Proceso de Reorganización Nacional* (PRN).

In the 1980s and 1990s, countries around the world were forced to confront the violence and trauma of military regimes and state repression that characterized the final decades of the Cold War. Within this context, Argentina's use of truth commissions alongside formal tribunals in the mid-1980s made it somewhat unique.[4] In 1985, those tribunals handed down prison sentences for the junta members who had led the coup and implemented the program of state terror. However, in 1989 and 1990, President Carlos Menem pardoned the convicted leaders as part of his platform of "national reconciliation" that emphasized what critics denounced as a "forgive and forget" approach. The rise of the Kirchners after 2003 reversed this emphasis on reconciliation—a code word under Menem for ending inquiries into state violence during the PRN—by restarting judicial proceedings and establishing official holidays such as the Dia de la Memoria y Justicia which commemorates the 1976 coup that inaugurated the military dictatorship.

Macri's election in 2015 raised fears among human rights advocates and Madres de la Plaza supporters, who opposed efforts to minimize the abuses of the past. Having scaled back their "marches of resistance" during the Kirchner era, segments of the Madres de la Plaza de Mayo returned to the streets in December 2015 to protest Macri's electoral win, and they continued their efforts during his presidency. On the 1st anniversary of Macri's election, for example, in a December 2016 march, they joined other protesters lifting banners declaring, "Solidarity and Struggle or Hunger and Repression," and accused the center-right government of being "an enemy" of social justice movements; weakening social supports for workers and the marginalized; and undermining human rights (Madres de la Plaza de Mayo concluyen, 2016; Argentina's march of resistance continues, 2016).[5] Given the decades-long struggle to confront the abuses of the past and the recent hard-won gains of human rights organizations, concerns about what might be lost with a Macri presidency were not unwarranted.

Being in Buenos Aires in March 2016 as citizens and educators from the United States also forced us to reckon with the complicated historical relationship between Argentina and the United States, a task made unavoidable by then-President Barack Obama's presence in Buenos Aires at that moment. Obama arrived on March 23 for a two-day visit meant to improve U.S. relations with Argentina after Macri's election. On the first day, he met with Macri, praising him for Argentina's new economic reforms to create "sustainable and inclusive growth" and to "reconnect Argentina with the world economy" (e.g., lifting price controls to support free exchange between the U.S. dollar and the Argentine peso) (Mason & Lough, 2016). The next day, March 24, Obama participated in a commemorative ceremony held at the Parque de la Memoria in Buenos Aires to honor the victims of the dictatorship. In his speech, he acknowledged the "controversy about the policies of the United States early in those dark days" and that the United States "has to examine its own policies as well, and its own past." He also confirmed the declassification of the U.S. State Department archives related to the period of state terror, including "for the first time, military and intelligence records" based on his belief that "we have a responsibility to confront the past with honesty and transparency" (Mason, 2016). The past that Obama referred to included the U.S.-sponsored counterinsurgency program, Operation

Condor, which provided training for and facilitated intelligence sharing among the military regimes in the Southern Cone countries of South America during the 1970s and 1980s.[6]

Project Sites and Core Arguments
Sites

During the past 20 years, Argentina has been at the forefront within Latin America in devising ways to preserve sites of violence and memorialize the dead and disappeared. In Buenos Aires alone, hundreds of grassroots markers register the breadth of the military government's "reign of terror" (Page, 2013). *Memories of Buenos Aires: Signs of State Terrorism in Argentina*, assembled by Memoria Abierta (an important Argentine human rights organization featured in Chapter 5), offers neighborhood by neighborhood descriptions of these memorials, marking many of these seemingly mundane or ordinary locations as "sites of state terrorism" (Page, 2013). As an iconic historical site in Buenos Aires, the Plaza de Mayo on March 24, 2016 centralizes the main concerns of this project. A nexus of mass commemorative activity, it brought together tens of thousands of voices and perspectives of people from across the city, country, and beyond, filling the streets with chants, songs, speeches, and a diverse array of signs, posters, and banners. Each of these texts staked a claim about the meaning and significance of the day's events, each interpreting memories of the traumatic past through present-day perspectives. Of the many perspectives at the Plaza de Mayo, in this book, we highlight the voices and ideas of people who came to the Plaza from three sites in Buenos Aires: a university, a Catholic church, and a former naval base and clandestine detention center.

We were deliberate in choosing our path to and through these sites. We prioritized a return to the same university space—the Facultad de Filosofía y Letras (Filo), a college within the University of Buenos Aires (UBA)—which James visited in 2006. This decision stemmed from James's familiarity with this space, contacts with faculty members there, and the data he had collected in this location during the 30th anniversary commemoration of the 1976 coup. In addition, we selected another UBA site for data collection and analysis, the Facultad de Ciencias Sociales (CS) after being invited by Fortunato Mallimaci, a CS faculty member, to attend a special commemorative ceremony there on March 21, 2016. We also wanted to gain a comparative perspective on Filo. Methodologically, the primary analysis of this chapter was shaped by a literacy studies orientation, James's background, and a close reading of the visual texts at these university sites.

The Church of Santa Cruz was another key site in our project for two reasons. One of our team members who traveled to Buenos Aires with us, Liliana Barro Zecker, grew up in the San Cristóbal neighborhood and was a member of the Santa Cruz parish. She was also a high school friend with the sister of Francisco Murray, who became Father Francisco, the parish priest at Santa Cruz when we were there in 2016. Through Liliana, we made contact with Fr. Francisco, who granted us an extended interview and walking tour of the church sanctuary and grounds on March 21. He also invited us to be special guests for a church vigil held two days later to commemorate the lives of 12 people from the Church of Santa Cruz who were disappeared in December 1977. While our team was collectively taken by the depth of Fr. Francisco's warmth and kindness, we did not foresee the extent to which we would become central to this commemorative vigil on March 23, 2016, the evening before the national holiday. We also selected the Church of Santa Cruz because religion is Loren's area of expertise. James's own upbringing and education in the Catholic faith offered another entry point. Loren's specific work centers on Islam, Middle Eastern Christianity, and Palestinian identity in religious and secular communities (Lybarger, 2007, 2020), but his sociological grounding in the areas of ritual and memorialization provided a foundational entry point to engage with the meaning-making practices at Santa Cruz. Not surprisingly, then, the analysis in this chapter is shaped by particular approaches in religious studies that have animated Loren's work for the past two decades.[7]

The third site we selected for our inquiry was the ex-ESMA, a former naval base and clandestine detention center and torture site during the *Proceso*, preserved since 2004 as an official "space for memory and for the promotion and defense of human rights" (Espacio para la Memoria y para la Promoción y Defensa de los Derechos Humanos). The site is located in the northern part of Buenos Aires in the Núñez neighborhood. Our selection of this site was perhaps the most straightforward given the deep historical significance of the ex-ESMA for Argentines and the site's expressed purpose to remember "that dark chapter of history" and affirm the call of "Never Again." We also interviewed an artist, Nico Arrué, and viewed his exhibit called "Presencias," which was located on the grounds of the ex-ESMA in the Casa De Nuestros Hijos, a small building managed by Las Madres De La Plaza De Mayo—Línea Fundadora.[8] Liliana was again instrumental in establishing this connection, since Nico was her cousin. In terms of framing and analysis, this chapter points more in Edward's direction, as his expertise and his understanding of this site's historical development and importance played a prominent role in our meaning-making with the ex-ESMA.

Significantly, these three public sites—the two University of Buenos Aires (UBA) areas, the Church of Santa Cruz, and the ex-ESMA—possess deep historical ties to the period of state terror. The UBA was a prime target of state repression, which resulted in numerous students and faculty being disappeared. The Church of Santa Cruz also became a target of the security forces. Regime operatives spray painted threatening graffiti and set off bombs in front of the church gates just six weeks after the military coup in 1976. Also, 12 community members with ties to the church, including two French nuns and several founding members of the Madres, had disappeared in December 1977. And the ESMA was the largest detention center during the time of state terror and has remained a site of political debate and contestation. As these sites continue to play an active role in the commemorative events pertaining to March 24, each can be understood as a distinct "community of memory" where participants are involved in an "interminable renewal of their understanding and assessment of past events" through ongoing deliberations and decisions about what community members deem necessary to pass on (Simon & Eppert, 1997, p. 186).

These sites, however, do not represent the entire range of views in Argentina about the history of the last military dictatorship and the perceived significance of the March 24 *Día de la Memoria por la Verdad y la Justicia*. Some sectors of the population hold positive views of the dictatorship and its self-declared program to "restore morality and efficiency" and unify the country by stamping out all activities deemed "subversive." Some Argentines even oppose the March 24 public holiday as inappropriate for commemoration and celebration. The UBA, the Church of Santa Cruz, and the ex-ESMA are situated at the other end of this spectrum. Each of these sites is deeply rooted in the commitment and call to action encapsulated by the phrase *Nunca Más!* Consequently, our account here explores the commemorative practices and memory mobilizations of voices resolutely critical of the dictatorship. This fact reflects our particular connections to these voices and to the sites in which they register.

Arguments

This book advances three main arguments. Our first assertion is that **literacy practices of commemoration, what we call "commemorative literacies," mobilize memory of the past to advance present-day concerns**. This is a well-established thesis in historical and memory studies and in the sociology of memory. Literacy practices refer to the access and use of a range of semiotic resources, including print, images, speech, and embodied performance, such as chants, songs, and participation in vigils, to communicate ideas or construct meanings. Across our three research sites, these literacies differed considerably. At the two UBA locations, visual texts created and disseminated by students linked memories of past impunity for leaders of the military dictatorship to present-day concerns that the Macri government was engaged in repressive practices. These practices, through the links created within these texts, were seen as stemming from actions from the period of state terror or from the policies and actions of the succeeding democratic administrations, which were also deemed to be repressive in some way. At the Church of Santa Cruz, images of sacred and secular martyrs, as well as a commemorative ritual, invoked memories of past atrocities, linking them to possibilities for present-day peace and human rights commitments. At the ex-ESMA, the work of artist Nico Arrúe, situated spatially in one of the buildings called *La Casa de Nuestros Hijos* (The House of Our Children), conjured familial memories of loss that linked a tragic personal story of disappearance to a national narrative of pervasive, insidious injustice.

18 Setting the Stage

In sum, the commemorative processes across these three sites, as political scientist Katherine Hite (2012) has pointed out, were "more than symbolic exercises to understand the past" but instead reflected a goal to "transform the meanings of the past and mobilize the present" (p. 4). Elizabeth Jelin's concept of "labors of memory," which locates humans as "actively involved in the process of symbolic transformation and elaboration of meanings of the past" (2003, p. 5), is also relevant in this regard as memory is mobilized at specific moments and in specific contexts.[9] Marguerite Feitlowitz, in her book about language use during the dictatorship, *Lexicon of Terror: Argentina and the Legacies of Torture*, echoes this point, stating, "memory is unstable—elusive, even inaccessible, then suddenly explosive" (2011, p. 323). Each of these observations underscores our point that commemorative work appropriates the past for purposes of interpreting and mobilizing action around social and political concerns in the present.

Our second related assertion is that these **commemorative literacies function spatially to enact different labors of justice.** Each site retained the unwavering perspective that the policies and practices during the military dictatorship were criminally unjust. Commemorative literacies across these sites in March 2016—expressed through signs, posters, banners, poems, images, displays, and rituals—were steadfast in their dedication to the call of "Nunca Más!", reflecting and articulating concerns for human rights. Yet, the angle and trajectory of this devotion differed across the sites. At the UBA, the prevailing theme was *justice as resistance*. The visual texts in the hallways and classrooms pointed to the need for struggle against present-day injustices with roots in the past—the need, that is, to oppose any policies that restricted or threatened hard-won freedoms, especially policies of the Macri administration.

The form and quality of justice labor at the Santa Cruz Church was less about resistance and more about *justice as reconciliation* with two facets of reconciliation framed through a particular Catholic lens. One was reconciliation of the religious and political; the other was a reconciliation of the relationship between Argentina and the United States as expressed and embodied in the interaction between Santa Cruz parishioners and our research team from the United States. Our use of the term reconciliation here differs markedly from how it is typically understood in Argentina. As noted above, the concept of reconciliation has been most often associated with the policies of Carlos Menem in the 1990s, which built on a foundation of "oblivion" (Roniger & Sznadjer, 1998). This is especially true for the Argentine left, whose perspectives dominated the three sites of this project. The push for reconciliation became closely tied to a "forgive and forget" approach toward reconciliation, to which the political left responded with the slogan, "Ni olvido, ni perdón!" (Neither forgetting nor forgiveness!).

At the ex-ESMA, we discerned three layers of *justice as recovery*. The first was an *individual layer* that centered on the work of an artist to recover a relationship with his father, who had been disappeared; the second was a *societal layer* that connected this type of individual account to wider, collective human rights struggles; and the third was a distinct *spatial layer* connected to the reclamation, development, and evolution of the ex-ESMA as a physical site of memory, truth, and justice. Finally, it is also essential to note that while we outline these three labors of justice as distinctive, one corresponding to each of our three focal sites, they overlap and intersect in different ways. A case could even be made that all three labors of justice coexisted in at least some form at each of the sites. Nonetheless, at each research site, our findings indicated one predominant interpretation, which is why our analysis pairs a specific emphasis with a particular case study.

Our final assertion builds from the previous two to stipulate that **commemorative literacies that seek to address injustices have transnational resonances.** Over the past three decades, debates around "memory politics" have gained momentum at local and national levels in Argentina and have become increasingly divisive (Robben, 2018). The implications, at both levels, remain fiercely contested, as competing tendencies argue over what the dictatorship meant and how it should be remembered. As subsequent chapters demonstrate, the implications are transnational for several reasons. First, commemorative literacies at each site in Buenos Aires indexed people, places, and institutions beyond the borders of Argentina. The textual landscape at the university, for example, included links to the plights of Palestinians and Syrian refugees and criticism of Russian leader Vladimir Putin and Bashar al-Asaad of Syria. Second, since the beginning of the twenty-first century, competing memory narratives and mobilizations in Argentina have been increasingly shaped by transnational and cosmopolitan discourses of human rights. These discourses can be traced to a shift from framing memory politics in Argentina after redemocratization in 1983 with concepts like "dirty war" and the so-called "two demons" theory toward frameworks that emphasize state terrorism and genocide, with the latter gaining significance during the Kirchner era (Robben, 2018, p. 61). The term "dirty war" suggested erroneously that two sides were mutually engaged in a conflict, and the "two demons theory" equated the actions of armed leftist organizations with the widespread repression and violence committed by the state. Analyzing the dictatorship through the lens of state violence shifts responsibility to the military-led government and invokes comparisons to genocides around the world.

The labors of justice at the UBA, Santa Cruz, and the ex-ESMA mobilized memory for the purpose of reminding Argentines and the world—including those of us from the United States—of the duty that the living have to the victims of unjust repression. This duty includes remembrance and bearing witness to testimonies of suffering but also the requirement to act to transform the present and future so that past injustices do not continue or reappear and new injustices do not occur. Roger Simon and Claudia Eppert (1997) suggest this bearing witness entails a "commemorative ethics" in which testimonial accounts are admitted "into a contemporary moral community in ways that make an active claim on one's present and future actions in ways that do not simply reduce the terms of this admittance to projections of one's own identities and desires" (p. 178). We reflect further on the implications of commemorative ethics in Chapter 6.

Key Concepts and Terms
Commemorative Literacies for Justice: An Emerging Framework

We have invoked several key concepts and terms that require further elaboration. One of our central ideas is "commemorative literacies." To commemorate is to actively recall something in the past and mark it through some type of observation or ceremony. Practices of commemoration, then, are embedded in the ways births, deaths, and anniversaries, for example, are commemorated in personal friend and family circles, and in the ways significant cultural and historical events are commemorated within and across communities, states, and countries (Damico & Lybarger 2016; Frost & Laing, 2013). Objects or forms of commemoration also vary and can be found or expressed in, for example, coins, furniture, and clothing or in museums, monuments, and memorials. Purposes and modes of commemoration also differ and can involve festive celebration or somber, solemn reflection such as when flags are raised and saluted, small explosives are set off, or moments of silence are observed. What is especially important is how a larger public commemorative event "constitutes the event as an objective fact of the world…with a social significance and emotional implication of objectively large magnitude" (Frijda, 1997, p. 111). As such, practices of commemoration tied to collective, public events can also be heavily contested and difficult if not impossible to resolve (Frost & Laing, 2013). Moreover, as Di Paolantonio (2011) has argued in the Argentine context, imperatives such as "Nunca Más!" frame what there is to value, learn, and remember about a horrific past.

Our primary goal in this project was to understand meaning-making and justice-focused practices across our three main sites in Buenos Aires during events tied to the 40th anniversary of the 1976 coup. With this objective in mind, we developed the concept of commemorative literacies as a tool to make sense of the expressions and concerns about justice enacted at each of our sites. We clarify the key elements of this framework in what follows.

Literacy

We work with a view of literacy as sociohistorical, critical, and consequential. In contrast to what Brian Street (1984) has called an "autonomous model" of literacy, which understands literacy as the acquisition of discrete, decontextualized, or "neutral" reading and writing skills, we frame literacy in terms of the highly context-dependent ways people make meaning, what Street calls an "ideological model" of literacy. In other words, literacy is a set of social processes with cultural and historical roots as people enter spaces with diverse personal experiences or "funds of knowledge" (Moll, 1994) and create unique communities of meaning (Bakhtin, 1981; Gee, 1992; Guerra, 2008; Gutiérrez, 2008). This places an emphasis on sociological rather than psychological perspectives of reading (Luke & Freebody, 1997) because literacy, again, exists "in the relations between people, within groups and communities, rather than as a set of properties residing in individuals" (Barton et al., 2000, p. 8) and these relations are always steeped in power (Bloome et al., 2008; Macedo, 2003). The centrality of sociohistorical conditions and context also harmonizes theoretically with geosemiotics, which Ronald and Suzanne Scollon define as "the study of the social meaning of the material placement of signs and discourses in the material world" (2003, p. 2). Scollon and Scollon, in particular, emphasize "place semiotics," which they consider to be "the central thesis of geosemiotics" because "exactly where an action takes place is an important part of its meaning" (2003, p. 19).

Critical perspectives in literacy, or critical literacy, draw from a range of traditions, including critical social theory and the work of Brazilian scholar and educator Paulo Freire as well as post-structural perspectives of discourse and power (Cervetti et al., 2001). Critical literacy has also developed through feminist, postcolonial, critical race theory, cultural studies, and critical linguistics (Luke, 2014). In terms of on-the-ground applications, Comber (2013) defines critical literacy as an "evolving repertoire of practices of analysis and interrogation which move between the micro features of texts and the macro conditions of institutions, focusing upon how relations of power work through these practices" (p. 589). Geertz (1975) called this type of movement between the micro and macro a "continuous dialectical tacking between the most local of local detail and the most global of global structure in such a way as to bring both into view simultaneously" (p. 52). The metaphors of excavation and elevation can also be used to describe the complicated process of discerning how texts and discourses work (Baildon & Damico, 2011).

"Doing literacy," then, involves working in particular places with a wide range of texts, which comprise different semiotic resources, such as words, images, sounds, and movement. These resources offer different representations or versions of reality based on how a text is selected and organized (Janks, 2018). Given the focus of this book's inquiry, namely, commemorative literacies to advance justice, we appeal to two distinct yet compatible conceptions of *text*. The first is text as *liturgy*. Beginning with the customary definition of liturgy as a form of public worship performed by a religious group, we then appeal to a more secular interpretation from the Greek root, *leitourgia*, which translates roughly as "work of the people." Liturgy, in this sense, encompasses a set of practices that enact shared ideals, symbols, and narrative. As such, liturgy constitutes "the sacred"—in the sense "of things set apart and forbidden" or "things deemed special" and in relation to which a moral community forms (Durkheim [1912] 1995; Taves, 2009). The liturgies at the Plaza de Mayo that invoke and recall the 30,000 disappeared and that declare their presence "now and always," for example, enact the sacred for the Argentine political left. The 30,000 are sacrosanct for this moral community: the figure is symbolic and constitutive of who and what the left is. The number is beyond question and any attempt to cast doubt on it elicits profound anxiety and sharp denunciations of the transgressors. Set apart and forbidden, the 30,000, their invocation, call forth the moral community of those who commit to the memory of the disappeared and the responsibility to ensure that "never again" will there be a similar atrocity.

Text can also be understood as *testimony* or *testimonio*, defined as a narrative that denounces violence, especially violence of the state, and displays subaltern resistance (Gonzalez et al., 2003). Testimonio has been central to political resistance efforts throughout Latin America, allowing victims to narrate their experiences of terror and violence. This was a central practice in Argentina during the transition to democracy after 1983. The findings from the La Comisión Nacional sobre la Desaparición de Personas (National Commission on the Disappearance of Persons, CONADEP) report, *Nunca Más* (Sabato, 1984), exemplified this concern by publishing harrowing personal testimonies of Argentine victims of repression and torture, including oral testimonies of survivors, relatives and friends of the disappeared, and eyewitnesses (Robben, 2010). In this way, testimonial accounts are modes of instruction which carry the injunction to "listen and remember" and produce ethical and epistemological considerations for those bearing witness to these accounts (Simon & Eppert, 1997). According to Alicia Partnoy (2006), human rights activist, scholar, poet, and former political prisoner in Argentina during the dictatorship, testimonios can also "construct a discourse of solidarity" in ways that empower victims while prompting others to end large-scale injustices and that there is also a need for greater attention to the "relations woven within and around" testimonios (2006, p. 1665).

For our purposes with this book, we engage with testimonios somewhat differently. For the most part, we focus less on testimonial accounts from individuals about their experiences, or experiences of their loved ones, and more on the ways testimonios work spatially within and across sites in Buenos Aires. Among a wide range of testimonios in Buenos Aires in March 2016 were posters and banners spotlighting oppressed and marginalized groups, including signs and posters at the UBA that voiced concerns for gender equity and indigenous rights; a ritual ceremony at the Church of Santa Cruz, where parishioners recited the names of victims disappeared from the church; and the art installation at the ex-ESMA, featuring testimonial truth-telling and the recovery of lives lost to state violence. The ex-ESMA, as we demonstrate in Chapter 5, itself functions as material testimony tied to the dictatorship. To Partnoy's point, our research sites highlighted the "relations woven within and around" these testimonios as each pointed to or indexed related past or contemporary stakeholders, such as political leaders or groups, or events.

Finally, sociohistorical and critical perspectives of literacy are consequential. They involve direct engagement with the world—what Paulo Freire called reading the word and reading the world. In these engagements, there are explicit goals to critique and transform "dominant ideologies, cultures and economies, institutions, and political systems" for the purpose of understanding "how texts and discourses work, where, with what consequences, and in whose interests" (Luke, 2014, p. 22). This emphasis on consequences of how people work with or respond to texts engenders questions like: *what work in the world does our response to texts do?* (Damico et al., 2009).

Memory

The development and deployment of memory as an analytical tool is central to this project. Our experiences across different sites in Buenos Aires leading up to and through March 24, 2016 forced us to confront multiple forms of memorialization and commemoration and to locate individual memories within social and historical frameworks. Drawing from a broad interdisciplinary literature, we contend that memory always and necessarily functions at multiple temporal scales, illuminating not only the past but also our present moment (Confino, 1997; Connerton, 1989; Halbwachs, 1992; Jameson, 1991; Kansteiner, 2002). In the 1990s and 2000s, as scholars looked back on the twentieth century and saw both the proliferation of state-sponsored repression and the promises of modernity in apparent crisis (such as the failure of human rights enforcement, the return of violent ethnic nationalism and genocide, the collapse of democratic institutions, the rise of religious fundamentalisms globally), investigations into the politics of memory exploded in what came to be called the memory studies boom (Terdiman, 1993; Blight, 2009). This research generated new theoretical approaches that considered memory beyond the individual frame, elaborating notions of collective memory, postmemory, and intergenerational memory.

This book builds from the debates and discussions of the memory boom but uses two particular approaches to define our understanding and use of memory. First, we draw on Argentine sociologist Elizabeth Jelin's concept of "labors of memory" to argue that individuals and groups engage in the work of memory for different purposes. Jelin (2003) writes that analyzing memories as "subjective processes anchored in experiences and in symbolic and material markers" underscores that, both individually and collectively, the construction and transmission of memories cannot be considered objective and that memories carry meanings beyond what can be derived from a single person's recollections (p. xv). Memories must be interrogated historically because the significance of the past evolves alongside complex social and political processes. Following Jelin, we understand memories as "objects of disputes, conflicts, and struggles," an approach that requires both historical contextualization and an engagement with the present-day power relations in which memories are situated and transmitted (Jelin, 2003, p. xv). Engaging in the work of memory, particularly when tied to traumatic historical events, also involves a great deal of emotional, physical, and mental or psychological labor. This is critical to our reading of the commemorative literacies that we witnessed around the 40th anniversary of the coup and how these practices reflected contemporary political exigencies.

The second pillar of our framework for engaging memory is the work of historian Steve Stern, especially his groundbreaking trilogy exploring memory and repression in Chile around the dictatorship of Augusto Pinochet (Stern, 2004, 2006, 2010). Stern's metaphor of the "memory chest" as a socially constructed collection of scripted "albums" that document and shape understandings of key moments along the lines of family photo albums provides a visual representation for understanding collective memory processes. This memory chest sits "in the living room, not the attic," and allows community members to access memories even if the person exploring the chest, or an album within the chest, did not experience or was not directly implicated in a specific past event (Stern, 2004, p. xxvii). Stern argues that contentious memory (and/or remembering) is "a process of competing selective remembrances, ways of giving meaning to and drawing legitimacy from human experience" (Stern, 2004, p. xxvii). Importantly, the albums within the memory chest do not necessarily complement one another—indeed, they are often at odds. These contradictions expose what Stern describes as contesting forms of "emblematic memory," the broader frameworks within which individuals locate and create meaning from their personal memories. Stern deployed this concept of emblematic memory to show how, for example, Chileans could alternatively view the Pinochet dictatorship positively, within a framework of *memory as salvation* (Pinochet as having saved the country from socialism or communism), or negatively, emphasizing the violence and terror of the period, underscoring *memory as persecution and awakening* (Stern, 2004). That these competing memory narratives around the same event(s) could coexist within Chile's national memory chest illustrated the complexity and inherent tensions of memory as an analytical tool.

We draw on Stern's metaphor of a memory chest in this work but in doing so emphasize one specific form of emblematic memory. Several other types of emblematic memory exist in Argentina, including a form of "memory as salvation" with respect to the *Proceso*, which is similar to positive Chilean constructs of regime violence during the Pinochet era. We, however, engage with one part of the Argentine memory chest, those albums "filled with scripted photos ('emblematic memory') and scattered prints and messages ('lore')" that condemn the ideologies and actions of the dictatorship and the post-dictatorship denials offered by supporters of the *PRN* (Stern, 2004, p. 245). Our approach also differs in our focus on three specific sites—the UBA, the Church of Santa Cruz, and the ex-ESMA. Each of these sites has its own "scripted albums," and its own "lore." We engaged these albums and lore as guests who were invited to engage with the contents of the larger Argentine memory chest. This invitation allowed us to identify practices of memory mobilization that advanced justice work in three forms: as resistance, as reconciliation, and as recovery. Recognizing memory mobilization as a central aspect of justice work also reinforces Jelin's conceptualization of the "labors of memory," pointing to significant work that memory processes entail.

Space

British geographer Doreen Massey challenges the conventional view that space is a flat, inert area, as "land out there," and instead posits that space is a "product of interrelations," a "sphere in which distinct trajectories coexist" that are dynamic, indeterminate, and "always under construction" (2005, p. 9). Space, in her view, is a "simultaneity of stories-so-far" (p. 5), "always in the process of being made" through intersecting trajectories (Massey, 2005, p. 24). Space, then, can be understood as agentive, actively being formed through social interaction and the relations of power that condition that interaction.

As we considered space in this way, we became aware of the multiplicity of stories at each site and across sites in Buenos Aires during the March 2016 remembrance of the period of state terror. There was a relational mixing of stories in and through these spaces. The sites we visited and the texts we considered offered stories about their geographic locales which were particular to each site and ever changing. As we will see, for example, the ex-ESMA featured a dedicated archive and memorial for the assassinated Argentine Bishop Enrique Angelelli (1923–1976). Angelelli also featured centrally in the memorials at the Church of Santa Cruz. This overlap constituted a link between these sites and in doing so forged a common moral space and community—a shared conception of the "sacred"—even though the ex-ESMA was an explicitly non-religious, non-sectarian context while Santa Cruz was an overtly Catholic one. But these sites also had links to other spaces. Santa Cruz, for instance, as a Catholic-identified space, connected with a global religious community in ways that were not the case for the ex-ESMA or the UBA. Thus, a site could be a node in a network of multiple, intersecting spaces. For this reason, space, as we encountered and conceptualized it, was dynamic. There were potentially as many Santa Cruzes as there were individuals passing through and interacting with it.

At the same time, however, the spaces we navigated in Buenos Aires, as with all spaces, were not arbitrarily constructed sites. Rather, they constituted specific distillations of the past pertaining to the period of state terror but inclusive of other memories as well. The UBA, Santa Cruz, and the ex-ESMA were distinct spaces of memory that evoked and instituted distinct communities of memory with distinct commemorative literacies. These spaces evolved continuously through the ongoing interaction of people and groups with the memories constituted already within them. This dialectic or dialogic process produced a range of narratives about that past in relation to differences of class, gender, generation, religion, and political alignment (Massey, 2005). Santa Cruz, for example, constituted specific narratives through its visual texts that commemorated the disappeared and also through its status as a Catholic church. The individuals engaging with this space, however, brought their own narratives into conversation with the church. In Argentina, since the dictatorship's end, the continuum of such spaces of remembrance and the narratives that have formed within them have been manifold. We must include our own narrative in this manifold. As we passed through these sites and endeavored to interpret them, we added to their possible meanings. Our interpretation does not replace other meanings or stand in as the "truer" meaning. Our three sites constituted specific and diverse lines of narrative trajectory. Even as we passed through them, bringing to the spaces our own individual and collective memories—as U.S. citizens, for example—we did so in conversation with the texts, images, and practices that were already present within, and definitive of, these particular sites.

These three concepts—literacy, memory, and space—are the key pillars for our framework of *commemorative literacies*. Put simply, *commemorative literacies* refer to meaning-making with texts—understood broadly to include all types of semiotic resources—tied to specific historical events. Of particular interest is public and collective meaning-making, how "communities of memory" (Simon, 2005; Simon & Eppert, 1997) negotiate and navigate memories of past atrocities within and across space in the present moment to advance their own causes and concerns. These concepts—literacy, memory, space—are not always oriented toward justice. However, given that the commemorative events in Buenos Aires in March 2016 were grounded in calls for justice, we needed to interpret commemorative literacies with a justice lens—to link these three concepts to broader ideas of justice.

Justice

In *Justice and the Politics of Difference*, feminist scholar Iris Marion Young makes a case that injustice refers primarily to two "forms of disabling constraints, oppression and domination" (1990, p. 39) and outlines five distinct forms or "faces" of oppression: exploitation, marginalization, powerlessness, cultural domination, and violence. For Young, justice is tied to the social conditions necessary for non-domination and non-oppression, which shifts the focus from distributive justice (the allocation of material goods) to decision-making processes, culture, and divisions of labor. With this "enabling conception of justice" Young argues that justice needs to center on the "institutional conditions necessary for the development and exercise of individual capacities and collective communication and cooperation" (1990, p. 39).

One way to apply this emphasis on the enabling conditions of justice to places that experienced severe state repression like Argentina is to examine transitional justice in terms of governmental, institutional, or other macro-level events and processes, such as trials, truth commissions, and reparations. Since the transition to democracy in Argentina began in 1983, attempts to address the atrocities of the dictatorship have been marked by shifts in transitional justice policies and accompanying memory narratives (Lessa, 2013). Francesca Lessa identifies three critical junctures to account for these shifts over time. The first juncture, what she calls "Truth and Limited Justice," covers the initial post-dictatorship years from 1983 to 1985 when memory narratives emphasized findings revealed in the CONADEP report and trials and prosecutions of military leaders. This reflected an approach to justice that was more retributive than restorative as the goals of truth, guilt, accountability, and punishment were advanced (Robben, 2010). While this path led to trials and convictions of key military leaders in the early years after the dictatorship, continued economic instability and growing opposition from the Armed Forces led to the second juncture, what Lessa calls, "Impunity Laws and Pardons: Challenging Oblivion," which spanned the years 1986–2002.[10] This time period was marked by pardons and amnesties for military leaders as the state attempted to focus on the future rather than relive or litigate the past. For Lessa, the third critical juncture, "The Return of Prosecutions and Memory," covers the years 2003–2012, when criticism targeted amnesty laws and called for a return to prosecutions. In an analysis of memory as national contestation in Argentina, anthropologist Antonious Robben identifies 2005–2016 as a time of "accountability and revision" when the resumption of trials "occurred in the midst of a discursive shift" from naming past atrocities as acts of state terrorism to calling it genocide (2018, p. 28). This discourse of genocide resulted in greater calls for accountability of civilians complicit with the dictatorship, such as journalists, businessmen, judges (and Argentina as a whole), and reflected the expanding influence of transnational and cosmopolitan discourses of human rights (p. 58).

These more macro-level framings of transitional justice interact dynamically at the local level. Evolving communities of memory at specific sites might invoke a similar emblematic memory of past trauma and injustice—for example, the wide scope of severe state repression and slaughter of thousands of people—to engage in varied forms of justice work. In literacy studies, Allan Luke (2014) draws on feminist philosopher, Nancy Fraser's three concepts of social justice— redistributive, recognitive, and representative—to frame the "uses of literacy for social justice" particularly in marginalized or disenfranchised communities (p. 21). For Luke, redistributive social justice requires ensuring all groups have access and opportunity to use all valued literacy practices; recognitive social justice is about inclusivity that uses of literacy comprise texts and knowledge of historically marginalized communities; and with representative social justice, literacy represents the values, interests, and perspectives within and across communities.

Nancy Fraser's work conceptualizing justice in three dimensions—redistribution, recognition, and representation—helps frame issues of justice as transnational. Fraser (2008) has argued that disputes about justice have traditionally taken place within nation states as citizens worked through two "major families of justice claims"—claims for redistribution of socioeconomic resources and claims for cultural or legal recognition. Whether the justice concern was mostly about redistribution or recognition, it was adjudicated by the modern territorial, or geographically bounded, state. Fraser introduces a third dimension of justice, representation, further centralizing concerns for "participation parity" to ensure that individuals and groups are actively engaged in decision-making related to economic (redistribution) and cultural (recognition) dimensions of justice. Misrepresentation, then, is when some people are denied the possibility of equal participation. Accentuating the importance of this third dimension, Fraser (2008) sums up the central concern as "no distribution or recognition without representation" (p. 282).

This more comprehensive understanding of justice is responsive to rapid globalization and the expanding influence of transnational corporations and organizations as well as the rise of transnational social movements, including human rights activists and international feminists. These developments require a remapping of political space in ways that render "undivided state sovereignty [as] no longer plausible" because "a sharp division between domestic and international space" is increasingly questionable. In her remapping of political space, ideas of transnational solidarity and emancipatory border-crossing projects are central to justice. The commemorative literacies we encountered in Buenos Aires also suggest a mapping of political space that includes other places—the United States, Vietnam, South Africa, Syria and Palestine, for example—and in doing so invites transnational connections between the remembrance of the Argentine period of state terror and justice struggles elsewhere.

Based on our effort to discern commemorative literacies as "uses of literacy for social justice" (Luke, 2014) at three focal sites in Buenos Aires, we argue that overlapping and distinct justice foci at these local sites center on resistance, reconciliation, and recovery. This justice emphasis on the uses of literacy anchors broader discussions of human rights in the practices of actual communities. Moreover, just as memory is fluid, capable of being mobilized and shaped by narrative, justice is also "an ongoing, dynamic process, of which storytelling is a vital part" (Phelps 2004, p. 9).

The Relevance of Commemorative Literacies

The concept of commemorative literacies as developed and applied in this book together with the grounded fieldwork, textual analysis, and historical method we have implemented has relevance for researchers across a broad range of disciplines and areas of inquiry. Most immediately, the idea of commemorative literacies encourages literacy studies researchers to grapple with how, at the local level, communities appropriate the past to make sense of and advance justice concerns in the present. Our fieldwork bridges distanced textual analysis and grounded ethnography by focusing on a specific historical conjuncture—the commemoration of the start of the period of state terror in Argentina—and on specific locales of that conjuncture—a university, church, and former concentration camp/memory space. This method, which is perhaps most aligned with geosemiotics (Scollon & Scollon, 2003), helps ground the analysis of meaning-making processes in direct observation of texts as they are emplaced or enacted within specific sites.

Our method is also comparative, which aids in documenting shifts in meaning and in justice work across spaces. The appropriation of the past through textual processes is always a polyvocal and polysemous phenomenon. Our cross-site comparisons within a tight focus on a single historical/commemorative conjuncture reveal key differences in the repurposing of the past within the Argentine moral and political milieu that demands accountability for the 30,000 disappeared. We suggest that this method might bear fruit in other contexts. In Chapter 6, we show how this approach could work, as we apply our method to understanding the commemoration of Dr. Martin Luther King, Jr. in the United States.

Beyond literacy studies, researchers in other fields, such as memory studies, area studies, and religious studies, might find a commemorative literacies framework useful in their investigations on the agentive qualities of specific sites. One of our key contributions in this regard lies in our notion of texts as liturgical and testimonial. Drawn from the religious studies and human rights fields, the concepts of liturgy and testimony render texts dynamic and formative: they not only express but also shape justice concerns by linking past and present within meaningful, enacted narratives that constitute particular kinds of spaces and particular kinds of interventions (in our case, as spaces/interventions of resistance, reconciliation, and recovery). In religious studies, for example, scholars have analyzed liturgies in terms of their interventive, moral, and discursive/interpretive properties: liturgies call upon the gods/spirits/ancestors to prevent or mitigate or overcome crises; they establish ethical modes of conduct required to live justly (and prevent crises), and they make sense of crises by placing them within a larger dramatic narrative, for example, of sin and salvation or, in other approaches, of the profane and the sacred (Durkheim 1995 [1912]; Riesebrodt, 2010; Spiro, 1966; Taves, 2009). While particular historical context undeniably distinguishes cases from one another, this commemorative literacies approach might also be useful in Latin American Studies broadly, given the wide range of debate and discussion around the importance of testimony, witness, and memory following the violence of the mid-twentieth century (Menchú, 1983; Stephens, 2017; Stoll, 1999).

More broadly, with respect to human rights concerns, for instance, testimony forms part of the liturgical enactment, linking the individual's experience of suffering and demand for restitution and accountability to the appeal for solidarity and assistance in changing the circumstances that have created injustice. The commemorative literacies frame focuses analysis across these diverse fields on liturgical enactments and interventions that span a spectrum of memory and space in situations of social trauma and political fracture. In doing so, it opens up new insight into how liturgical and testimonial practices can shape meaning making within a wider community.

Conclusion

In this chapter, we have introduced our main arguments and outlined our framework of *commemorative literacies as labors of justice*. We have provided an initial description of the Argentine context, including sketches of our three focal sites. We have introduced historian Steve Stern's metaphor of a societal "memory chest," which resides in the "living room" and contains scripts, photo albums, and other memory lore, to help conceptualize our engagement with our three fieldwork sites. Drawing out Stern's metaphor further, we think of ourselves as invited guests, ushered into three historically significant sites in Buenos Aires to engage first-hand with the multilayered commemorative literacies and labors of justice across these spaces. In doing so, we witnessed the ways in which these sites appropriated and mobilized particular historical memories from across the preceding four decades to advance contemporary justice initiatives.

In the next chapter, we offer a more substantive historical grounding by tracing significant political and economic events in Argentina. This historical context provides a sturdy foundation for our examination of commemorative literacies as labors of justice at the three sites (Chapters 3–5).

Notes

1 The origins of the term "Nunca más" are contested. Argentine historian Emilio Crenzel attributes it to one of the members, Gerardo Taratuto, of the CONADEP (*Comisiòn Nacional sobre la Desapariciòn de Personas* or National Commission on the Disappearance of Persons) involved in the 1984 report, *Nunca Más*; others claim an American Rabbi, Marshall Meyer, who lived and worked in Buenos Aires, came up with it, with some reference to the Jewish uprising in the Warsaw Ghetto. Neither seems to suggest a direct connection, though it's hard to imagine that the CONADEP members were ignorant of the "Never Again" connotations.
2 Since independence in 1810, the conflict between the capital city of Buenos Aires and the rest of the country has been one of the definitive tensions of Argentina's political and social history. Approximately ⅓ of Argentines live in Gran Buenos Aires (the capital and its immediate surroundings), making it the largest metropolitan area by far. However, the idea of Buenos Aires as a metonym for the whole country continues to provoke debates. While our case studies are centered in the city of Buenos Aires, we recognize the diversity of experiences and perspectives outside of the capital.
3 Fernández de Kirchner was constitutionally prohibited from running again and chose a successor, Daniel Scioli, to run on her platform.
4 Unlike South Africa, Argentina's truth commission did not aim at reconciliation but rather was a preliminary step in the process of post-dictatorship tribunals and justice. See Teitel (2003).
5 The connection between the victims of past repression, embodied by the Madres, and the perception of current political exigency, represented by criticism toward proposed austerity measures, illustrated one of the central elements of our experience in Argentina, namely the overlap between past and present. We will explore this matter more fully in each of the three case-study chapters, and we will return to it again in the conclusion.
6 The "Southern Cone" refers primarily to Argentina, Chile, and Uruguay. Other countries, chiefly Brazil, Bolivia, and Paraguay, are sometimes included. Operation Condor

involved intelligence sharing between all six nations from the 1970s forward. The United States, however, never directly intervened in Argentina like it had in Chile.
7 We have published initial findings and analysis centered on Santa Cruz (Lybarger et al., 2018). Our chapter focusing on this church draws from this earlier work and the underlying data from our fieldnotes and interviews.
8 The original group of Madres has experienced various splits. One of its branches, La Asociación Madres de Plaza de Mayo, led a renewal of its protests following the rise of Argentine President Mauricio Macri. The other branch, the Las Madres de la Plaza—Línea Fundadora, has maintained a continuous protest since the start of the original movement in the late 1970s ("Madres de la Plaza concluyen," 2016).
9 Memory is not always actively mobilized but also works passively or subliminally. Much research and theoretical reflection, going all the way back to the foundational texts of sociology, demonstrates the importance of educative practices that instill and routinize (render as taken-for-granted) shared dispositions, knowledge, and memory. Bourdieu and, before him, Mauss got at this through the concept of habitus. Elias expressed the same thing in his study of the history of manners and "the civilizing process." Space and ritual process, as these studies show, inculcate memory in ways that do not involve any sort of active mobilization or agency. We absorb memory/ways of acting in the world at levels that become "rote" and "unthinking." And, this fact raises questions about "agency" if what we mean is a conscious engagement or manipulation or active transformation of the past. The past, we need to remember, also acts on us unawares. See Bourdieu (1992); Mauss (1973); Elias ([1994] 2000).
10 While the military's refusal to submit to civilian justice procedures was critical to the breakdown of these efforts, the inability of the democratic government to control Argentina's financial freefall ultimately deprived it of the legitimacy that might otherwise have allowed those trials to continue.

References

Argentina's march of resistance continues protest against Macri. (2016, December 9). *TeleSur*. https://www.telesurenglish.net/news/Argentinas-March-of-Resistance-To-Honor-Fidel-Protest-Macri-20161208-0020.html

Baildon, M. & Damico, J.S. (2011). *Social studies as new literacies in a global society: Relational cosmopolitanism in the classroom*. Routledge.

Bakhtin, M.M. (1981). *The dialogic imagination: Four essays*. University of Texas Press.

Barton, D., Hamilton, M., & Ivanic, R. (Eds.). (2000). *Situated literacies: Reading and writing in context*. Routledge.

Blight, D.W. (2009). The memory boom: Why and why now?. *Memory in mind and culture*, 238–251.

Bloome, D., Carter, S.P., Christian, B.M., Madrid, S., Otto, S., Shuart-Faris, N., & Smith, M. (2008). *On discourse analysis in classrooms: Approaches to language and literacy research*. Teachers College Press.

Bourdieu, P. (1992). *Language and symbolic power*. Polity Press.

Cervetti, G., Pardales, M.J., & Damico, J.S. (2001). A tale of differences: Comparing the traditions, perspectives, and educational goals of critical reading and critical literacy. *Reading Online*, 4(9), 80–90.

Comber, B. (2013). Critical literacy in the early years: Emergence and sustenance in an age of accountability. In J. Larson & J. Marsh (Eds.), *Handbook of research in early childhood literacy* (pp. 587–601). London: SAGE/Paul Chapman.

Confino, A. (1997). Collective memory and cultural history: Problems of method. *The American Historical Review*, 102(5), 1386–1403.

Connerton, P. (1989). *How societies remember*. Cambridge University Press.
Damico, J.S., Campano, G. & Harste, J. (2009). Transactional and critical theory and reading comprehension. In S. Israel and G. Duffy (Eds.), *Handbook of research on reading comprehension* (pp. 177–188). Lawrence Erlbaum.
Damico, J.S. & Lybarger, L.D. (2016). Commemoration, testimony, and protest in Argentina: An exploration of response and responsibilities. *Ubiquity: The Journal of Literature, Literacy, and the Arts*, 3, 7–44.
Di Paolantonio, M.D. (2011). Interrupting commemoration: thinking with art, thinking through the strictures of Argentina's Espacio para la memoria. *Discourse: Studies in the Cultural Politics of Education*, 32(5), 745–760. doi:10.1080/01596306.2011.620756
Durkheim, E. (1995; 1912). *The elementary forms of religious life*. Translated by Karen E. Fields. The Free Press.
Elias, N.(1994; 2000). *The civilizing process: Sociogenetic and psychogenetic investigations*. Blackwell.
Feitlowitz, M. (2011). *A Lexicon of terror*. Oxford University Press.
Fraser, N. (2008). *Scales of justice: Reimagining political space in a globalizing world*. Columbia University Press.
Frijda, N. (1997). Commemorating. In J.W. Pennebaker, D. Paez, & B. Rimè (Eds.), *Collective memory of political events: Social psychological perspectives* (pp. 103–127). Lawrence Erlbaum.
Frost, W. & Laing, J. (2013). *Commemorative events: Memory, identities, conflict*. Routledge.
Gee, J.P. (1992). *The social mind: Language, ideology, and social practice*. Bergin & Garvey.
Geertz, C. (1975). On the nature of anthropological understanding. *American Scientist*, 63(1), 47–53.
González, M.S., Plata, O., García, E., Torres, M., & Urrieta, L. (2003). Testimonios de immigrantes: Students educating future teachers. *Journal of Latinos and Education*, 2(4), 233–243. doi:10.1207/S1532771XJLE0204_4
Guerra, J.C. (2008). Cultivating transcultural citizenship: A writing across communities model. *Language Arts*, 85(4), 296–304.
Gutiérrez, K.D. (2008). Developing a sociocritical literacy in the third space. *Reading Research Quarterly*, 43(2), 148–164.
Halbwachs, M. (1992). *On collective memory*. University of Chicago Press.
Hite, K. (2012). *Politics and the art of commemoration: Memorials to struggle in Latin America and Spain*. Routledge.
Jameson, F. (1991). *Postmodernism, or, the cultural logic of late capitalism*. Duke University Press.
Janks, H. (2018). Texts, identities, and ethics: Critical literacy in a post-truth world. *Journal of Adolescent & Adult Literacy*, 62(1), 95–99. doi:10.1002/jaal.761
Jelin, E. (2003). *State repression and the labors of memory*. University of Minnesota Press.
Kansteiner, W. (2002). Finding meaning in memory: A methodological critique of collective memory studies. *History and Theory*, 41(2), 179–197.
Lessa, F. (2013). *Memory and transitional justice in Argentina and Uruguay: Against impunity*. Palgrave Macmillan.
Luke, A. (2014). Defining critical literacy. In J.Z. Pandya & J. Àvila (Eds.), *Moving critical literacies forward: A new look at praxis across contexts* (pp. 19–31). Routledge.
Luke, A. & Freebody, P. (1997). The social practices of reading. In S. Muspratt, A. Luke, & P. Freebody (Eds.), *Constructing critical literacies: Teaching and learning textual practice* (pp. 185–226). Hampton Press.
Lybarger, L.D. (2007). *Identity and religion in Palestine: The struggle between Islamism and Secularism in the Occupied Territories*. Princeton University Press.

Lybarger, L.D. (2020). *Palestinian Chicago: Identity in exile*. University of California Press.

Lybarger, L.D., Damico, J.S., & Brudney, E. (2018). Religion and the commemoration of the disappeared in Argentina 40 Years after the dictatorship: A study of martyrological memory at the Church of Santa Cruz. *Journal of Religion and Society, 20*.

Macedo, D. (2003). Literacy matters. *Language Arts, 81*(1), 12.

Madres de la Plaza de Mayo concluyen una nueva "marcha de la resistencia." (2016, December 10). *Agencia EFE*. https://www.efe.com/efe/cono-sur/sociedad/madres-de-la-plaza-mayo-concluyen-una-nueva-marcha-resistencia/50000760-3120924

Mason, J. (2016, March 24). Obama honors Argentina's 'dirty war' victims; Faults U.S. on human rights. https://obamawhitehouse.archives.gov/the-press-office/2016/03/24/remarks-president-obama-and-president-macri-argentina-parque-de-la

Mason, J. & Lough, R. (2016, March 23). Obama Praises Argentina's 'Man in a hurry' Macri for Reforms. *Reuters*. https://www.reuters.com/article/us-usa-argentina-idUSKCN0WP0B3

Massey, D.B. (2005). *For space*. SAGE.

Mauss, M. (1973). Techniques of the body. *Economy and Society, 2*(1), 70–88.

Menchú, R. (1983). *I, Rigoberta Menchú*. Verso.

Moll, L. (1994). Literacy research in community and classroom: A sociocultural approach. In R. Ruddell, M.R. Ruddell, & H. Singer (Eds.), *Theoretical models and processes of reading* (4th ed., pp. 179–207). International Reading Association.

Page, M. (2013). *Memories of Buenos Aires: Signs of state terrorism in Argentina*. University of Massachusetts Press.

Partnoy, A. (2006). Cuando vienen matando: On prepositional shifts and the struggle of testimonial subjects for agency. *PMLA, 121*(5), 1665–1669.

Phelps, T.G. (2004). *Shattered voices: Language, violence, and the work of truth commissions*. University of Pennsylvania Press.

Riesebrodt, M. (2010). *The promise of salvation: A theory of religion*. S. Rendall (Trans.). University of Chicago Press.

Robben, A. (2010). Testimonies, truths, and transitions of justice in Argentina and Chile. In A.L. Hinton (Ed.), *Transitional justice: Global mechanisms and local realities after genocide and mass violence* (pp. 179–205). Rutgers University Press.

Robben, A.C.G.M. (2018). *Argentina betrayed: Memory, mourning, and accountability*. University of Pennsylvania Press.

Roniger, L. & Sznadjer, M. (1998). The politics of memory and oblivion in redemocratized Argentina and Uruguay. *History & Memory, 10*(1), 133–169.

Sabato, E. (1984). Report of CONADEP: National commission on the disappearance of persons. *El Proyecto Desaparecidos*.

Scollon, R. & Scollon, S. (2003). *Discourses in place: Language in the material world*. Routledge.

Simon, R.I. (2005). Remembering otherwise: Civic life and the pedagogical promise of historical memory. In *The touch of the past: Remembrance, learning, and ethics* (pp. 1–13). Palgrave Macmillan.

Simon, R.I. & Eppert, C. (1997). Remembering obligation: Pedagogy and the witnessing of testimony of historical trauma. *Canadian Journal of Education / Revue canadienne de l'éducation, 22*(2), 175–191. doi:10.2307/1585906

Spiro, M.E. (1966). Religion: Problems of definition and explanation. In M. Barton (Ed.), *Anthropological approaches to the study of religion* (pp. 85–126). Tavistock Publications.

Stephens, L. (2017). Bearing witness: Testimony in Latin American anthropology and related fields. *Journal of Latin American and Caribbean Anthropology, 22*(1), 85–109.

Stern, S.J. (2004). *Remembering Pinochet's Chile: On the eve of London, 1998.* Duke University Press.

Stern, S.J. (2006). *Battling for hearts and minds: Memory struggles in Pinochet's Chile, 1973–1988.* Duke University Press.

Stern, S.J. (2010). *Reckoning with Pinochet: The memory question in democratic Chile, 1989–2006.* Duke University Press.

Stoll, D. (1999). *Rigoberta Menchú and the story of all poor Guatemalans.* Columbia University Press.

Street, B.V. (1984). *Literacy in theory and practice.* Cambridge University Press.

Taves, A. (2009). *Religious experience reconsidered: A building-block approach to the study of religion and other special things.* Princeton University Press.

Teitel, R.G. (2003). Transitional justice genealogy. *Harvard Human Rights Journal, 16,* 69–94.

Terdiman, R. (1993). *Present past: Modernity and the memory crisis.* Cornell University Press.

Young, I.M. (1990). *Justice and the politics of difference.* Princeton University Press.

2
HISTORICAL BACKGROUND

Introduction

Conceptualizing this book as a transdisciplinary project has meant considering how and where to incorporate diverse approaches. Among the most difficult challenges was determining what context we needed to provide within and across our case study chapters to ensure readers could follow our analysis. With an intended audience beyond Buenos Aires, including those less familiar with Argentina, we all agreed that providing sufficient historical grounding was critical, but the question of how much remained a sticking point. A strictly historical study would have meant engaging with the complex historiographical debates that have shaped the narration of Argentine history over the previous five decades. Such a study might have also worked to situate Argentina's experiences within a broader regional or transnational context, focusing on the Cold War in Latin America. However, our emphasis on literacy studies—and specifically the interplay of texts (broadly conceived), context, and processes of meaning-making—suggested different priorities with respect to historical grounding. This chapter addresses those priorities, introducing the particularities of Argentina's recent past while only tangentially participating in broader historiographical conversations. The narrative presented here reflects our attempt to avoid general or facile references to context and instead take seriously the specific historical dynamics that continue to influence local and national power relations. The project's transdisciplinary nature brought us to the conclusion that only through such a treatment could we highlight the uniqueness of Argentina's experience while also considering possible points of connection with struggles over memory and justice around the globe.

DOI: 10.4324/9781003184195-3

Our time in Buenos Aires and our subsequent analysis of the multiple sites and forms of justice work are grounded in a much longer historical trajectory. Making sense of the events around the 40th anniversary commemorations in March 2016 requires exploring how this complex and multivocal past has shaped and informed the texts and practices with which we engaged. Although there are multiple valid ways to approach contemporary Argentine history, in this chapter, we emphasize three themes that are critical to understanding the book's subsequent discussions. First, the rise of Peronism in the 1940s and the violent backlash it provoked brought two lasting consequences: a new conception of justice—and particularly social justice—and a willingness to use force as a political tool. Both of these trends would culminate in the *Proceso de Reorganización Nacional* during the 1970s. Second, over the latter half of the twentieth century, Argentina experienced a combination of economic dependency and political instability, which by the 1970s led conservative sectors to embrace free-market liberalism as a potential solution to both. The debate between greater state intervention and laissez-faire economics played a key role in the events of March 2016. Finally, as Argentina struggled to cope with the trauma of the *Proceso*, the 1990s witnessed the development of a discourse of "national reconciliation" that emphasized forgetting and forgiving—a discourse that dissipated after 2003 but would reemerge with the election of Macri in December 2015. The relationship between trauma and commemoration remains a central feature of Argentina's political sphere. In highlighting these themes, this chapter unpacks the origins for the conceptions of justice considered in subsequent chapters through our analysis of the commemorative literacies and spaces of memory.

Justice and Violence

1943 and the GOU

The history of the *Proceso* has many possible starting points, but the rise of Peronism in the mid-1940s offers an appropriate entry into this longer trajectory. In 1930, a coup d'état led by conservative Generals José Félix Uriburu and Agustín Pedro Justo marked the first successful overthrow of an elected government in Argentina. Over the following decade, a succession of military and civilian rulers held the presidency, maintaining their authority via fraudulent elections and repressive measures (Juareche, 1983). By mid-1943, most sectors of society disapproved of the government of then-President Ramón Castillo, including the military. Another military intervention, this time led by a collection of younger officers calling themselves the "Grupo de Oficiales Unidos" (Group of United Officers or GOU), pre-empted the next scheduled elections. Instead, the GOU seized power and installed themselves as the de facto authorities (Potash, 1971). Although the end of the so-called Infamous Decade (1930–1943) brought cautious applause from most of Argentine society, many remained wary about what this new military regime would mean.

In the wake of the coup, as the spoils were divided between military officials, a young colonel named Juan Domingo Perón claimed for himself the relatively obscure post of Secretary of Labor. Despite this obscurity, Perón saw something in the Secretariat that he could utilize. The previous 50 years had brought a massive influx of immigrants—mostly from Eastern and Southern Europe—together with the growth of the country's industrial sector. By the early 1940s, a new class had emerged, encompassing hundreds of thousands, if not millions, of workers. To what extent Perón fully understood the political potential of this nascent working class remains debated. Some claim that the new Secretary of Labor used his office to manipulate and use the workers as a political base, while others argue that it was the rank-and-file who pushed the political positions that Perón later adopted (Luna, 2012; Germani, 1955; James, 1988). The end result proved the same: Colonel Perón's meteoric rise from a background figure to the most popular member of the government by 1945. Indeed, his mass appeal became a cause for concern both domestically and internationally.

Perón in Office

Perón's fellow officers, many of them traditional conservatives (as were most military officers), felt increasingly threatened by his popularity and in particular the prospect of welcoming previously marginalized actors—the urban working classes—into the political sphere (Luna, 2012). Simultaneously, the U.S. Ambassador in Argentina, Spruille Braden, took an aggressively anti-GOU stance, intensified by his personal dislike of Perón.[1] In concert with established conservative interest groups like the Argentine Chamber of Commerce, Braden sharply criticized the GOU generally and Perón specifically. Meanwhile, fears within the Armed Forces culminated in the removal of Perón as Secretary of Labor and his imprisonment in October 1945. However, both Braden and the GOU had dramatically underestimated the connections Perón had forged during his time as Secretary. On October 17 and 18, tens of thousands of workers occupied the Plaza de Mayo and demanded Perón's immediate release (James, 1988; Luna, 2012; Torre, 2005). Bowing to popular pressure, the government ordered Perón freed, and on the evening of October 18, Perón addressed the packed Plaza de Mayo from the balcony of the Casa Rosada (the residence of Argentina's President), thanking them for their support. Having effectively lost its legitimacy over the course of the Perón saga, the GOU announced that presidential elections would take place in February 1946.

The next five months witnessed an intense struggle between the ascendant forces of Peronism and Argentina's conservative "old guard," comprising the urban elite and sectors of the middle classes, military leadership, and large employers. Into this fray stepped once again Spruille Braden, whose distrust of Perón and anti-unionism motivated him to interfere aggressively in Argentina's domestic political scene. Braden campaigned openly against Perón, attempting to rally the country's middle class. His actions, however, provoked the opposite result, as Perón skillfully reframed the presidential campaign around the issue of US interference and behind the slogan "Braden o Perón" easily won election as president.[2] This confluence of nationalism and trade-unionism would become a hallmark of the Peronist administration and Peronism as a movement.

Perón's first administration (1946–1952) dramatically reshaped Argentina's social, political, and economic landscapes. His experiences as Secretary of Labor and his connections to the country's trade unions provided not only a willing political base but also a ready partner in the remaking of social citizenship. The integration of workers into the national polity meant that the political rights and social privileges of citizenship extended to working men (and, after 1949, women) across Argentina for the first time. The name that Peronism adopted in 1946—the *Partido Justicialista* or Justicialist Party—reflected this emphasis. Social justice provided the platform for incorporating and uniting formerly excluded groups and pursuing a specific political program built around the expansion of citizenship (James, 1988). This rhetorical foregrounding of justice would become a hallmark of Peronist political philosophy and remains a critical element of contemporary Argentine political culture, as the subsequent chapters explore. However, *justicialismo*'s upending of the country's traditional power dynamics deepened the divisions between Peronist and anti-Peronist forces, setting the stage for political struggle throughout the remainder of the twentieth century.

From the middle of the 1940s, Argentina's economic fortunes continued to rise as Import Substitution Industrialization (ISI), introduced in the 1930s, expanded dramatically under Perón. Manufacturing from the United States and Europe arrived to take advantage of a relatively skilled, but still low-paid, workforce. The destruction of European economies during World War II meant that Argentina's exports—chiefly wheat and beef—brought high prices and drove further investment. During these first years, Peronism also counted on important allies—namely the Armed Forces and the Catholic Church—who viewed *justicialismo* as a bulwark against Marxism. For the Peronist base, these were exciting, if complicated, years. Social, political, and economic improvements within the working class came alongside the formalization of labor regimes that allowed Perón and his chosen subordinates—particularly his wife Eva (Evita)—to wield increasing control over the movement. Peronism's verticalist orientation, which emphasized a rigid hierarchy and relied on the organizational capacity of the General Confederation of Labor (CGT), harnessed the power of the masses while shutting off alternative avenues for their political participation.

The Rise of Anti-Peronism

The post-war boom began to collapse with the introduction of the United States' Marshall Plan, which effectively froze Argentina out of the lucrative European markets after 1948.[3] Perón weathered the country's economic downturn in part due to his wife's fight to enfranchise women, further expanding his political base. The country's deteriorating financial situation did not prevent Perón from easily winning reelection in 1952. However, the following months witnessed a dramatic shift in Peronist fortunes. Evita's untimely death at 33 deprived Perón of his most important ally and the only political figure in Argentina capable of matching his star power. Tensions between Peronism and the Catholic Church steadily mounted, culminating in Perón's support for a legislative package that included the legalization of prostitution and divorce, the suppression of religious education, and the formal separation of Church and State (Luna, 1985). Meanwhile, the Armed Forces viewed Perón with growing distrust, wary of what they considered his demagogic tendencies. By 1954, the Church and the military had mostly abandoned their early support for Peronism and allied themselves with the landed oligarchy and urban elites to form an anti-Peronist alliance.

The showdown between Peronism and anti-Peronism reached a climax over the second half of 1955. On June 16, during a failed coup attempt, factions of the Armed Forces bombed the Plaza de Mayo in the middle of the afternoon, leaving hundreds of civilians dead and injured. Perón survived the attempt on his life, but the attack was a watershed moment in Argentine history because of the indiscriminate use of violence against civilian populations. Following the assault, Peronist supporters responded by burning and looting several Catholic churches, accusing the clergy of having incited the failed coup (Cichero, 2005; Potash, 1980). The President's grasp on the country was slipping.

The Revolución Libertadora

Indeed, when the end arrived a few months later, Perón made clear his choice not to fight his removal, urging his supporters to refrain from violence and accepting his exile (Potash, 1980). In September 1955, the Armed Forces orchestrated Perón's ouster and the new regime, initially under the direction of General Eduardo Lonardi (Ret.), adopted the name "Revolución Libertadora," or "Liberating Revolution." As part of the negotiations, Lonardi, a Catholic nationalist, proclaimed that there would be no punishment for Peronist supporters and that this revolution would have neither victors nor victims (James, 1988, p. 43). Meanwhile, despite an initial call to arms by the secretary general of the CGT, workers largely opted not to take to the streets in defense of Perón, instead mirroring the leader's apparent resignation. This relative peace lasted less than two months before General Pedro Aramburu, an extreme right-wing nationalist, forced Lonardi from office and assumed control.

The Aramburu Presidency

Between November 13, 1955, when Aramburu installed himself as de facto head of state, and May 1, 1958, when he stepped down, the government dedicated itself to undoing the so-called "hecho maldito" ("damned occurrence") of Peronism. The "heretical" nature of Peronism—its challenge to traditional order and established power relations—made it anathema to the newly installed anti-Peronist forces, who focused their attention on rolling back the economic, political, and social reforms implemented under *justicialismo*. This included amending the Constitution in 1958 to invalidate many of the changes that Perón had introduced in 1949, while laws prohibiting the Peronist/Justicialist Party and banning the names Juan and Eva Perón sought to erase the previous decade from public memory. The most immediate question, however, was how to handle the Peronist unions (Munck et al., 1987). Aramburu proved willing to use the state's security apparatus to quell dissent, most notably in the aftermath of an attempted uprising by military personnel loyal to Perón in 1956.[4] The regime arrested labor leaders, occupied union headquarters, and suspended key rights—including the right to strike—to prevent the development of organized working-class resistance (Rubens, 1974). This repression typified the new approach of the Armed Forces vis-à-vis the maintenance of "order." Aramburu's tactics evidenced a new commitment to violence as a political tool, and state repression would resurface with increasing intensity during the following three decades.

"Democratic" Interlude

In 1958, Aramburu retired from the military and dedicated himself to becoming a full-time politician. The *Revolución Libertadora* had been intended to provide a "reset" for the political sphere that would allow the country to move forward without Peronism, not to hold power indefinitely. Elections were held, but tellingly the Justicialist Party was prohibited from participating. This "democratic process" went forward only under the continued suppression of Argentina's largest political movement. The military's decision to extend the proscription of Peronism suggests that even their most optimistic evaluation of the Liberating Revolution recognized that it had fallen short of expectations.

The eight years from 1958 to 1966 witnessed two "free" elections in 1958 and 1963 (albeit with Peronism banned from participating) and a third transfer of power that established a semi-de facto regime from 1962 to 1963. During this stretch, the country's anti-Peronist forces continued their efforts to reverse Peronism's impact but had limited success. By 1965, the alliance between the Radical Party (Argentina's second-largest political party, which won those elections in which Peronists could not compete), elites, and the Armed Forces had frayed considerably. President Arturo Illia, elected in 1963 when Peronists and even sectors of the Radical Party had refused to cast ballots in protest, called legislative elections on March 14, 1965, and lifted the proscriptions on all political tendencies. The Peronist Party won handily, taking 38% of the national vote as compared to 30% for Illia's party (Munck et al., 1987, p. 160). For conservatives, this result proved that the democratic experiment had failed. Given the impending presidential elections scheduled for 1967—and the probability that a Peronist candidate would triumph—the military began laying the groundwork for another coup. With labor unrest continuing to cause social and political turmoil, and an increasingly intransigent Peronist legislature blocking Illia's agenda, a group of generals decided in June 1966 that the moment had come.

Cyclical Instability

The Revolución Argentina

The self-titled "Revolución Argentina" (Argentine Revolution) fit within a longer trajectory of military interventions in Argentina, but it differed in one key respect from both the 1955 *Revolución Libertadora* and the 1976 onset of the *Proceso de Reorganización Nacional*. In those cases, the country faced moments of profound economic instability, which exacerbated political and social unrest. In 1966, however, Argentina was enjoying one of the longest sustained periods of economic growth in national history (Gerchunoff & Llach, 2010, pp. 304–305). That the military seized power—and that the public largely accepted this development (at least initially)—underscores the depth of anti-Peronist sentiment that predominated among certain sectors of the Armed Forces and civil society.

Seeking to learn from the failure of Aramburu, who perhaps surrendered power before accomplishing the primary goal of eliminating Peronism, the new de facto President General Juan Carlos Onganía announced that the revolution did not have "timelines, but rather objectives" (Gerchunoff & Llach, 2010, p. 302). This time around, the military understood its role as more than simply a placeholder that would shortly give way to authentic democracy. Instead, the *Onganiato* (the first phase of the dictatorship) had more ambitious aspirations: the disciplining of the labor movement, the rationalization of the economy, and the modernization of the state (James, 1988, p. 216). Accomplishing these would require that the Armed Forces assume more direct control over the country's political apparatus than previous de facto regimes—and to make use of repression to a far greater extent.

The Onganiato

General Onganía saw himself as uniquely capable of bringing about these changes. Although the Argentine Revolution began cautiously and was even initially celebrated by some Peronist leaders, the regime quickly revealed its true character. Just weeks after the coup d'état, students and professors at public universities around the country occupied school buildings in protest against a proposed measure to rescind the *Reforma Universitaria* (University Reform) of 1918 that established university autonomy. The Onganía government's response became known as the "Noche de los bastones largos" or "Night of the Long Batons." Police and security forces stormed the universities and savagely beat students and professors. Hundreds were arrested and the dictatorship severely curtailed the independence of the university system, imposing new regulations on course materials and forcing dozens of professors to resign (Morero et al., 2002). This incident was notorious for the scope of state violence, but similar measures were aimed at sectors of the labor movement and the political parties as the government sought to assert its dominance over all aspects of civil society that might potentially challenge its authority.

Nor was Onganía content to simply cow possible opponents. He appointed the economically liberal Adalbert Krieger Vasena to head the Ministry of Economy, signaling a dramatic change in the dominant mode of capital accumulation in Argentina.[5] Krieger Vasena suspended existing collective bargaining agreements, established strict wage controls, encouraged foreign investment, and lowered protective tariffs (Rock, 1987, pp. 347–348). These laissez-faire policies initially produced positive results, promoting economic growth while keeping prices and salaries relatively steady and gaining favor with sectors of the Argentine Right. Although the situation provoked widespread worker discontent, a faction of the labor movement found common cause with the Onganía regime on certain economic and political issues and worked out a tense but largely functional accord from 1967 into 1969.[6] The "transformation" of Argentine society promised after the 1966 coup seemed increasingly possible.

Popular Responses

However, just beneath the surface, a wellspring of anger had been bubbling up, waiting for the right moment to explode. A series of smaller student demonstrations, occasionally accompanied by union activists and politicians, in early 1969 provoked severe government repression and resulted in deaths of two students (Ramírez, 2009). The real moment arrived at the end of May 1969, with a series of popular mobilizations and riots in Argentina's second-largest city, Córdoba. The *Cordobazo* began as a repudiation of anti-labor policies and police abuses, organized by two prominent labor leaders. As workers massed on the morning of May 29 to march through the city, university students rushed to join them, and soon thousands of demonstrators were moving toward the center of Córdoba, clashing with police and security forces along the way. The size of the mobilization was both unexpected and unprecedented. The alliance of workers and students, united in their opposition to the *Onganiato*, seized control of large areas of the city, and held them for more than two days, until the military forcibly dislodged them late on May 31 (Brennan, 1994). Although the protests were ultimately put down, they exposed the fragility of the military's control and set the stage for Onganía's resignation less than a year later.

During the next two years, more than a dozen popular uprisings shook cities all around the country. Like the *Cordobazo*, they frequently involved students and workers acting together against the military regime. However, they also brought people into the streets around other issues, as during the *Mendozazo* (1972) when thousands protested a 300% rise in electricity costs (Jiménez & Jiménez, 2018). Alongside these mobilizations, targeted political violence became increasingly visible, further undermining the *Revolución Argentina*. On May 29, 1970, a new armed leftist group, the Montoneros, kidnapped former de facto President Pedro Aramburu, drove him to a farmhouse in rural Buenos Aires province, tried him for crimes committed during his mandate, and summarily executed him several days later. This operation dramatically announced the Montoneros' presence on the national stage. From his exile in Spain, Perón backed the Montoneros, reasoning that the more unrest they sowed the more likely his return would be. Shortly thereafter, the Marxist *Ejército Revolucionario del Pueblo* (Revolutionary Army of the People) began armed operations, as did a handful of other Peronist guerrilla organizations (Gillespie, 1982; Lewis, 2002). Counterrevolutionaries on the right—many who also identified as Peronists—responded by forming paramilitary groups, often composed of off-duty security forces, and targeting suspected leftists. During the early 1970s, these death squads tortured, disappeared, and killed people with increasing frequency, with these practices predating the period of state terror that began in 1976.[7] By 1973, facing turmoil and protest on all sides, the Armed Forces prepared to do what had long been unthinkable: pave the way for Perón's return.

"Vuelve Perón"

From 1971 to 1973, the Argentine Revolution attempted to set the terms for the transition to democracy, and particularly the relegitimation of Peronism after 18 years of proscription. After Onganía's resignation in 1970 (hastened by the killing of Aramburu), the country descended further into political and economic turmoil as the military government's remaining legitimacy evaporated. Regime leaders began negotiations with politicians and union leaders around the restoration of civilian rule, but these concessions did not appease the newly militarized Left. The Armed Forces found themselves increasingly committed to a conflict against "subversion," an amorphous term that included the various guerrilla organizations but also their sympathizers and even segments of the labor and student movements (Rock, 1987, pp. 356–357). Even as the dictatorship surrendered power, the military remained wary of another Peronist administration. Indeed, the Armed Forces attempted to prevent (or delay) his return to power by implementing a residency clause for the upcoming March 1973 elections. Although the Peronist Party could stand for office, this effectively excluded Perón.

To circumvent this restriction, Perón designated a stand-in, Héctor Cámpora, to run in his stead. However, over the previous 18 years, the meaning(s) of Peronism had evolved considerably. His long exile had allowed different groups to invest Peronism with their own hopes and dreams. Thus, the conservative trade-union bureaucracy imagined a return to the glory days of the 1940s and 1950s; the business community saw Perón as a safeguard against the rising tide of Marxism; and the left, with Perón's encouragement, read him as a bringer of national liberation (Rock, 1987, p. 359). Cámpora's convincing victory in March inspired the *Juventud Peronista* (Peronist Youth, JP)—which encompassed Peronism's younger and more radical sectors—to imagine the General's return as a step toward Argentine socialism. The JP had close ties to the *Montoneros* as well as other Peronist guerrilla organizations (James, 1988, pp. 242–243). Meanwhile, union leaders worried that Perón in power would compromise the authority and autonomy they had established over the past two decades (James, 1988; Torre, 2004). Tensions within Peronism that could be ignored while the movement was in the opposition now risked boiling over. The battle over what Peronism would mean threatened to tear the country apart before Perón even reached Argentina.

As president, Cámpora quickly struck down the military's prohibitions on residency, declared that he would step aside, and scheduled another election for September 1973. In June, Perón formally returned to Argentina to proceed with his campaign. His arrival, planned as a celebratory event, provided an ominous preview of the difficulties that awaited. On June 20, thousands of people headed to Ezeiza airport outside Buenos Aires to show their support. The gathering was dominated by young leftists, including many Montoneros and their supporters, who hoped their demonstration of allegiance would push Peronism toward their objectives. Instead, hours before Perón's plane landed, right-wing Peronists allied with the trade-union leadership occupied the podium and then opened fire on the crowd. At least a dozen people were killed and hundreds more injured (Gambini, 2008). The Ezeiza massacre definitively fractured the Peronist movement—not even Perón himself could reunite the disparate elements under a single banner.

The Third Peronist Government

The violence at the airport foreshadowed what was to come, but it did not prevent him from pursuing a third presidential term. With his third wife María Estela Martínez de Perón (known as Isabel) as his vice-president, Perón ran at the head of a loose coalition of Peronists, elements of the Radical Party, the Christian Democrats, and the Socialists. Perón won overwhelmingly, amassing more than 7,000,000 votes, which exceeded 60% of the total turnout (Cantón & Jorrat, 1980). This mass support, however, failed to provide the new government with a solid foundation from which to pursue legislative action. Instead, Perón confronted distrust from business leaders and segments of the trade-union hierarchy, while also facing the growing disillusionment of the *justicialismo*'s younger and more radical members. Despite these obstacles, Perón managed to negotiate a temporary truce between the various groups. Dubbed the "Pacto Social" (Social Pact), the agreement froze prices and wages, demanding sacrifices of employers and workers to stabilize the economy and establish a base for continued growth. Yet the Pacto contained the seeds of its own collapse. Even as it reinforced the authority of the union bureaucracy, the agreement severely limited their ability to defend their members' interests, so that when the Pacto was inevitably violated and prices rose, the leadership found itself penned in by competing imperatives (Gerchunoff & Llach, 2010, pp. 342–345; James, 1988, pp. 244–246). Perón's expulsion of the Montoneros and their allies from the Plaza de Mayo during a May Day speech in 1974 marked the permanent rupture of the tenuous Peronist alliance. Once again, domestic political uncertainty combined with financial upheaval to reinforce Argentina's dependent—and unstable—place in the global economic arena.

Perón's Death and the Isabel Government

On July 1, 1974, Perón died of heart failure at 78, leaving his widow and vice-president, 43-year-old Isabel, to assume the presidency, despite having no prior political experience. Whether Perón could have navigated the difficulties facing Argentina is unlikely; with Isabel, it was impossible. Following Perón's death, Peronism's internecine struggles burst into the open as conservative union leaders tried to drive shop-floor militants out of the factories and radicalized sectors of the rank-and-file responded with wildcat strikes and spontaneous direct actions (James, 1988; Torre, 2004, p. 127). The *Montoneros* resumed their attacks on security forces and right-wing labor leaders. In response, the Minister of Social Welfare, José López Rega, founded the Argentine Anticommunist Alliance (*Alianza Argentina Anticomunista*, or Triple A), the most infamous right-wing paramilitary group of the pre-coup era, targeting not just leftist guerrillas but anyone who could potentially be labeled "subversive."

Isabel surrendered much of her authority to close advisors, including Lopez Rega as the worsening economic outlook exacerbated social and political turmoil. Assassinations, bombings, strikes, factory occupations, and mass demonstrations regularly rocked the country, creating an atmosphere of uncertainty and fear (Carassai, 2014). With Perón gone, the Armed Forces believed themselves the only institution capable of reasserting control, and by late 1974, military leaders began planning another intervention. Isabel contributed by declaring an *estado de sitio* (state of siege/state of exception) in November 1974, partially suspending the Constitution. This declaration responded to the growing perception that the state had lost its legitimacy and gave the military permission to conduct operations against domestic enemies.[8] The Army, under General Jorge Rafael Videla, wasted little time exercising this new authority. In February 1975, they launched

"Operation Independence" in Tucumán province, a counterrevolutionary offensive that became the first theater for the period of coordinated state terror. The detention, torture, disappearance, and murder of thousands of civilians—most of whom had only tangential connections (if any) to guerrilla activity—served as a test-run for the repressive tactics that would become widespread after March 24, 1976 (Lewis, 2002).

Meanwhile, Argentina's economy continued its precipitous decline. A decade of growth from 1963 to 1973 was followed by the Oil Crisis and the outbreak of global stagflation in the early 1970s (Gerchunoff & Llach, 2010, p. 309, 378). The collapse of the *Pacto Social* meant rising prices and depressed wages, crippling purchasing power. In June 1975, newly appointed Minister of Economy Celestino Rodrigo—a close ally of López Rega—announced his plan to shock the economy from its current state. Overnight, he approved a currency devaluation on the order of 100% which more than doubled the cost of public services and utilities. The *Rodrigazo*, as it became known, devastated the national economy, wiped out the life savings of millions, and dramatically increased working- and middle-class precarity (Gerchunoff & Llach 2010, pp. 347–348). Within days, Rodrigo had resigned in disgrace and López Rega, who had pushed for his appointment, was forced to flee the country. During the next nine months, five people held the post of Economy Minister, desperately trying to undo the damage of the *Rodrigazo*, but no one succeeded in repairing the national economy. As monthly inflation topped 35% and political violence seemed to worsen by the day, most of Argentina looked to the impending military coup with either hope or fatalistic acceptance. The question now was not "if" but "when."

Repression and Trauma
March 24, 1976

The *golpe de estado* that deposed Isabel Perón began just after midnight on March 24, 1976. By 3:00 a.m., the Armed Forces had seized control of the government, detained the former president, and announced to the country that another period of military rule was underway. In his address to the nation, de facto President Videla declared that the coup marked the definitive closure of one historical cycle and the opening of another.[9] During the months leading to March 24, the military had carefully planned its operations, while waiting as popular faith in civil government deteriorated. Thus, when they finally acted, they encountered little actual resistance, and indeed, many sectors of civil society—including sectors of the political world and the trade-union apparatus—either tacitly or openly supported the coup (Novaro & Palermo, 2003, p. 33). For most Argentines, this seemed to be simply another in a long line of military interventions. That assumption would quickly prove tragically misguided.

War Against Subversion

The first ruling junta comprised the heads of the three divisions of the Armed Forces: General Jorge Rafael Videla (Army), Admiral Emiliano Eduardo Massera (Navy), and Brigadier Orlando Ramón Agosti (Air Force). Each man had a vision for the future Argentina that the *Proceso de Reorganización Nacional* (Process of National Reorganization, PRN) should create, but those visions generally failed to overlap. Instead, factions within the military competed for power and direction over the political and social strategies of the dictatorship, leaving most of the PRN's ambitious agenda foundering (Canelo, 2008).

The various elements did agree on two things, however. First, they understood the failure of earlier dictatorships, especially the *Onganiato*, as a lesson to learn from—they would not surrender control before they were done. Second, a broad consensus existed across the different branches and factions of the Armed Forces that subversion, in all of its forms, must be stamped out with severity. This objective, more than any other, gave the dictatorship a semblance of coherence during the first two years as the state's security forces pursued their campaign of terror. Between March 24, 1976 and the end of 1983, tens of thousands of people disappeared or were killed by the regime, with thousands more detained and tortured. The exact number remains unknown, because Argentina's military and police forces have never officially recognized their role in this repression nor, with few exceptions, opened their archives to researchers.[10] The highest confirmed estimate comes from mid-1978, when members of Intelligence Battalion 601 produced a report that acknowledged more than 22,000 deaths attributable to state security forces.[11] Human rights activists have long claimed that the total is closer to 30,000.

This violence developed naturally from the repression and paramilitary activity of the previous government. The jump from the Triple A (Argentine Anticommunist Alliance) and Operation Independence to a coordinated nation-wide effort to eradicate subversion was fairly simple (Novaro & Palermo, 2003, pp. 80–81). The Armed Forces established dozens of clandestine detention centers (CCDs), often in the middle of busy urban environments. Operations teams surveilled targets and abducted people off the street, in their homes, or at work. All of this contributed to an atmosphere of fear and uncertainty that helped unravel the social compact. During this period, the infamous phrase "algo habrá(n) hecho" ("she/he/they must have done something") circulated among those who witnessed, directly or indirectly, acts of state violence. This phrase had two purposes. First, it allowed people to separate themselves from the violence by creating an "us" that obeyed norms and a "them" that violated norms, and thus deserved their punishment. Second, in addition to assigning blame, "algo habrá(n) hecho" simultaneously made the state responsible and thus became a mechanism by which the speaker could abdicate her or his own responsibility to act. For many, this distancing proved a critical tool in coping with the violence that Argentine society experienced during this period, though for many the lingering trauma remains unhealed.

Climate of Terror

An important and intentional corollary of this "war against subversion" was the creation of a broader climate of terror that crossed nearly all strata of Argentine society. The concept of "algo habrá hecho" not only allowed people to separate themselves from the state's repression as described above but also contributed to an environment in which neighbors no longer trusted neighbors, in which the bonds that sustained social relations began to fray and break. The act of witnessing the state's security forces grab someone off the street became in itself a mortal danger to be mitigated. Silence might protect the individual, but it simultaneously reinforced the pervasive sense that violence lurked around every corner. The military actively played up this uncertainty and fear, both through the brutality of their tactics and via their manipulation of language and information. The practice of disappearing people—whether guerrillas, suspected subversives, or merely those in the wrong place at the wrong time—reflected a deliberate plan to not only eliminate an internal enemy but to leave an open wound in the lives of everyone connected to that person. It was a public spectacle of terror, evidence that the Armed Forces could do more than take people's lives—they could erase them from being (Taylor, 1997). The intent mattered, insofar as it demonstrated the dictatorship's belief that its actions would have consequences for years, and perhaps generations, to come.

At the same time, the regime also toyed with language and policy in almost Orwellian fashion. Marguerite Feitlowitz's *A Lexicon of Terror* (1999) chronicles the rhetorical tactics used by the PRN to sow fear and uncertainty among the Argentine people. While they are too broad to cover here, two examples—one well known, one much less so—help illustrate the larger pattern. In 1978, Argentina faced mounting international criticism from human rights organizations around the use of extralegal repression. That June and July, the country hosted the World Cup, an opportunity for the dictatorship to demonstrate its accomplishments on a global stage. To combat what conservative Argentines dubbed an "anti-Argentine campaign," the government coined a new slogan: "Los argentinos somos derechos y humanos" ("We Argentines are right and human"), a macabre play on the language of human rights. The slogan became the official answer to the critiques facing Argentina and was parroted by media outlets throughout 1978 and 1979, especially during the 1979 visit by the Inter-American Commission on Human Rights (Gutman, 2015). The second example has more to do with the manipulation of policy and the disconnect between the law and its implications. In 1976, shortly after seizing power, the PRN relegalized the death penalty, contributing to the broader climate of fear by making it appear that the regime wielded the power of life and death. However, in an overt perversion of justice, not one person was ever officially put to death, despite the tens of thousands killed (Serra, 2008). This break between the "legitimate" function of the state and its actions reinforced the terror that was per se a central goal of the *Proceso*. Indeed, terror—not simply violence—played a pivotal role in the regime's broader effort to "reorganize" the Argentine nation.

Collapse of the Proceso

The Armed Forces shared the desire to eliminate subversion, but their priorities diverged on nearly every other major issue. The economy, labor policy, and redemocratization quickly became flashpoints for internal conflict and provoked sharp divisions with the regime. Paula Canelo has demonstrated that the "lucha antisubversiva" ("antisubversive fight") served two key purposes: it provided the regime with legitimation and it covered up the deep fissures between factions of the Armed Forces around policy and politics (Canelo, 2008). However, the dictatorship did its job too well. Within months of the coup, military operations against the country's guerrilla organizations had effectively eliminated the "subversive" threat. The defeat was overwhelming and by the start of 1977, the operational capacity of Argentina's armed leftist groups was almost completely destroyed. This left the PRN in a difficult situation. On one hand, the war against subversion was a central objective of the *Proceso* and required visible demonstrations of success. Thus, reports of "confrontations" with guerrillas that included the number of militants killed and captured were critical for the regime. On the other hand, defeating subversion so quickly risked eliminating a—perhaps *the*—primary justification for the dictatorship's continued existence, and so new rationales had to be found or invented (Canelo, 2008). One of these involved extending the definition of subversion to include tens of thousands of people with political views considered "undesirable," regardless of their connection to guerrilla movements. Expanding the scope of the antisubversive operation allowed it to remain part of the PRN's agenda well into 1978. However, this was not enough to ensure continued coherence, and indeed after 1976, internal discord grew rapidly precisely because of the vacuum that the end of the war against subversion left behind.

The dictatorship's economic policy exemplifies these internal contradictions. The Minister of Economy, José Alfredo Martínez de Hoz, pursued an aggressive free-market strategy that clashed with the nationalist and developmentalist positions of many within the Armed Forces.[12] Martínez de Hoz eliminated protective tariffs, tried to privatize state-owned industries, and courted foreign investment, especially via global financial institutions like the International Monetary Fund (IMF). Within six months of the 1976 coup, the IMF authorized loans of $100 million and then $260 million, among the largest ever for a Latin American nation (Cooney, 2007). Some on the left sharply criticized the neo-imperial impulse behind this kind of financing, as did—somewhat paradoxically—some right-wing nationalists within the military.[13] Yet, for Argentina's economic elite, including the family of future president Mauricio Macri, these policies meant the triumph of the "patria financiera," and a new way to increase their wealth. In the short term, disagreements within the PRN around economic policy undermined the regime's efforts to effect lasting change. In the long term, these loans intensified a cycle of indebtedness that would culminate in the largest sovereign debt default in history in 2001.

The de facto presidency of General Videla (March 29, 1976–March 29, 1981) was the high point of the regime's authority. While various obstacles hamstrung most of its "refoundational" goals, this five-year span saw the PRN govern with relative stability.[14] After Videla, however, the dictatorship's control crumbled rapidly. Between March 29, 1981 and December 10, 1983, when democratically elected President Raúl Alfonsín was sworn in, seven people exercised—at least temporarily—the powers of head of state.[15] Human rights organizations, political parties, and labor unions, especially after 1980, threatened the regime's integrity and created a series of intractable problems. These were compounded by continued economic decline, which the PRN had been largely unable to arrest. Growing discontent within diverse sectors of Argentine society put increased pressure on the regime. Videla's successor, General Roberto Viola, served just eight months before being removed from office by General Leopoldo Galtieri, who succeeded him as President. It was Galtieri who decided to invade the Islas Malvinas/Falkland Islands on April 2, 1982. His desperate gambit briefly united the country behind the PRN, as a wave of nationalist enthusiasm temporarily drowned out criticism. However, Galtieri had miscalculated badly, first by assuming that the United States would support Argentina rather than the United Kingdom; and second, in thinking that Margaret Thatcher would simply cede the islands. Thatcher's decision to send a fleet to retake the Malvinas/Falklands sealed the PRN's fate. The actual conflict was short, lasting less than three months. With the Argentine military suffering a humiliating defeat, the last vestiges of the regime's authority evaporated (Lorenz, 2012). The focus shifted dramatically, as the Armed Forces attempted to set the terms for the transfer of power to a civilian administration. Although nearly all the *Proceso*'s most ambitious objectives remained unmet, the counter-revolutionary campaign had "succeeded" insofar as the violence unleashed against the Argentine Left eliminated the viability of armed struggle and effectively broke a generation of militancy and activism (Sidicaro, 1996). It would be nearly two decades before the Left managed to reconstitute itself.

Redemocratization, Memory, and Human Rights

The Alfonsín Presidency

The final year of the dictatorship witnessed fierce negotiations between a regime devoid of authority, a resurgent political front, and a renewed labor movement. The first presidential elections in ten years were held on October 30, 1983.

Since 1946, only the Peronist Party had won free elections, but 1983 produced a shock as Raúl Alfonsín, the Radical Party candidate, triumphed with nearly 52% of the vote.[16] Over objections from the military, the Alfonsín administration launched an investigation into human rights violations during the PRN, empowering the National Commission on Disappeared Persons (CONADEP, Comisión Nacional sobre la Desaparición de Personas) five days after taking office. For ten months, the Commission collected testimonies and evidence from thousands of people before issuing a final report, which came to be known as the *Nunca Más* ("Never Again") Report. *Nunca Más* detailed the crimes committed by the security forces and set the number of verifiable casualties (meaning killed and disappeared) at nearly 9,000, though the report cautioned that many more cases could not be confirmed (Crenzel, 2008).

Nunca Más became the basis for judicial proceedings against high-ranking military officers, including Videla, Massera, and Agosti, in the mid-1980s. The Alfonsín government prosecuted and convicted the members of the different juntas that had exercised power during the PRN. The so-called "Judgment of the Juntas" proved to be a judicial landmark: it was the first time that the members of a dictatorship were compelled to appear before the civil authorities of their own nation and tried for their crimes. The *Nunca Más* Report and the television broadcast of the court proceedings obliged many Argentines who had attempted to ignore or deny the PRN's repression to confront the scope of its violence (Lira & Morales, 2005). By the start of 1986, when the Supreme Court upheld the convictions, it seemed that Argentina was on the road to recovery.

However, the final years of Alfonsín's presidency belied this optimism. Even before the trial of the leaders of the *Proceso* had ended, the problem of what to do with the thousands of soldiers of different ranks who had participated in the detention, torture, disappearance, and murder of their fellow citizens risked fracturing the still-fragile nation. The possibility of expanding judicial proceedings to include mid-level and low-ranking officers and soldiers provoked a series of barracks uprisings in 1987, 1988, and 1990. The new commanders of the Armed Forces, meanwhile, warned the government that continuing the trials down the ranks would be, in their view, unacceptable. Few missed the threat implicit in the military's position (Pion-Berlin, 1991). The government was forced to accept two measures, the Full Stop Law (which established a fixed date after which new prosecutions could not be opened) and the Law of Due Obedience (which protected lower-ranking officers from prosecution on the grounds that they had been following orders) (Engstrom & Pereira, 2012).

Under different conditions, the Alfonsín government might have been able to assert itself and continue its work, but the country faced a difficult conjuncture. Even after 1983, the loans made by the IMF to the dictatorship in the 1970s continued to weigh heavily on the Argentine economy and created conditions for the imposition of austerity measures. During this period, we encounter the origins of what David Harvey has described as "vulture capitalism," an "unholy alliance between state powers and the predatory aspects of finance capital forms…that is as much about cannibalistic practices and forced devaluations as it is about achieving harmonious global development" (Harvey, 2003, p. 136). By the late 1980s, Argentina found itself in the middle of a catastrophic hyperinflation crisis which eventually sparked popular riots. Meanwhile, the Peronist labor unions adopted an increasingly confrontational stance toward the Radical administration, hamstringing much of its agenda with a series of general strikes (Teunissen & Akkerman, 2003). This combination of factors effectively ended Alfonsín's efforts to carry forward justice work against members of the PRN.

The Menem Years

Circumstances had prevented Alfonsín from accomplishing all he hoped in the arena of human rights; his successor, Carlos Menem, rapidly rolled back whatever progress had been made during the 1980s. The country's economic and social turmoil obliged Alfonsín to transfer power to President-elect Menem several months before the scheduled transition. Menem, who won the 1989 elections for the Peronist Party, wasted little time pushing an ambitious strategy to transform Argentina. This included two rounds of *indultos* (pardons) issued in 1989 and 1990 that released the members of the different juntas from prison and allowed them to return to private life. These pardons also covered several leftist guerrillas convicted of crimes committed during the 1970s (Langan, 1991; Pion-Berlin, 1994). The government argued that violence had been used by both sides and that the country needed to move past the dictatorship period in order to heal. The so-called "theory of the two demons" (*teoría de los dos demonios*) equated the repression of the military state with the terrorism of armed leftist organizations and assigned blame to both sides for the horrors of the 1970s and 1980s.[17] The idea of reconciliation became associated with Menem's efforts to minimize the atrocities of the PRN era and, per his explanation, find a path forward. Although human rights groups continued their fight throughout the 1990s, they found few allies within the Menem administration and consequently faced an uphill battle for recognition and relevance.

The Menem government also proved willing to abandon Peronist orthodoxy on the economic front. Despite Peronism's history of protectionism and defense of working-class interests, Menem almost immediately began aggressive privatization of Argentina's largest state enterprises. Between 1989 and 1992, the administration sold off the national telecommunications company (1990); the national airline (1991); the national gas utility (1991–1992); the electric utilities for the city of Buenos Aires (1992); the railroads (1993); and deregulated the oil industry (1991–1993) (Calvert, 1996; Goldstein, 1998). These privatizations responded to a confluence of factors, including the state's desperate need for steady capital to combat the ongoing financial crisis and a general move away from the mid-century developmentalist philosophies that had dominated until the 1970s. On the one hand, Menem's policies provided short-term benefits. Inflation fell sharply, prices stabilized, and capital accumulation seemed to recover by the middle of the 1990s. With support from the World Bank and the IMF, Argentina appeared to have corrected course. On the other hand, this success came at a steep price. By the late 1990s, nearly 20% of the economically active population was unemployed and some 42% of Argentines lived at or below the poverty level (Montes Cató, 2004). The so-called "Plan Cavallo," after Menem's Minister of Economy Domingo Cavallo, deregulated currency exchanges and lowered trade barriers, flooding Argentina with cheap imports and setting the conditions for capital flight (Cooney, 2007, p. 24). Thus, despite the popular narrative, the country's recovery was far more tenuous than most admitted, and the potential for disaster lurked just below the surface.

Kirchnerismo

That disaster struck at the end of 2001. Much of Argentina's "success" during the Menem years had been fueled by easy credit, artificially inflated currency, and large loans from international finance organizations and private financiers. A severe recession hit Argentina starting in 1998, and by late 2001, the country faced a dire economic outlook. A decision by the IMF to cut off further funding prompted a mass exodus of capital which the government proved unable to control. Consumer confidence in the existing system evaporated within days, and in the chaotic aftermath, both President Fernando de la Rúa and his interim successor Adolfo Rodríguez Saá were forced to resign (Cortés Conde, 2003; Goddard, 2006). Popular disgust with the entire political and economic system crystallized in the chant "Que se vayan todos!" ("Get rid of them all!").

The power vacuum that followed the 2001 crisis—the largest sovereign debt default in history—left Argentina directionless at the beginning of the new millennium. Presidential elections were scheduled for 2003 and an interim president was appointed to oversee the transition. The 2003 elections featured a broad slate of candidates, including Carlos Menem, who actually won a plurality in the first round of balloting. However, he did not reach the threshold necessary to avoid a runoff, and during the following months, it became apparent that Argentine society was coalescing behind his challenger, Néstor Kirchner, who had placed second in the initial vote. Prior to the runoff, Menem chose to withdraw instead of face defeat, leaving Kirchner as president-elect (Sanches, 2005). He had received just 22.2% of the popular vote.

From this inauspicious beginning, Kirchner proved himself an exceptionally capable politician. Over the next four years, he built up an alliance of Peronists, human rights activists, leftists, and elements of the center-left. This *Frente para la Victoria* (Front for Victory, FpV), Kirchner's electoral coalition, endured through the 2003 election and became the foundation for a powerful political movement. A central plank of Kirchner's strategy involved challenging the country's dependence on international finance organizations. In 2005, his government spearheaded efforts to renegotiate Argentina's debts from the 2001 collapse. Although he persuaded most foreign holders of this debt to accept discounted payments, some 9% of creditors refused to negotiate and demanded full repayment. These "holdouts" created significant problems for Argentina vis-a-vis the global financial system, complicating the country's access to credit, but they also gave Kirchner a perfect target for popular frustration (Guzman & Stiglitz, 2006). Most of the holdouts were hedge funds in the United States, and Kirchner used the opportunity to employ a fiercely nationalist rhetoric that criticized not only the debt holders, but also the IMF and the World Bank. Maristella Noemí Svampa has argued that this approach allowed the Kirchner administration to consolidate a sort of "middle-class" populism that built bridges between Peronism's traditionally working-class supporters and the urban middle classes, who tended to belong to more diverse (but largely center-left and left) political parties (Svampa, 2013).

Kirchnerismo's other main policy pillar was its commitment to human rights and justice work. Within months of his inauguration, the FpV alliance in Congress had struck down the Alfonsín-era Full Stop Law and the Law of Due Obedience, opening the door to renewed prosecution of crimes committed during the *Proceso*. During the next four years, Kirchner appointed human rights activists to prominent positions in his administration and gave strong government backing to various related projects.[18] This included, most notably, pursuing legal cases against hundreds of people who had participated in state terrorism during the 1970s and 1980s.

Néstor was not alone in this effort. His wife, Cristina Fernández de Kirchner, served as Senator from their home province of Santa Cruz from 2001 to 2005, before being elected to the Senate as a representative of Buenos Aires province in 2005 and served until 2007. In 2007, she ran for President at the head of the FpV and won handily, nearly doubling the second-place candidate. Cristina continued many of Néstor's policies, including the commitment to the political cause of human rights. Alliances with groups like the Madres de la Plaza de Mayo, the Abuelas de la Plaza de Mayo, and H.I.J.O.S. (Hijos e Hijas por la Identidad y la Justicia contra el Olvido y el Silencio; Sons and Daughters for Identity and Justice against Forgetting and Silence) solidified the association between particular notions of justice work and *kirchnerismo* as a political movement (Barros, 2012). Many suspected that the Kirchners' plan was to alternate at the top of the ticket, in order to circumvent Argentina's term limits. However, Néstor's unexpected death in 2010 threw the FpV into confusion. Ultimately, Cristina decided to run again in 2011 and, with the support of the country's powerful trade unions and prominent human rights organizations, won handily with more than 54% of the vote.

During her second term, however, the FpV coalition began to show cracks. Forces on the political left of this alliance ran into resistance from institutionalized centers of power, such as employers and even Peronist trade unions, who began to push back against some of the administration's economic measures. Following the *Kirchnerista* line, Cristina railed against the holdouts in the United States who continued to demand full repayment, labeling them "vulture funds" (*fondos buitres*) after their practice of cannibalizing the debt of foreign nations. A broader economic slowdown created additional difficulties, and despite the Ministry of Economy's efforts to control inflation, prices rose steadily after 2012. Although Cristina's government attempted to set exchange rates for the peso vis-à-vis the dollar, demand so outstripped supply that a black market for dollars flourished throughout her second term (Bercovich & Rebossio, 2013). This parallel economy undercut the administration's efforts to spur growth and contributed to a general distrust, both domestic and international, of the Ministry of Economy's data related to the health of the national economy. Argentines increasingly displayed their frustrations around financial uncertainties and social problems. By 2015, Cristina—prohibited from running for president for a third successive term—and the Frente para la Victoria appeared weak and fractured.

The Right Turn

The 2015 elections saw the candidate of the Frente para la Victoria, former Vice President and then-Governor of Buenos Aires Province Daniel Scioli, lose in a runoff to Mauricio Macri, the candidate of the center-right alliance "Cambiemos" ("Let's Change"). Similar to past political transformations during the twentieth century, this transition from center-left to center-right was not an isolated moment within Argentina, but rather part of a broader trend across Latin America that saw the "Pink Wave" of the mid-2000s roll back before conservative reactionism (Cannon, 2016; Santos & Guarnieri, 2016). If the parliamentary coup against Brazilian President Dilma Rousseff and subsequent election of Jair Bolsonaro marked the high-water mark of this right turn, Macri's 2015 ascendancy in Argentina was nonetheless a significant development within this larger regional shift. The heir to a massive commercial and industrial empire, known as the Grupo Macri, Mauricio Macri represented much of what Carlos Menem had promoted during the 1990s: free enterprise, finance capitalism, and the desire to put the dictatorship—and the associated justice work—squarely in the past. This was, at least in part, personal for Macri: his father, Francesco Macri, had steered the company through the 1970s and 1980s and was among those private citizens who benefitted the most from the PRN's economic policies, as the Grupo Macri grew considerably during the dictatorship ("Los Macri y sus negocios," 2015).[19] Promising a return to "normality" following eight years of Kirchnerist rule, Macri sought to reintegrate Argentina into the global economic network by agreeing to negotiate with the "vultures" who held the country's debt (Guzman & Stiglitz, 2006). This enraged his critics on the left, but Macri's political and economic stances reflected the longer history of Argentine conservatism, especially the general disgust with and distrust of Peronism, which had been the driving forces behind the Frente para la Victoria.

After the 2015 elections, the Macri government made little effort to hide its lack of support for the human rights movements. March 24, which became a national holiday under Néstor Kirchner in 2006, remained a day of popular mobilizations and protest, but the government no longer participated. Between 2016 and 2019, no official representative addressed the march—as both Néstor and Cristina had done each year since 2004. Moreover, Macri himself publicly called into question the number of disappeared and dead under the PRN, refusing to accept the figure of 30,000 that most human rights organizations believe to be an accurate total (Goñi, 2016). The 40th anniversary of the coup in 2016 brought hundreds of thousands to the Plaza de Mayo in Buenos Aires in defense of the human rights and justice work begun during the Kirchner administrations and in repudiation of the seemingly reactive policies of the Macri government.

The overlap(s) between acknowledging past events and reinvesting them with contemporary meaning was one of the principal factors that inspired our current project and provides a foundation for the subsequent chapters. The above historical background will intersect with the specific contexts in Chapters 3, 4, and 5 to frame our readings of the diverse texts and experiences encountered during and around the 40th anniversary of March 24, 1976.

Notes

1 Braden's pro-business political stance usually reflected his own economic interests, as a partial owner of copper mining concerns in Chile, a shareholder in the United Fruit Company in Central America, and an agent of Standard Oil in Bolivia (Bosoer, 2011).
2 Braden later resurfaced as a paid lobbyist for the United Fruit Company at the end of the 1940s and was a key organizer in the U.S.-backed coup d'état against Jacobo Arbenz in Guatemala in 1954 (Bosoer, 2011). This is relevant to the anti-U.S. sentiment that we observed in Buenos Aires on and around the 40th anniversary of the March 24 coup.
3 The United States and Argentina were competing with respect to Argentina's principal exports, grains and beef. For the United States, ensuring that their allies and defeated foes purchased these commodities from U.S. producers was a key component of their post-war economic strategy (Dorn, 1999).
4 This incident, during which the Aramburu regime authorized the summary execution of 29 military and civilian personnel, was later used as justification by the leftist guerrilla organization the Montoneros for the trial and execution of Aramburu in 1970.
5 In this chapter, the use of the word "liberal" reflects the definition accepted outside of the United States, namely supporting free-market reforms, deregulation, and limited government intervention in the economy.
6 This cooperation incensed both leftist workers and many who remained loyal to the exiled Perón and would directly contribute to the founding of a combative labor confederation, the CGT de los Argentinos, in May 1968 (James, 1988).
7 This pre-*Proceso* violence figures into our discussion in Chapter 4 of the assassination of Fr. Carlos Mugica in 1974. Mugica's image appeared in a large poster on a wall in the Church of Santa Cruz, one of the three sites of our fieldwork. This violence also

figures into Chapter 5 when we consider the memory work of artist Nicolás Arrúe, whose father was disappeared in 1975 before the coup.
8 This perception that the state had "lost control" was used on the Right to justify direct military intervention, up to and including a coup. However, violence perpetrated by right-wing death squads, often with the tacit or open support of elements of the Peronist government, far outstripped violence committed by leftists. Thus, if we accept that the state had lost control over the legitimate exercise of violence, it was more likely surrendered to paramilitary and extra-legal organizations on the Right than taken by force by groups on the Left.
9 "30 de marzo: Discurso pronunciado al asumir la Primera Magistratura de la República Argentina, exponiendo al Pueblo de la Nación los fundamentos del *Proceso* de Reorganización Nacional emprendido el 24 de marzo de 1976," (*Mensajes Presidenciales*, 1977, pp. 7–8).
10 One important exception is the archive of the Intelligence Division of the Police Department of Buenos Aires Province, known as the Archivo DIPPBA, which was given over to the Commission for Memory in La Plata, Buenos Aires Province, in 2005.
11 Hugo Alconada Mon, "El Ejército admitió 22.000 crímenes," *La Nación* (March 24, 2006).
12 Developmentalism is an economic theory that attempted to resolve the perceived "underdevelopment" of non-Global North countries through state support for internal markets and domestic industrialization. Developmentalism flourished in Latin America during the mid-20th century (Cardoso & Faletto, 1979).
13 Rodolfo Walsh, the leftist journalist and Montonero, famously attacked the IMF in his "Open Letter" to the Military Junta in 1977 (Walsh, 2007).
14 This does not mean that there were not major challenges to the authority of the military dictatorship. Two prime examples are the long-running conflict between Admiral Massera and General Videla, which lead to Massera's resignation in 1978 and his subsequent attempt to mount an electoral challenge against Videla; and an attempted palace coup against Videla led by Army hardliners in 1979, who were angry with what they saw as the regime's "concessions" on human rights in the face of international pressure (Canelo 2008; Novaro & Palermo, 2003).
15 From March 24, 1976 to December 10, 1983, the following people acted as head of state: Jorge Rafael Videla (March 29, 1976–March 29, 1981); Roberto Eduardo Viola (March 29, 1981–November 21, 1981); Horacio Tomás Liendo (November 21, 1981–December 11, 1981); Carlos Alberto Lacoste (December 11, 1981–December 22, 1981); Leopoldo Fortunato Galtieri (December 22, 1981–June 18, 1982); Alfredo Oscar Saint-Jean (June 18, 1982–July 1, 1982); Reynaldo Benito Bignone (July 1, 1982–December 10, 1983); Raúl Alfonsín (December 10, 1983–July 8, 1989).
16 The reasons for this victory are complex and go beyond the scope of this chapter. However, one critical factor was the circulation of rumors that Peronist labor and political leaders had made a deal with the military to effectively grant them amnesty for crimes committed over the previous eight years.
17 The "theory of the two demons" has since been widely criticized for drawing a false equivalency between the violence of the military state and the violence of leftist guerrillas, and mostly discarded (Franco, 2014).
18 Much of this work will be explored in more detail in the subsequent chapters.
19 We will revisit this question in more detail in Chapter 3.

References

Barros, M. (2012). Los derechos humanos, entre luchas y disputas. In M.S. Bonetto & F. Martínez (Eds.), *Política y desborde: Más allá de la democracia liberal*. Eduvim.
Bercovich, A. & Rebossio, A. (2013). *Estoy verde. Dólar. Una pasión argentina*. Aguilar.

Bosoer, F. (2011). *Braden o Perón: La historia oculta*. El Ateneo.
Brennan, J. (1994). *The labor wars in Córdoba, 1955–1976: Ideology, work, and labor politics in an Argentine industrial city*. Harvard University Press.
Calvert, P. (1996). Privatisation in Argentina. *Bulletin of Latin American Research, 15*(2).
Canelo, P. (2008). *El proceso en su laberinto: La interna militar de Videla a Bignone*. Prometeo Libros.
Cannon, B. (2016). *The right in Latin America: Elite power, hegemony, and the struggle for the state*. Routledge.
Cantón, D. & Jorrat, J.R. (1980). El voto peronista en 1973: Distribución, crecimiento marzo-setiembre y bases ocupacionales. *Desarrollo Económico, 20*(77), 71–92.
Carassai, S. (2014). *The Argentine silent majority: Middle classes, politics, violence, and memory in the seventies*. Duke University Press.
Cardoso, F.H. & Faletto, E. (1979). *Dependency and development in Latin America* (M. Mattingly Urquidi, Trans.). University of California Press.
Cichero, D. (2005). *Bombas sobre Buenos Aires. Gestación y desarrollo del bombardeo aéreo sobre Plaza de Mayo*. Vergara.
Cooney, P. (2007). Argentina's quarter century experiment with neoliberalism: From dictatorship to depression. *Revista de Economia Contemporânea, 11*(1), 7–37.
Cortés Conde, R. (2003). La crisis argentina de 2001–2002. *Cuadernos de economía, 40*(121), 762–767.
Crenzel, E. (2008). *Investigar el pasado. La CONADEP y la elaboración del Nunca Más*. Siglo XXI Editores.
Dorn, G. (1999). Bruce Plan and Marshall Plan: The United States's disguised intervention against Peronism in Argentina, 1947–1950. *The International History Review, 21*(2), 331–351.
Engstrom, P. & Pereira, G. (2012). From amnesty to accountability: The ebbs and flows in the search for justice in Argentina. In L. Payne & F. Lessa (Eds.), *Amnesty in The Age of Human Rights Accountability: Comparative and International Perspectives*. Cambridge University Press.
Feitlowitz, M. (1999). *A Lexicon of terror: Argentina and the legacies of torture*. Oxford University Press.
Franco, M. (2014). La 'teoría de los dos demonios', un símbolo de la posdictadura en la Argentina. *A Contracorriente, 11*(2), 22–52.
Gambini, H. (2008). *Historia del peronismo. La violencia (1956–1983)*. Javier Vergara Editor.
Gerchunoff, P. & Llach, L. (2010). *El ciclo de la ilusión y el desencanto: Un siglo de políticas económicas Argentinas* (2nd ed.). Emecé.
Germani, G. (1955). *Estructura social de la Argentina*. Raigal.
Gillespie, R. (1982). *Soldiers of Perón: Argentina's Montoneros*. Oxford University Press.
Goddard, V. (2006). "This is history": Nation and experience in times of crisis—Argentina 2001. *History and Anthropology, 17*(3), 267–286.
Goldstein, A. (1998). The politics and economics of privatization: The case of Argentina. *Canadian Journal of Latin American and Caribbean Studies, 23*(45).
Goñi, U. (2016, August 29). Blaming the victims: Dictatorship denial is on the rise in Argentina. *The Guardian*. https://www.theguardian.com/world/2016/aug/29/argentina-denial-dirty-war-genocide-mauricio-macri
Gutman, D. (2015). *Somos derechos y humanos. La batalla de la la dictadura y los medios contra el mundo y la reacción internacional frente a los desaparecidos*. Editorial Sudamericana.

Guzman, M. & Stiglitz, J. (2006, April 1). How hedge funds held Argentina for ransom. *The New York Times.* https://www.nytimes.com/2016/04/01/opinion/how-hedge-funds-held-argentina-for-ransom.html

Harvey, D. (2003). *The new imperialism.* Oxford University Press.

James, D. (1988). *Resistance and integration: Peronism and the Argentine working class, 1946–1976.* Cambridge University Press.

Jiménez, U. & Jiménez, J. (2018, April 4). Mendozazo: Cuando tembló el poder de los de arriba. *La izquierda diario.*

Juareche, A. (1983). *FORJA y la Década Infame.* A. Peña Lillo.

Langan, M. (1991). Argentine President Carlos Menem's first pardons: A comparative analysis of coverage by Buenos Aires' leading dailies. *Canadian Journal of Latin American and Caribbean Studies, 16*(31), 145–156.

Lewis, P. (2002). *Guerrillas and generals: The Dirty War in Argentina.* Praeger.

Lira, E. & Morales, G. (2005). *Derechos humanos y reparación. Una discusión pendiente.* LOM Ediciones.

Lorenz, F. (2012). *Las guerras por Malvinas, 1982–2012.* Editorial Edhasa.

Los Macri y sus negocios durante la dictadura Argentina. (2015, November 13). *Telesur.* https://www.telesurtv.net/news/Los-Macri-y-sus-negocios-durante-la-dictadura-argentina-20151112-0008.html

Luna, F. (1985). *Perón y su tiempo. II. La comunidad organizada.* Editorial Sudamericana.

Luna, F. (2012). *El 45: Crónica de un año decisivo* (2nd ed.). Editorial Sudamericana.

Mensajes Presidenciales: Proceso de Reorganización Nacional 24 de marzo de 1976, Tomo 1. (1977). Buenos Aires: Imprenta del Congreso de la Nación.

Montes Cató, J.S. (2004). The impact of labor flexibility on the Argentine telecommunications sector (R. Stoller, Trans.). *Latin American Perspectives, 31*(4), 32–44.

Morero, S., Eidelman, A. & Lichtman, G. (2002). *La noche de los bastones largos* (2nd ed.). Nuevohacer.

Munck, R., Falcón, R., & Galitelli, B. (1987). *Argentina: From anarchism to Peronism. Workers, Unions, and Politics, 1855–1985.* Zed Books Ltd.

Novaro, M. & Palermo, V. (2003). *La dictadura militar (1976–1983): Del golpe de estado a la restauración de la democracia.* Paidós.

Pion-Berlin, D. (1991). Between confrontation and accommodation: Military and government policy in democratic Argentina. *Journal of Latin American Studies, 23*(3), 543–571.

Pion-Berlin, D. (1994). To prosecute or to pardon? Human rights decisions in the Latin American Southern Cone. *Human Rights Quarterly, 16*(1), 105–130.

Potash, R. (1971). *El ejército y la política en la República Argentina (1928–1945).* Sudamericana.

Potash, R. (1980). *The army and politics in Argentina, 1945–1962.* Stanford University Press.

Ramírez, A.J. (2009, April 24). *Campos de protesta, acción colectiva y radicalización política. Un estudio sobre las pueblades de los setenta.* III Jornada Académica Partidos Armados en la Argentina de los Setenta, Universidad Nacional de San Martín.

Rock, D. (1987). *Argentina, 1516–1987: From Spanish colonization to Alfonsín* (2nd ed.). University of California Press.

Rubens, Í. (1974). *Historia del movimiento sindical* (Vol. 4). Editorial Ciencias del Hombre.

Sanches, O. (2005). Argentina's landmark 2003 presidential election: Renewal and continuity. *Bulletin of Latin American Research, 24*(4), 454–475.

Santos, F. & Guarnieri, F. (2016). From protest to parliamentary coup: An overview of Brazil's recent history. *Journal of Latin American Cultural Studies, 24*(4), 485–494.

Serra, J. (2008). *Fusilados: Historia de condenados a muerte en Argentina.* Sudamericana.
Sidicaro, R. (1996). El régimen autoritario de 1976: Refundación frustrada y contrarrevolución exitosa. In H. Quiroga & C. Tcach (Eds.), *A veinte años del golpe: Con memoria democrática.* Homo Sapiens Ediciones.
Svampa, M. (2013). La década Kirchnerista: Populismo, clases medias y revolución pasiva. *LASA Forum, 44*(4), 14–17.
Taylor, D. (1997). *Disappearing acts: Spectacles of gender and nationalism in Argentina's "Dirty War."* Duke University Press.
Teunissen, J.J. & Akkerman, A. (Eds.). (2003). *The crisis that was not prevented: Lessons for Argentina, the IMF, and globalisation.* FONDAD.
Torre, J.C. (2004). *El gigante invertebrado: Los sindicatos en el gobierno, Argentina 1973–1976.* Siglo XXI Editores.
Torre, J.C. (2005). *Diecisiete de Octubre de 1945.* Lumiere.
Walsh, R. (2007). Carta abierta de Rodolfo Walsh a la Junta Militar. *Veredas do Direito, 4*(8), 137–156.

3
LABORS OF JUSTICE AS RESISTANCE ACROSS TWO UNIVERSITY SITES

It is late afternoon Monday, March 21, 2016. We meet Fortunato Mallimaci, a noted sociologist and former dean (1998–2002) of the Facultad de Ciencias Sociales (CS) at the Universidad de Buenos Aires (UBA)[1]*, in a cafe across the street from the university entrance. He tells us there is little unity about the past, especially now in the aftermath of the election that has brought the center-right Macri government to power. President Macri will not attend the mass rally in the Plaza de Mayo later in the week that marks the memory of the victims of the military dictatorship. Many view the decision as a sharp repudiation of the previous Kirchner administrations, which had established March 24 as a day of remembrance and revived judicial proceedings against government figures who had perpetrated the policies of abduction, torture, and disappearance during the period of state terror. In such a situation, Mallimaci observes, there is anxiety about the past and a demand to reassert it as part of a politics in support of justice, accountability, and human rights. Mallimaci concludes our conversation by inviting us to attend a formal commemoration of the disappeared at the Facultad de Ciencias Sociales later that evening. Adolfo Pérez Esquivel, the 1980 Nobel Peace laureate, will speak. Representatives of the Madres de la Plaza will be honored. The disappeared students and faculty from CS will be remembered.*

Later, with evening approaching, we walk toward the CS building and see a young man scribbling notes on a card (Figure 3.1).[2] *He is leaning against a "New Movement Toward Socialism" poster. The poster calls on its readers to take to the streets on March 24th, the 40th anniversary of the coup, to protest against "the reactionary Macri government."*

The poster lists three demands: (a) Obama out of Argentina, (b) No to [the Macri administration's] repressive protocols, and (c) Not one peso to the venture capitalists. The demands refer to U.S. President Obama's planned visit to Buenos Aires

DOI: 10.4324/9781003184195-4

62 Labors of Justice as Resistance

on the 24th, the regulations limiting public protest that Macri's administration has enacted, and the agreements negotiated between the Macri administration and Argentina's private creditors, many of them U.S. "vulture capitalist" firms that bought up Argentina's debt after the 2001 default. Black spray-painted graffiti on a low wall nearby reinforces the sentiment, demanding, "Yankee get out of Latin America!"

We enter Ciencias Sociales and walk to the auditorium in which the evening commemoration is to occur. People have packed the lobby in front of the assembly hall. A long line has formed for coffee at the concession table. Posters and photographs of the disappeared cover the walls. Students operate tables with leaflets and placards. We walk into the auditorium and find open seats. A presenter on stage declares the opening of the ceremony and then welcomes the honored guests—the members of the Madres, representatives of the families of the Faculty's disappeared, and Esquivel. The presentations begin and speeches are made. Family members of the disappeared receive commemorative gifts.

Esquivel then stands to speak. He talks briefly, emphasizing the need to preserve the memory of the period of state terror, especially for those born after 1983. There is energy, he says, a desire among the youth to know and to resist efforts to elide those memories. He notes the necessity of placing what has happened in Argentina within the context of U.S. policy in Latin America. The United States has a long history of intervening in the domestic affairs of countries across the region; and from the 1960s through the 1980s, the U.S. military trained armed forces in Central America, Brazil, and the Southern Cone in the practices of torture and supported the military regimes that seized power during that period.[3]

Following Esquivel's comments, several members of Las Madres walk on stage to receive commemorative awards and certificates. The women take the microphone. They urge the audience to never forget the disappeared and to resist the Macri government's efforts to minimize the number of victims. They then lead the gathered attendees in the chant, "Presente, Ahora y siempre!"

The connections at Ciencias Sociales between commemorations of the period of state terror and calls to oppose the Macri government underscore the key theme of *justice as resistance* that emerged in our engagement with two University of Buenos Aires sites in March 2016. These sites were the Ciencias Sociales (CS) and the Facultad de Filosofía y Letras (Filo). Our primary aim was to document the commemorative literacies as expressed in the visual texts—signs and posters—at these public institutions leading up to the events at the Plaza de Mayo on March 24. We view these signs and posters to be *liturgical texts*, drawing from the Greek root, *leitourgia*, or "work of the people." Liturgy involves practices that invoke and enact shared ideals and narratives that help comprise "the sacred," a sense "of things set apart and forbidden" or "things deemed special" and in relation to the ways a moral community forms (Durkheim 1995 [1912]; Taves, 2009). While the Ciencias Sociales and Filo spaces are distinct, we jointly consider them in this chapter rather than treat each site separately. We made this decision primarily because the visual texts at both sites were strikingly similar in their critiques of recently elected Argentine President Mauricio Macri and of U.S. President Barack Obama. We were also more interested in visual texts with this macro-level—national, transnational, or global—focus than those with a local emphasis specific to either UBA institution. This decision aligned with our broader goal, as well, to identify and examine the interplay of narratives across the three main sites of this book project: the UBA, the Santa Cruz Church, and the ex-ESMA. Alongside our focus on visual texts, we spoke with faculty and, in the case of Ciencias Sociales, attended planned commemorative events. These activities complemented and enriched our analyses of the visual texts.

In this chapter, we first consider the historical context of these university sites, located both on the left of the political spectrum with established and spirited traditions of student activism. We then attend to a specific set of emblematic texts at the UBA. Before proceeding, however, an essential proviso is in order. Both UBA sites were densely populated with hundreds of visual texts. Although we attempted to capture the polyvocal complexity at each site through our 500+ photos of these texts, we make no claims that our analysis engages all of this complexity. Researchers with other interests and questions would generate different interpretations and findings.

Our analysis across the two university sites reveals how commemorative literacies mobilized memory of the past for particular present-day purposes that reflected an articulation of justice labor as *resistance*. We define resistance as a deliberate act of non-compliance with, or non-acceptance of, something or an equally deliberate attempt to thwart or counteract an action or state of affairs. In our analysis, we discerned two primary overlapping themes that expressed an articulation of justice as resistance. The first theme involved resistance to state-level repression that linked the Macri government to the 1976 coup and impunity for the junta's military leaders. The second theme emphasized resistance to unjust economic policies and programs, both domestic and transnational. These two themes moved between the past and present in different ways, as the signs and posters worked across the time of state terror (1976–1983) and other intervening historical events leading up to the 2016 commemorations. Put another way, the students at each university site accessed the Argentine societal memory chest for the albums, scripts, and lore related to state tactics of repression and impunity for military leaders tied to the 1976 coup, as well as material related to adverse effects of economic policy in the aftermath of the 2001–2002 economic crisis. Further, they understood this material in relation to the ways universities in Argentina have long been a site of protest in the country, as the next section highlights. The commemorative literacies and labor of justice as resistance also had transnational resonances of solidarity with Syrian refugees and Palestinians, linking the remembrance of the Argentine period of state terror with justice struggles elsewhere.

Historical Background of UBA

Argentina's university system dates to the colonial era and the founding of the Universidad de Córdoba in 1613. The university, among the oldest in the Americas, operated for nearly two centuries, first under the Jesuits and later run by the Franciscans, as the Viceroyalty of the Río de La Plata's only such institute. The independence movements of the early 1800s coincided with new attitudes toward higher education that questioned its religious character and looked to Europe for guidance on how to establish a "modern" university. The Universidad de Buenos Aires (UBA), established via decree on August 9, 1821, was intended to follow this example and implement a new educational system. The UBA quickly became the focal point for national debates around the mission, structure, and governance of the university in Argentina. From the mid-nineteenth century, aspects of the UBA's internal administration slowly evolved, including the advent of faculty councils (known as "facultades") charged with overseeing the admissions policies, plans of study, evaluations, and daily operations of the university.[4] Almost from the start, different authorities within and outside of the system competed for this control.

The waves of mass immigration from Europe at the end of the 1800s exacerbated these tensions and raised questions about higher education's role in Argentine society.[5] In 1896, partly in response to these debates over the university's purpose, the High Council of the University of Buenos Aires inaugurated the Facultad de Filosofía y Letras (Faculty of Philosophy and Letters), commonly known as "Filo." The following year, the National University of La Plata (UNLP) came into existence, imagined as a model for the future expansion of the higher education system ("Historia de la Universidad de la Plata," 2019). This period also witnessed a sharp rise in student activism, as an increasingly diverse (within the broader limitations of the middle and upper-middle classes) population argued for greater student involvement in the administration of the universities. In 1906, the national government responded by passing a reform package that revoked lifetime tenure for members of the faculty councils and restructured evaluative procedures, among other measures (Buchbinder, 2005). While the 1906 reforms overhauled operations at the UBA and the UNLP, the University of Córdoba—an older and far more conservative institution—resisted changes. Students fought back against this reticence, and in 1918, the reformist President Hipólito Yrigoyen intervened the University of Córdoba and forced through a set of new policies—the University Reforms of 1918. These gave the students a more powerful political voice and ensured their place alongside the faculty councils (Buchbinder, 2005). Their critique of the previous structure reflected discontent with the elite approach to the university and promoted a more democratic—yet still undeniably professional—vision.

During the next 25 years, the country's three universities (UBA, UNLP, and Córdoba) largely maintained their autonomy despite the heated political climate and undemocratic governments of the Década Infame.[6] The GOU's seizure of power in 1943, and the Peronist regime that followed, marked a new era. As largely middle- and upper-middle-class spaces, the universities strongly opposed Peronism's populist message, especially the extension of social citizenship rights to the lower and working classes. Perón, in turn, viewed the UBA, the UNLP, and the University of Córdoba as hostile, and after he won the 1946 election, numerous professors were fired or resigned their positions. Infamously, Argentina's most celebrated intellectual Jorge Luis Borges, who had opposed Peronism prior to 1946, was removed from his post at the Miguel Cané library and named inspector of poultry and rabbits at the municipal market of Buenos Aires.[7] Even as Peronism transformed much of Argentine society during the 1940s and 1950s, the universities remained distinctly anti-Peronist spaces. The new government repealed many of the key aspects of the 1918 University Reforms, increasing state control at the expense of university autonomy. Students and faculty largely disapproved of Peronism's perceived "revolutionary" tactics, instead reaffirming their commitment to the reformist (or conservative, from the Peronist perspective) attitudes that characterized higher education from the end of the nineteenth century.

The 1955 coup that inaugurated the *Revolución Libertadora* once again dramatically altered the path of Argentina's universities. Despite Peronism's policies toward higher education, the UBA, the UNLP, and the University of Córdoba had grown dramatically over the previous decade, from less than 52,000 students in 1947 to approximately 140,000 in 1955 (Buchbinder, 2005).[8] This massive influx of students once again raised the question of what the universities' mission should be. From 1955 to 1966, military and civilian administrations attempted to "de-Peronize" higher education, removing faculty with ties to or sympathy toward the previous government, with some initial success.[9] In December 1955, Decree 6,403 restored and expanded university autonomy, giving much of the decision-making power back to the faculty councils (Buchbinder, 2005). The same decree also permitted the establishment of the first private universities, which opened the door to the return of Catholic universities after a long prohibition. Meanwhile, the total population of students continued to grow rapidly as interest in higher education increased, further stressing the system's existing capacity. This moment of relative optimism, marked by the restoration of autonomy and renewed commitment to the university mission, was cut short by the 1966 coup d'état. The transformation of the global political context over the previous decade—notably the 1959 Cuban Revolution—caused the new military regime to take an aggressive approach toward the universities, authorizing their intervention soon after the coup. Those universities that resisted—including the UBA—suffered fierce repression as troops were dispatched to remove students and faculty who had occupied various buildings, in the so-called "Night of the Long Batons."

The concerns of the military regime were not necessarily misplaced. The massification of the university system had meant the ingress of tens of thousands of new students, many of whom did not share the traditionalist ideas of the early twentieth century. By the late 1960s, again in concert with global trends, Argentina's universities had become increasingly radicalized and, in a somewhat paradoxical twist, affinity between students and a particular brand of leftist Peronism grew precipitously. The return of democracy (and Peronism) in 1973 brought what would have been unthinkable just two decades earlier: a favorable university reception, as the new government claimed its mission would be to put the universities "at the service of the people" (*Mensaje del presidente*, 1973). However, this attitude would last only until the death of Perón in July 1974, after which rightist elements seized power. In October 1974, the government intervened the universities once again, expelling leftists and suspected subversives. This would preview the repression that followed the 1976 coup. The dictatorship severely persecuted students and faculty, both through legal measures like Law 21,276 (which placed all universities under control of the Executive) and through extralegal means including arrests, disappearances, and murder (Buchbinder, 2005; Rodríguez & Soprano, 2009). The regime slashed the university budget, with specific majors most associated with "subversion"—including psychology, sociology, and anthropology—as special targets.[10] Intellectualism itself became a threat to the military's reactionary cosmovision (Feitlowitz, 1999). Nevertheless, despite the PRN's violence, the university population continued to rise, topping 400,000 by 1983. These years also saw a sharp rise in the number of students enrolled at private universities, although they remained the minority.

The consequences of the restoration of democracy in the 1980s for Argentina's universities were not immediately clear. On the one hand, the Alfonsín government reintroduced statutes that had been suspended since 1966 promoting university autonomy and student participation in governance. On the other hand, extreme economic and political instability defined the post-dictatorship decade, throwing doubt on the solvency of the university system. The mid-1980s also witnessed another massive surge in student population, which reached 700,000 by 1987 (Buchbinder, 2005). The following year, the UBA inaugurated the Facultad de Ciencias Sociales. By the 1990s, and the Menem administration's large-scale privatization combined with student population growth and budgetary uncertainty called into question the very foundations of higher education. However, in 1995, the government passed Law 24,521, which established new parameters for all institutes of higher education, authorized each university to determine its own specific standards and statutes, recognized university autonomy, and reaffirmed the state's fundamental responsibility in supporting higher education ("Ley No 24.521," 1995). Since the mid-1990s, university autonomy and the student body's centrality in daily governance have been regularly reaffirmed through political participation and mobilizations. These have taken the form of mass demonstrations, posterings, strikes, and other direct actions in response to both internal and external conflicts and demands.

While three key groups of stakeholders—students, faculty, and alumni are responsible for shaping and directing institutional policy and university life, most germane for our purposes here is that students retained primary responsibility for the visual texts that adorned the hallways and classrooms.[11] As Nicolás Sillitti, who spent 12 years at Filo as a student and instructor, explained: "Without some foothold with the students, something that you hung up on the walls wouldn't last more than five minutes" (2019).[12] The dominant political orientation among students at both Ciencias Sociales and Filo is strongly left-leaning and is frequently framed through firm commitments to social and economic justice.

Justice as Resistance at UBA

Our analysis of visual texts across the two university spaces revealed two overlapping themes that underpinned the broader articulation of justice work as resistance: 1) resistance to state repression and impunity of military leaders and 2) resistance to unpopular economic policies tied to Argentina's dependence on transnational capital, namely the International Monetary Fund (IMF). These two themes moved between the past and present in different ways, as the texts worked from the period of state terror (1976–1983); encompassed intervening historical events from the 1990s and 2000s; and culminated in critiques related to the present moment, just prior to the March 2016 commemorations.

State Repression and Impunity from 1976 Coup to 2016

Critique of Macri and the policies of his center-right government were central to the justice work as resistance at these two sites. A slim margin of the Argentine voting public elected Macri in the November 22, 2015 run-off. His inauguration took place 18 days later. By March 2016, the new government had implemented a series of measures that had provoked strong reactions from Macri's critics.

At the UBA, sometimes the critique of Macri remained general, naming no specific injustices. Figure 3.2, for example, called people to the streets (a las calles!) on March 24 (24/03) at 3:00 pm at the Argentine National Congress (15HS Congreso) to protest Macri's reactionary government (gobierno reaccionario de Macri!). The sponsor of this poster—Nuevo Mas (Movimiento Al Socialismo)—was the same organization that sponsored the poster (Figure 3.1) discussed at the start of this chapter (the two texts used nearly identical language).

Other visual texts linked Macri to more specific injustices. Figure 3.3, for example, emphasized women's rights and gender equality. The March 8 date (8/3) refers to a major women's strike that commemorated International Women's Day in Argentina two weeks earlier with the text stating "thousands of us women

FIGURE 3.1 Critical of Macri government

stood against Macri" (Miles de mujeres nos plantamos contra Macri). March 8 has since continued to be an occasion for protest against Macri's economic policies, which activists connect to rising domestic violence as state support for social programs benefiting middle- and working-class families declined. The visual text in Figure 3.3 called for abortion rights, making abortions free, legal, and safe (libre, legal, seguro y gratuito); the end of violence against women and femi-nicide; and an end to the sex trade and sexual exploitation. (In late December, 2020, Argentina's Senate approved a bill to legalize abortion, a historic victory for abortion rights advocates.)

More often, visual texts indexed specific measures taken by the Macri government. Among them, a new set of rules about use of public space—collectively referred to as "Security Protocols"—established new guidelines for police responses to street mobilizations. Security forces were given wide leeway to use force to dislodge protesters, while punishments for unsanctioned demonstrations included up to two years in prison for "impeding, obstructing or disturbing the normal development of land, water or air transportation or public services of communication, water supply, electricity or energetic substances" ("Sin capuchas, ni palos," 2016; "Limitación del derecho a la protesta," 2016; "Argentina: President Macri Orders Crackdown on Protests," 2016; Castilla, 2016). These punishments

Labors of Justice as Resistance **69**

FIGURE 3.2 To the streets to protest the government!

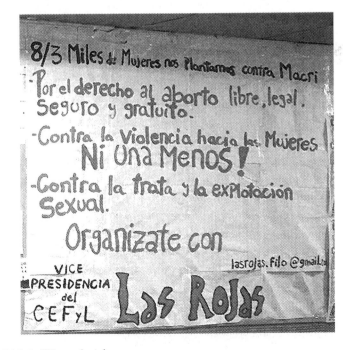

FIGURE 3.3 Women's rights

70 Labors of Justice as Resistance

FIGURE 3.4 Critical of vultures, Obama, repressive protocols

effectively criminalized protest by providing a legal justification for the use of security personnel to forcibly remove people who were blocking the streets.[13] The protocols also imposed restrictions on journalists covering protests. The third and fourth lines ("No al protocolo represivo!" [No to the repressive protocols!]) in the poster (Figure 3.4) highlight concerns about these measures.

The visual texts in the UBA spaces also suggested an intersection of past and recent concerns about impunity for those involved in state-sponsored repression. These concerns invoked historical accounts of repression during the coup and connected them to more recent cases of state officials not being held accountable for similar offenses.

The large banner (Figure 3.5), for example, declared, "Let's march with EMVyJ against the impunity of yesterday and today!" EMVyJ stands for Encuentro Memoria, Verdad y Justicia, a coordinating body that brings together a range of human rights organizations, women's groups, student groups, labor unions, and other similarly aligned movements. The Frente de Izquierda (Front of the Left) and Izquierda Socialista (Socialist Left) signed this poster.

The EMVyJ formed in 1996 to mobilize civil society for the commemoration of the 20th anniversary of the start of the period of state terror. The organization has since continued to take political stands in defense of human rights and

Labors of Justice as Resistance **71**

FIGURE 3.5 March against Obama and impunity

against the failure to investigate and bring to justice the perpetrators of a long list of assassinations, abductions, and bombings, including those that occurred during the 1976–1983 dictatorship as well as those that have taken place since the return to democracy.[14]

The group's publications and the text in Figure 3.5 reference impunity and recall President Raul Alfonsín's 1986 enactment of the controversial *Ley de Punto Final* that curtailed investigations and prosecutions of those accused of acts of repression during the most recent dictatorship. The *Ley de Obediencia Debida*, passed a year later, exempted all military personnel except top commanders from legal punishment for crimes carried out during the period of state terror because they were just obeying orders from their superiors. In 1990, then-President Carlos Menem, Alfonsín's successor, issued a blanket pardon that freed military officials who had been tried and convicted under Alfonsín's presidency prior to 1986. After 2003, the Kirchner governments subsequently reversed these pardons, reinstituting the process of accountability for the abuses of the regime.

Macri's election raised fears of a return to the policy of pardons and suspended investigations. EMVyJ took direct aim at Macri, decrying his government's negative impact on the cause of justice. The student call to march in solidarity with EMVyJ translates this critique into a call to resist through direct action

FIGURE 3.6 Neither forget nor forgive

(i.e., through participation in the march on the Plaza de Mayo during the March 24 commemoration). The addition of "Fuera Obama" (Obama out!) highlighted their opposition to U.S. support for Macri's government and its policies.

Texts at the UBA also linked impunity concerns to the more recent past. The image in Figure 3.6 features a blank face on a head with a cap (bottom right).

The featureless face appears between two question marks. Beneath the image is the caption, "10 años sin Lopez" (ten years without Lopez). The reference is to Jorge Julio López, a bricklayer who was abducted in October 1976 and imprisoned and tortured until June 1979. Lopez was kidnapped while testifying against the former Director of Investigations of the Buenos Aires Provincial Police Miguel Etchecolatz in 2006 (during Nestor Kirchner's presidency). The Etchecolatz trial was the first to occur after the Kirchner administration overturned the Full Stop Law. Just hours before his final testimony, López was disappeared. The subsequent investigations were faulted for shoddy methods and follow-up. The case remained unsolved and had become a symbol of a return of impunity.

The case of López was also complicated because it occurred while the Kirchners occupied the presidency. Compared to previous administrations, the

Kirchners provided more public support and resources for human-rights organizations and efforts of groups like Las Madres. The Kirchners also reopened legal proceedings against former junta leaders to bring them to justice. Yet, the Kirchners were not beyond criticism, especially from left-leaning voices at the UBA who consistently questioned governmental involvement, ineptitude, or potential corruption with cases like that of Lòpez.

Figure 3.7 reflected more recent concerns about impunity. This mass-produced visual text included the headline "Against the impunity of yesterday and today" and the line "Cárcel común y efectiva a Pedraza" (Common and effective jail for Pedraza).

In 2013, José Pedraza, former head of the Railway Union, was convicted and sentenced to 15 years in prison for his role in the murder of Mariano Ferreyra, a member of the Workers' Party. Pedraza's sentence, however, was commuted to house arrest, ostensibly for health reasons and his age, being older than 70. This reminded many of Argentina's authoritarian past when many of the recent dictatorship's victims were young and had ties to the labor movement. The episode further resonated with President Menem's *indultos* (pardons) in the 1990s, which had invalidated convictions of top military officials for crimes committed between 1976 and 1983.

FIGURE 3.7 Mass produced poster against impunity

Interlude

The temporal intersections between the 1976 coup d'état and the 2016 commemorations highlight how anxieties around impunity and state violence during the 1970s and 1980s were (re)interpreted through fears about the political moment leading up to the 40th anniversary of the coup. Outrage over the recently announced (February 2016) "security protocols"—and specifically about forced evictions in the province of Buenos Aires and the suppression and arrest of protestors in Jujuy, a northwest province in the country—paralleled historical concerns over the security forces' repressive tactics (Castilla, 2016). However, worries about the return of impunity extended beyond the question of state repression to encompass the country's economic situation, as well.

Distinctions between state repression, financial crimes, and economic policy in Argentina during the second half of the twentieth century are often blurry, at best. The history of the Macri family—and its business interests—illustrates how difficult separating out these concepts can be. Mauricio Macri's father, Francisco (Franco) Macri, emigrated from Italy in 1949 and established himself in construction. His business took off during the Revolución Argentina, when his company won a series of state contracts during the de facto presidency of General Onganía (Vazquez, 2018). This would prove the onset of a broader pattern, one that intensified during the subsequent dictatorship, the Process of National Reorganization (PRN). Prior to the 1976 coup, the Macri Group's holdings consisted of seven businesses; by 1983, the group had grown to 47 total companies (Pertot, 2015). This rapid expansion reflected two key factors: the Group's aggressive strategy of taking over financially insolvent and bankrupt companies, and their close ties to military leaders, which allowed them to win a series of extremely profitable state contracts. In 1982, as the dictatorship broke down and the transition to democracy loomed, then-director of the Central Bank, Domingo Cavallo, arranged for the state to take on more than $170,000,000 of debt from the Macri Group, effectively transferring that debt to the state (Vazquez, 2018).[15] By the end of the 1990s, the value of the Macri Group was well over two billion dollars. While the Macri family was never accused of participating in extralegal repression—something that many prominent Argentine industrialists cannot claim—that their fortune came out of the most violent period of Argentine history has cast a long shadow on their activities.

These overlaps point to the complex processes of meaning making occurring in Buenos Aires, and specifically at the Facultades de Ciencias Sociales and Filosofía y Letras, in the days before March 24, 2016. First, the concerns of activists about impunity related to ongoing justice work dating back to the 1980s centered on holding members of the Argentine military accountable for crimes carried out against civilians during the Proceso. At the same time, these concerns were reinterpreted and reinvested with new significance in light of more recent instances of state repression, like the episodes involving Jorge Julio López and

Mariano Ferreyra. That these examples happened under Kirchner governments demonstrated, for many, the limitations of the Kirchners' commitment to justice work and, if nothing else, the challenges that such efforts face in Argentina. Third, as we will see in the next section, the Macri government's decision to negotiate with the "vulture funds"—effectively legitimizing what many viewed as the theft of national wealth by agents of the international finance class—echoed earlier financial misdeeds, like the history of the Macri family's accumulation of wealth and property during the 1970s and 1980s. That these actors were never held accountable—and indeed, that the family scion made it to the presidency— invested the fight against impunity with new meanings beyond those associated with the state's use of legal and extralegal violence. Concerns over unpunished and unacknowledged financial crimes intersected with fears about economic dependency on and subjugation to a global capitalist order that could undermine Argentina's very sovereignty as a nation. These concerns registered in the images we encountered at the two UBA sites, Ciencias Sociales and Filo.

Economic Policies: Domestic and Transnational Impact

The second key theme we discerned about justice work as resistance at these UBA sites centered on the social and economic impact of neoliberal policies and programs implemented by the Argentine government in collaboration with global financial institutions, primarily the International Monetary Fund (IMF), along with the United States. Soon after taking office in late 2015, Macri carried out economic reforms aligned with core tenets of neoliberalism. While neoliberalism can be a slippery term, we define it as the deregulation and privatization of public services in support of free-market solutions to problems.[16] This coincides with cutbacks in government spending along with, in the case of Argentina and other countries in the Global South, the infusion of capital from transnational lending institutions, like the IMF.

Macri instituted a series of measures to deregulate public services to be implemented starting April 1, 2016, with expected dramatic spikes in the cost of utilities and public transport. Macri also supported mass layoffs (despidos) of thousands of Argentines who were working primarily in the public sector. This included 500 dismissals in the Justice and Human Rights Ministry, which upset and angered the human rights community. Macri argued these steps, recommended by the IMF, were necessary to deal with high inflation and key to revitalizing the Argentine economy.

These measures were wildly unpopular at the UBA. Students strongly criticized Macri and identified neoliberalism as the threat or enemy. Figure 3.8 captured this sentiment. Here the image of Darth Vader symbolizes neoliberalism or "empire" through a direct link to the movie, *The Empire Strikes Back*. In our reading, this visual text names what happened in the recent past, after 2010, as a counterattack (contra ataca) against the "Pink tide" or leftward political turn

FIGURE 3.8 Neoliberalism counter-attack

in Latin America in the early-mid 2000's, when political leaders in Argentina, Bolivia, Brazil, Chile, Ecuador, Peru, Uruguay, and Venezuela, adopted a range of progressive economic policies intended to impugn, reform, or dismantle core tenets of neoliberal orthodoxy, such as de-regulation of public services and privatization (Isbester & Patroni, 2011). In the mid-2010s, neoliberal political forces in these countries reasserted their prominence or "counter-attacked" (contra-atacas), in, perhaps most notably, Brazil, Chile, and Argentina when elections resulted in centrist-right leaders wedded to market driven reforms gaining office. The 2015 election—in which Macri became president—signaled the arrival of this trend in Argentina and in just a few months into the Macri government the reversion to IMF-friendly neoliberal policies was firmly in motion (Goeury, 2018). It is this fact that resonates most immediately in the darkly humorous invocation of Darth Vader and the exclamation that "Neoliberalism strikes back (counter attacks)."

The sweeping critique of the Macri administration at these two UBA sites frequently invoked "los buitres" (the vultures). In terms of economic policy, among Macri's most contentious decisions was to negotiate and agree to settle with the "vulture fund" bondholders to end the country's existing default.[17] Figure 3.9, "Down with the pact with the vulture funds" (Abajo el pacto buitre), captures

FIGURE 3.9 Critical of pact with vulture funds

this criticism, naming Macri, the Argentine Congress, who approved Macri's plan to pay back the hedge funds, as well as Thomas Griesa, a United States District Judge of New York, who paved the way in court for Argentina's repayment to the hedge funds.

Many visual texts at these UBA sites linked criticism of the vulture funds to President Obama and a broader critique of neoliberalism or imperialism (see Figures 3.4 and 3.7). This was not a complete surprise given Obama's presence in Argentina on March 23 and 24, 2016 and controversy in Argentina about his visit. From the February 2016 announcement of his visit to up through his two-day stay on March 23 and 24, Obama's appearance provoked strong resistance in Argentina. Human rights activist Adolfo Pérez Esquivel, winner of the 1980 Nobel Peace Prize, captured the public reaction in an open letter to Obama prior to his visit. Esquivel stated that Obama was not welcome to visit on March 24, when Argentines would be commemorating the 40th anniversary of the military dictatorship, because the United States "has been and is behind all the destabilization attempts of popular governments of our continent" (Esquivel, 2016). Esquivel's language of "has been" and "is" underscored the perceived continuity between past and present acts of U.S. intervention and the continuing role of the United States as an imperial power in South America.

78 Labors of Justice as Resistance

The visual texts at the UBA engaged this continuity in different ways. In Figure 3.10, Obama's face appears in a circle with a line that crosses out his face, a powerful depiction that marks Obama—his face and person—for extinction (or, cancellation, at the very least). The image calls for Obama to leave Argentina ("Fuera Obama de Argentina") with a similar entreaty to end imperialism in Latin America. The sponsor of this reprinted visual text, La Izquierda Revolucionaria, is an organization with national and international concerns that has been highly critical of theories and practices of global capitalism.[18] The name of a second organization, Hombre Nuevo ["New Man"], also appears. This group, allied with La Izquierda Revolucionaria, is a student organization with limited sway beyond the Facultad de Filosofía y Letras.[19] The image of Che Guevara emphasizes a claim of continuity between these groups and the tradition of revolutionary Marxism in the region. The only temporal marker in this visual text is a call to march, on March 24, to the Plaza de Mayo (marchamos a Plaza de Mayo), the most iconic public space of protest and resistance in Buenos Aires. Thus, March 24 and, by implication, *memory* of this date, is used to promote an end to imperialism, led or shaped by the United States.

Concerning the claim in Figure 3.10 about the need to end U.S. imperialism, the United States has exerted significant economic influence in Argentina,

FIGURE 3.10 Critical of Obama

primarily through its association with the IMF and its lending policies. This association solidified during the time leading up to the 1976 coup and has remained strong through the present-day (see Chapter 2). Students' visual texts targeted this interventionism. With Figure 3.11, we see calls to not pay the debt (No al pago de la deuda) to the vultures (Ni un peso para los buitres) linked to resistance to Obama and the IMF.

Figure 3.12 offers a more visual depiction of the U.S.-backed vulture funds cast as an imperial power, looking down upon South America from the east in the form of an eagle perched on a branch with a U.S. flag draped to its back. The sponsor, La Mella Sociales, is a leftist student group, named after a popular martyr, Santiago Mella, and is a prominent group in Ciencias Sociales.[20]

The text and images employed in Figures 3.8 through 3.12 mobilize memory to narrate resistance to U.S. imperialism and to vulture capitalism more specifically.[21] Located at university sites with long-standing traditions of justice-seeking literacy and memory practices, the geospatial range of these visual texts that protest this state-private finance nexus, also implicates Europe (indirectly), with its conquest of the Americas, and the United States and all of Latin America (directly) in the continuing debt peonage of entire countries in the Global South. The transnational resonances registered in still other ways and in other images

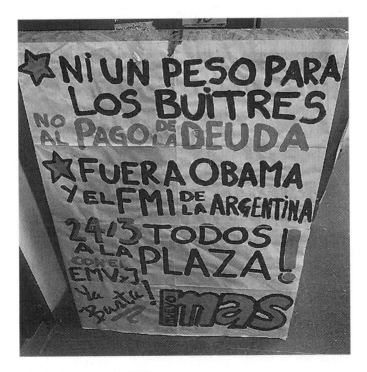

FIGURE 3.11 Vultures and the IMF

80 Labors of Justice as Resistance

FIGURE 3.12 Vulture with U.S. flag on tree branch by South America

that we encountered in these UBA spaces. For example, commemorative literacies at the UBA that expressed solidarity with Syrians and Palestinians reinforced this notion of connections between and across the Global South and expanded the critique of imperialism and neoliberalism beyond just the United States–Argentina relationship.

Transnational Solidarity: Syria and Palestine

An unsigned poster (Figure 3.13) that we encountered in UBA hallways declared, "Out with Obama, Perpetrator of the Massacre of the Syrian Masses / Obama + Putin + Al Assad = Genocide." Stenciled on the wall above the poster were the words, "Neither in Cuba, Nor in Argentina, Yankees Out of Latin America!" To the left of the poster (facing the image) was another poster, asking, "Never Again What? Counter-Repression Week, March 23–28," followed by a list of activities and events. Visible below the poster in bold red letters was the slogan, "Worker Democracy." Taken together, this complex tableau brought together the remembrance of the period of state terror ("Nunca más"/Never Again) with U.S. interventions in Latin America (Neither in Cuba, Nor in Argentina/Yankees Out of Latin America) and in Syria. The reference to Syria linked Obama to

Labors of Justice as Resistance **81**

FIGURE 3.13 Linking Obama, Putin, and Assad to genocide

Putin and Assad as perpetrators of the mass violence against the civilian population in Syria. In September 2013, President Obama threatened to bomb Syria in retaliation for the Assad regime's alleged use of chemical weapons against its own civilians. In the end, however, the Obama Administration avoided armed intervention by negotiating an agreement with Russia to destroy Syria's chemical weapons stockpiles. So, although U.S. intervention was perhaps not as direct as the poster claimed, the United States did support proxy forces like the PKK Kurdish militia in an effort to blunt Russian influence and the Assad government's capacity to act.[22]

Given this intervention as well as the history of U.S. support for Israel and the U.S. invasion of Iraq, which has served as a main catalyst for the deep instability in the Middle East, the poster's linking of Obama to the violence in Syria made sense even if, strictly speaking, the Obama Administration was neither responsible for the Iraq invasion nor for Syria's descent into civil war. The transnational gestures in this tableau—all of the images taken together—confront the viewer with a claim about oppressive power (and the struggle against it) operating on a global scale. One possible interpretation of this claim, grounded in the juxtaposition of the central, red poster, the stencil to the upper right demanding, "Yankees Out of Latin America," and the reference in the other, smaller poster invoking "Nunca

82 Labors of Justice as Resistance

Más," is that the forces that produced the period of state terror in Argentina were similar to those confronting Cuba, and indeed all of Latin America, as well as Syria and the global cause of "worker democracy." This force was imperialist, and it manifested in United States and post-Soviet Russian power as well as through local client states like Assad's Syria.

In another UBA text, a message of transnational solidarity was stenciled on a wall (Figure 3.14). "Todos somos la resistencia!" (We are all the resistance!) and, in Spanish and Arabic, "Refugiados Somos Todos"/ "*kullna laji'in*" (We are all Refugees!).

Alongside these connections to state repression in Syria, with the associated links to the United States, Russia, and the plight of Syrian refugees, calls for transnational solidarity with the Palestinian struggle also featured prominently in and around the UBA.

A large, vibrant mural further down toward the entrance to the UBA Ciencias Sociales area declares "Palestina Libre" [Free Palestine] (Figure 3.15). The words appear against a painted image of an enormous sun in the background and red and green terrain beneath it. Two roses blown by the wind appear in the foreground. There are also two human figures. One to the left facing the mural appears to be a woman kneeling in the soil. Her scarf, red in color, obscures her head and face, its long ends metamorphosing into crimson stems of flora. On the opposite edge

FIGURE 3.14 We are all refugees!

FIGURE 3.15 Palestina Libre

of the mural, a male figure appears in the classic iconography of Palestinian resistance: a kefiyya scarf obscuring his face except for his eyes, his arm, and fist raised to the sky. Between the figures, as if serving as a cord that binds them, is the slogan in Arabic and translated into Spanish (above the Arabic): "We shall return!" The slogan gives voice to the core Palestinian historical demand of the right of return as enshrined in United Nations resolutions. Human rights and international law have been core discursive frameworks for the Palestinian demand of restitution. On the man's shirt is a signature of sorts: "Muralismo Nómade en Resistencia," a reference to a network of artists devoted to transforming the public walls of Buenos Aires into canvases of political expression. Its Facebook site (https://www.facebook.com/pg/MuralismoNomadeEnResistencia/about/?ref=page_internal/ see also: https://forumnoticiasvalpo.blogspot.com/2017/10/violeta-le-canta-santiago-maldonado.html) explains:

> *Por que Muralismo nómade en resistencia?*
> *Las paredes son la imprenta de los pueblos, dijo Rodolfo Walsh, y creemos que vale también para una imagen. Elegimos el mural para transformar y ocupar el espacio público, las líneas para generar tensiones, los puntos para correrlos de las ies, los colores para llenar nuestros corazones, murales para expresarnos. Pintamos desde*

la alegre rebeldía, y pintamos organizados también, para denunciar, para contagiar la lucha, y nos gusta ser muchos, por eso decimos que todos podemos pintar. Por eso no solo pintamos, multiplicamos, y para poder multiplicar nos movemos como nómades. Construimos en pos de una estética anti patriarcal anti imperialista anti capitalista, desde abajo y a la izquierda. Con los pies en Latinoamérica.

Donde haya una necesidad, habrá un mural!!
Muralismo para el cambio social.
Why Nomade Muralism in Resistance?
Walls are the printing presses of towns, as Rodolfo Walsh has said, and we believe this is true of an image, as well. We chose the mural in order to transform and occupy public space—the lines to generate tensions, the dots to chase them from the i's, the colors to fill our hearts, murals to express ourselves.23 We paint from the happy rebellion, and we paint organized also in order to denounce, to make the fight contagious, and we wish to be many, that's why we say that we can all paint. That's why we not only paint, we multiply, and in order to multiply we move like nomads. We build in pursuit of an anti-patriarchal, anti-imperialist, anti-capitalist aesthetic, from below and to the left.

With feet in Latin America
Where there is a need, there will be a mural!!
Muralism for social change.

This invocation of the Palestinian struggle in mural form on the exterior walls of Ciencias Sociales expresses the idea of resistance as a global reality. It echoes, in this sense, what Collins (2011) refers to in his concept of "global Palestine" as a metaphor and a site of international solidarity across diverse justice struggles. The emergence of Palestine as such a metaphor has its roots in the forced, mass deterritorialization and dispersion of Palestinians during the war of 1948 and in the subsequent internationalization of the Palestinian national liberation movement in the form of the Palestinian Liberation Organization (PLO) following the war of 1967. During the post-1967 period, the PLO forged ties with Third World non-aligned and anti-colonial forces and especially with the liberation struggles in Northern Ireland and South Africa. Palestinian student groups and solidarity formations cultivated similar alliances and transnational politics, especially with the Black Power movement, in diaspora communities in the United States during the 1970s and 1980s (Feldman, 2015; Fischbach, 2019; Lybarger, 2020; Pennock, 2017). A further globalizing transformation occurred during the 1990s. This decade saw the rise of a broad-based justice movement targeting global capitalism and U.S. imperialism. Palestine and the Palestinians featured centrally as reference points for this movement. Collins cites the ubiquity of the keffiyeh scarf, the prevalence of references to "intifada" (uprising), and special sessions, workshops, artwork, and cultural events devoted to Palestine as part of the programing of major social justice conventions such as the U.S. Social Forum that was held in Detroit in June 2010 (Collins, 2011, p. 8).

Labors of Justice as Resistance   85

The demand to remember the disappeared of the period of state terror and to connect this demand to the rejection of U.S. vulture capitalism and the actions of Argentine "compradors" (i.e., the Macri Administration, the reactionary right wing) takes on a broad resonance through the invocation of Palestine as metaphor of the struggle against injustice, internationally. The Facebook statement of the mural artists amplifies this resonance, declaring the intent of their movement to struggle against patriarchy, imperialism, and capitalism "con pies en Latina America [with feet in Latin America]." There is a tension here between rootedness—in a region, notably, and not just in a single country (Argentina) or city (Buenos Aires) or neighborhood (the UBA area)—and movement, an idea carried in the very name of the group, "Nomads in Resistance." Resistance moves across borders because the forces of repression are globally ubiquitous. The currency of this movement is artistic expression, muralism. Image communicates beyond language; image connects: Argentine resistance becomes an instance of Global Palestine, and Palestine, an instance of a nomadic Argentina.

Elsewhere, inside the building's hallways, we encounter another expression of "Global Palestine." In this case, a poster declares in white lettering against a green background that "The Struggle (La Lucha) Will Conquer the Oppression of the Zionist State of Israel" (Figure 3.16). Two hands, cuffed in sleeves bearing the

FIGURE 3.16   La lucha

86 Labors of Justice as Resistance

insignias of the "USA" and the Star of David, clasp below the text. This poster appeared alongside two others demanding that Obama stay out of Argentina and that we, the readers, resist "the impunity of yesterday and today," and that we say no to Macri's neoliberal economic "adjustments." A second poster demanded that we also say no to vulture capitalism. An image of President Obama riding on the back of a menacing vulture accompanied this declaration. Taken together, these images signaled an orientation toward resistance. They created an immersive space that extended and developed this theme in myriad ways.

Another painted mural (Figure 3.17) targeted the state violence of Israel with a call to end the "massacre in Gaza" ("Frenemos La Masacre Israeli en Gaza"). Israel has carried out frequent devastating bombardments and invasions of the Gaza Strip and maintains a punishing blockade of the territory in an effort to weaken the Hamas movement, which controls the zone. The same poster offers a declaration of support for the Palestinian people ("Todo El Apoyo Al Pueblo Palestino").[24] The Centro de Estudiantes de Filosofía y Letras (CEFyL), a main organizational tribune for activist Filo students, signed the mural.

The above transnational resonances express clear solidarity commitments—expressions of shared struggle against repressive forces. The images we encountered forged connections between the state repression and injustice of the 1976

FIGURE 3.17 Mural in support of Palestine

coup and contemporary injustices and struggles that responded to them occurring elsewhere in the world.

Conclusion

Because understandings of the past evolve with complex, ongoing social and political processes, memories need to be investigated and contextualized historically vis-a-vis present-day power relationships (Jelin, 2003). Taken as a whole, the commemorative literacies we analyzed in this chapter emphasize memory mobilization as collective resistance toward repression and impunity between the past and present. It couples this mobilization with resistance to unpopular economic policies driven by commitments to neoliberal reforms that cut across nation-states—principally, Argentina and the United States—and across time, from the 1970s through the March 2016 commemorations. The Macri government's economic and political policies comprise the main targets of the visual texts in the lead up to the March 24, 2016 commemoration of the period of state terror. The United States and the IMF are also targets. The references to them cast Macri's administration as a recurrence of center-right tendencies that mortgage Argentina's independence to short-term economic measures. These measures, as the visual texts convey, benefit the national elite, U.S.-based hedge funds, and Washington DC's goals of maintaining hegemony in the region.

Put another way, the commemorative literacies at each university site accessed the Argentine societal memory chest for the albums, scripts, and lore related to state tactics of repression and impunity for military leaders tied to the 1976 coup, as well as material related to adverse effects of economic policy in the aftermath of the 2001–2002 economic crisis. The temporal and spatial contexts of the UBA spaces, calls to march, and invocations of the disappeared of "yesterday and today" serve further to deepen the critique of Macri: the current neoliberal shift is merely the latest instantiation of political tendencies that have exacerbated inequalities in Argentina at least since the 1976–1983 period. This historical-spatial reference to the period of state terror provides, as well, a powerful moral appeal: across the visual texts analyzed above, "neither forget nor pardon" arises in relation to "not one peso to the vultures" in a complex engagement with the past for purposes of critique and mobilization in the present. The problem of the debt and of limits to civil and political rights under Macri are this generation's core concerns among students at the UBA. But, these concerns connect to the remembered past as it is carried within organizations like EMVyJ and Frente Izquierda and in collective moments of remembrance of the 30,000 disappeared. The call to remember—in opposition to a president who desires to minimize and move on from the past—becomes a rallying cry of protest to the perceived regression to a violent past.

In this sense, the signs and posters are *liturgical*, invoking and enacting shared ideals, helping comprise "the sacred" or sense of "things set apart" in relation

88 Labors of Justice as Resistance

to how this community has formed (Durkheim [1912] 1995; Taves, 2009). The demands outlined in Figure 3.1, for example, *(a) Obama out of Argentina, (b) No to [the Macri administration's] repressive protocols, and (c) Not one peso to the venture capitalists,* constitute and activate "the sacred" for the Argentine political left: each of these demands become, in that particular moment, inviolable at, and definitive of, these university sites.[25] The texts across CS and Filo can also be read through a testimonial lens, as a "discourse of solidarity" that acknowledges and empowers victims of past as well as more contemporary repression and encourages actions to end other injustices (Partnoy, 1986). Finally, these texts can also be viewed through a lens of intergenerational memory as particular forms of spatial resistance took shape through this dynamic interplay between the past and present.[26] We will also see intergenerational memory at work in the next chapter at a more personal level when one Argentine woman at the Church of Santa Cruz reckons with the legacy of state terrorism vis-a-vis the relationship between Argentina and the United States.

Notes

1 Before the late 1980s, Ciencias was part of Facultad de Derecho y Ciencias Sociales. Loren had established the connection with Fortunato, who has published extensive sociological analyses of the role of Catholicism in Argentine society and politics, via email prior to our research trip to Buenos Aires.
2 All photographs in this book were taken by either James S. Damico or Loren D. Lybarger.
3 In our earlier conversation with him, Fortunato Mallimaci insisted that, in the case of Argentina, the United States was of less importance than forces specific to Argentine history and politics. Mallimaci did not discount the effects of U.S. policies in other Latin American countries. In Argentina, however, there were national precedents for authoritarian rule that predated the establishment of institutions like the School for the Americas, a notorious U.S. center that trained Latin American military officers in counter-insurgency techniques, including the use of torture in interrogations, and the U.S. Cold War "Operation Condor" policy. Esquivel's remarks were nevertheless relevant for seeing Argentina in a broad, regional perspective. HIs comments served as a reminder and as a political-ethical expression of the continuity of the Argentine human rights struggle with similar struggles elsewhere in Latin America, especially in Brazil and Honduras, where advocates of human rights had come under attack. They also had immediate relevance for U.S. President Obama's planned visit to Argentina on the occasion of the 40th anniversary of the period of state terror.
4 This summary obviously glosses over much of the nuance of the process through which Argentina's university system took shape (Buchbinder, 2005; Unzué, 2012).
5 These debates were closely tied to broader discussions of the so-called "social question." See Zimmerman (1992).
6 This oversimplifies the situation, obviously, and there were changes in how much autonomy and power the universities had at different moments (Buchbinder, 2005).
7 Borges, recognizing the insult, resigned the post a day later and remained a committed anti-Peronist for the remainder of his life (Williamson, 2004).
8 In 1949, the Peron-led government decreed the revoking of tuition and instead instituted free admission. This greatly expanded access to university education. Later, in 1973, the Peronist administration instituted open, unrestricted enrollment. Both of

these policies contributed to the massive enrollment expansion in the UBA system. Personal email communication, Fortunato Mallimaci, April 13, 2021.
9   Under Peronism, the faculty and administrative positions abandoned or otherwise vacated after 1946 had largely been filled with supporters and sympathizers (Sigal, 2002).
10 The focus on these disciplines reflected the dominant perspective within the Armed Forces that these schools of thought had undermined the traditional/conservative Christian social worldview. Victims of repression later recalled that their torturers would talk to them about the "three Jews" who had ruined civilization: Marx who had attempted to destroy the Christian idea of society; Freud who had attempted to destroy the Christian idea of family; and Einstein who had attempted to destroy the Christian idea of space and time. See Timmerman (1981). Also, we note that in 1974 the sociology major, in particular, had attracted the majority of students in the UBA system. Fr. Justino O'Farrell, a Catholic priest and dean of the Faculty of Philosophy and Letter (Filo), chaired the Sociology department (housed at Filo) at that time, shepherding it through the period of state terror. Personal email communication, Fortunato Mallimaci, April 13, 2021.
11 Interview with Nicolás Sillitti, February 5, 2019. At that time, Nicolás was a PhD candidate in history at Indiana University. Where students are able to place their visual texts is based on results of student elections as well as tradition. According to Sillitti, student groups that receive the majority of votes in elections to serve on boards or committees for UBA are rewarded more space to display visual texts. Of note, students run for positions as part of a group that represents certain ideas; they do not run as individuals. At Filo, tradition also plays a part with the constitution of the space as there is a long history of some student groups associated with a particular area of UBA. Also, in the highly democratized spaces of CS (Ciencias) and Filo, different political groups mobilize for department and university level meetings which are open to the public.
12 This political ethos contrasts sharply with the U.S. institutions in which we teach. On our campuses, administrative bodies retain strict control of public spaces, requiring prior authorization for the posting of any materials. Walls are also generally free of graffiti. When graffiti appears, it quickly becomes subject to removal (painting over or cleaning). In some cases, such as at Ohio University where Loren teaches, tradition and administrative agreement designate a single wall surface for student graffiti. University maintenance, however, will typically efface any expression deemed offensive. This retention of administrative authority to censor speech highlights the difference between our U.S. campuses and UBA spaces, where students retain the power to determine the use of public space for speech purposes.
13 Street protests, and especially the disruption of traffic (so-called "cortes"), have a long history in Argentina, and especially in Buenos Aires. For more on social protest in Argentina, and particularly the importance of public demonstrations (*El derecho a la protesta social en la argentina*, 2017).
14 The group lists these abuses at its website: https://encuentromvyj.wordpress.com/. See also their Facebook site at https://tinyurl.com/9bbk97fu.
15 Nor was the Macri clan the only beneficiary. During Cavallo's two-month tenure at the Central Bank, he allowed some 200 firms to transfer the majority of their collective $17 billion in debts to the state ("Ordenan investigar," 2011). Although Cavallo was later convicted of financial crimes committed during the Menem government, neither he nor the various industrialists involved in the 1982 debt transfer were ever punished.
16 In the previous chapter, we used the term "liberal" to refer to the laissez faire economic policies of different actors during the 1960s and into the 1970s. Neoliberalism, by contrast, generally refers to a reinterpretation of classical liberal ideas that became dominant starting in the 1970s, but really in the 1980s and 1990s. The "neo" prefix

speaks to this new system's focus on speculation and finance capitalism, as opposed to classical liberalism's primary emphasis on reducing tariffs and eliminating labor regulations. The two are closely related, and the difference might be productively thought of as one of scale, rather than of kind. For more, see Harvey (2007).
17 See Chapter 2 of this volume, specifically the section "The Right Turn," for a description of Argentina's relationship with these creditors.
18 Information about the Izquierda Revolucionaria, including history and current political projects, can be found at their website: https://www.izquierdarevolucionaria.net/.
19 Interview, Nicolás Sillitti. February 5, 2019.
20 Interview, Nicolás Sillitti. February 5, 2019.
21 Returning to the introduction of this section and Obama's meeting with Macri to ostensibly welcome Argentina back into the global economy, we can see the connection that Harvey (2003) makes between state-supported lending institutions like the IMF that seek to stabilize currency markets and international finance capital whose sole objective is profit maximization regardless of the impact on national societies.
22 The Obama Administration was deeply reluctant to involve U.S. troops directly in the Syrian conflict. Obama came to power promising—and, in the end, only partially succeeding—to end the U.S. presence in Afghanistan and Iraq. The Syria situation, however, presented Obama with a humanitarian disaster demanding action. Attempting to strike a balance, showing some willingness to act but holding the line against direct military deployment, the Administration threatened air attacks (in response to the use of chemical weapons) and made airdrops of food and weapons to Kurdish forces fighting Islamic State guerrillas in the Kobani region (Usher 2017; Baker, et al., 2015; Taddonio 2019).
23 The phrase "dots to chase them from the i's" is likely a reference to a Spanish language proverb about taking care while writing ("poner los puntos en los ies," "to dot the i's"). Here, the idea of the dots "chasing them" from atop the i's seems to suggest another form of rebellion against the accepted rules (in this case, of grammar).
24 For more on these bombardments and the prolonged blockade, Lipman (2019); Wilkins (2020); and "Confronting total collapse" (2021).
25 Former UBA student and active alumnus, Nicolás Sillitti, echoed this sentiment, stating, "Nobody would go to these classrooms praising the coming of Obama or Clinton or whoever." Moreover, there would be no consideration that the IMF is a good option. You wouldn't hear those kinds of debates in FILO or CS."
26 The concept of "intergenerational memory" is still being developed and debated, alongside "postmemory," which suggests a similar transmission of memories between generations and involving those who might not have personally experienced the events in question. See, for example, Hirsch (2012) and Aarons and Berger (2017).

References

Aarons, V. & Berger, A.L. (2017). *Third-Generation Holocaust representation: Trauma, history, and memory*. Northwestern University Press.
Argentina: President Macri Orders Crackdown on Protests. (2016, February 19). *TeleSUR*. https://www.telesurenglish.net/news/Argentinas-President-Macri-Orders-Crackdown-on-Protests-20160219-0005.html
Baker, P., Cooper H., & Sanger, D.E. (2015, October 30). Obama sends special operations forces to to help fight ISIS in Syria. *The New York Times*. https://www.nytimes.com/2015/10/31/world/obama-will-send-forces-to-syria-to-help-fight-the-islamic-state.html

Buchbinder, P. (2005). *Historia de las Universidades Argentinas*. Editorial Sudamericana.
Castilla, E. (2016, February 19). Bullrich, Macri y un protocolo represivo que ya entró en acción. *IzquierdaDiario.es* (February 19, 2016) at https://www.izquierdadiario.es/Bullrich-Macri-y-un-protocolo-represivo-que-ya-entro-en-accion
Collins, J. (2011). *Global Palestine*. Columbia University Press.
Confronting total collapse in Israeli-occupied Gaza: Division and Covid-19. (2021, January 25). *Informed Comment*. https://www.juancole.com/2021/01/confronting-collapse-occupied.html
Durkheim, E. (1995; 1912). *The elementary forms of religious life*. Translated by Karen E. Fields. The Free Press.
El derecho a la protesta social en la argentina. (2017). Centro de Estudios Legales y Sociales CELS.
Esquivel, A.P. (2016, March 6). Letter from Pérez Esquivel to Barack Obama in occasion of his travel to Argentina on March 24. *Common Dreams*. https://www.commondreams.org/views/2016/03/06/letter-perez-esquivel-barack-obama-occasion-his-travel-argentina-march-24#
Feitlowitz, M. (1999). *A Lexicon of terror: Argentina and the legacies of torture*. Oxford University Press.
Feldman, K.P. (2015). *A shadow over Palestine: The imperial life of race in America*. University of Minnesota Press.
Fischbach, J.W. (2019). *Black power and Palestine: Transnational countries of color*. Stanford University Press.
Goeury, H. (2018, April 22). Macri's Argentina has become a hotbed of neoliberalism and police violence. *Truthout*. https://truthout.org/articles/macris-argentina-has-become-a-hotbed-of-neoliberalism-and-police-violence/
Harvey, D. (2003). The 'new' imperialism: Accumulation by dispossession. *Socialist register*, 63–87.
Harvey, D. (2007). Neoliberalism as Creative Destruction. *The Annals of the American Academy of Political and Social Science*, 610, 22–44.
Hirsch, M. (2012). *The Generation of Postmemory: Writing and Visual Culture After the Holocaust*. Columbia University Press.
Historia de la Universidad Nacional de la Plata. (2019, August 9). Universidad Nacional de la Plata. https://unlp.edu.ar/historia/historia-de-la-universidad-nacional-de-la-plata-7946
Isbester, K. & Patroni, V. (2011). *The paradox of democracy in Latin America: Ten country studies of division and resilience*. University of Toronto Press.
Jelin, E. (2003). *State repression and the labors of memory*. University of Minnesota Press.
Ley No 24.521. (1995). http://servicios.infoleg.gob.ar/infolegInternet/anexos/25000-29999/25394/texact.htm
Limitación del derecho a la protesta. (2016, February 17). Centro de Estudios Legales y Sociales. https://www.facebook.com/notes/cels-centro-de-estudios-legales-y-sociales/limitación-del-derecho-a-la-protesta/960814430639734/
Lipman, D. (2019, August 28). In Focus: Israel's Gaza Wars. *Honest Reporting*. https://honestreporting.com/israels-gaza-wars/
Lybarger, L.D. (2020). *Palestinian Chicago: Idenitty in exile*. University of California Press.
Mensaje del presidente de la nación argentina Dr. Héctor José Cámpora al inaugurar el 98º periodo ordinario de sesiones del honorable congreso nacional. (1973). Buenos Aires: Congreso de la Nación.

Ordenan investigar si Cavallo debe devolver 17.000 millones de dólares. (2011, September 16). *La Nación*. https://www.lanacion.com.ar/politica/ordenan-investigar-si-cavallo-debe-devolver-17000-millones-de-dolares-nid1406673/

Partnoy, A. (1986). *The little school: Tales of disappearance and survival*. Cleis Press.

Pennock, P.E. (2017). *The rise of the Arab American left: Activists, allies, and their fight against imperialism and racism, 1960s-1980s*. The University of North Carolina Press.

Pertot, W. (2015, October 26). Un empresario de la política. *Página/12*.

Rodríguez, L.G. & Soprano, G. (2009). La política universitaria de la dictadura militar en la Argentina: Proyectos de reestructuración del sistema de educación superior (1976–1983). *Nuevo Mundo, Mundos Nuevos*. http://journals.openedition.org/nuevomundo/56023

Sigal, S. (2002). Intelectuales y Peronismo. In J.C. Torre (Ed.), *Nueva Historia Argentina* (Vol. 8). Sudamericana.

Sin capuchas, ni palos: Los 17 puntos salientes del protocolo antipiquetes. (2016, February 17). *Infobae*. https://www.infobae.com/2016/02/17/1790861-sin-capuchas-ni-palos-los-17-puntos-salientes-del-protocolo-antipiquetes/

Taddonio, P. (2019, October 9). Flashback: How US-backed Kurds defeated ISIS in Kobbani, Syria. *Frontline*. https://www.pbs.org/wgbh/frontline/article/flashback-how-us-backed-kurds-defeated-isis-in-kobani-syria/

Taves, A. (2009). *Religious experience reconsidered: A building-block approach to the study of religion and other special things*. Princeton University Press.

Timmerman, J. (1981). *Prisoner without a name, cell without a number* (T. Talbot, Trans.). Alfred A. Knopf.

Unzué, M. (2012). Historia del origen de la Universidad de Buenos Aires. *Revista Iberoamericana de Educación Superior*, 3(8), 72–88.

Usher, B.P. (2017, January 13). Obama's Syria legacy: Measured diplomacy, strategic explosion. *BBC News*. https://www.bbc.com/news/world-us-canada-38297343

Vazquez, C. (2018, March 23). Los Macri, el golpe de 76 y los orígenes de su fortuna. *La Izquierda Diario*. https://www.laizquierdadiario.com/Los-Macri-el-golpe-del-76-y-los-origenes-de-su-fortuna

Wilkins, B. (2020, August 25). As Israeli bombing of Gaza continues, US media show little interest. *Common Dreams*. https://www.commondreams.org/news/2020/08/25/israeli-bombing-gaza-continues-us-media-show-little-interest

Williamson, E. (2004). *Borges: A life*. Viking.

Zimmerman, E.A. (1992). Intellectuals, universities, and the social question: Argentina, 1898–1916. In J. Adelman (Ed.), *Essays in Argentina labour history 1870–1930*. Palgrave Macmillan.

4
LABORS OF JUSTICE AS RECONCILIATION AT THE CHURCH OF SANTA CRUZ

It is Monday morning, March 21, 2016, our first full day in Buenos Aires. Seven of us travel in taxicabs to the Church of Santa Cruz.[1] The address is Estados Unidos 3119 located in the district of San Cristóbal. The eighth member of our team, Liliana, meets us in front of the church. We are here because of Liliana. She grew up in this neighborhood, attended this church through her childhood and youth, and is a friend of the priest, Father Francisco. Liliana and Francisco have remained in contact through the decades. At the time of the coup in March 1976, Francisco was in the novitiate.

The church rises above the street behind a high wall. As we walk into the courtyard on our way to Fr. Francisco's office, we notice trees and a garden to our left. Fr. Francisco greets us with a wide, endearing smile, handshakes, and hugs. We soon make our way into the center of the church near the altar to begin the interview. Loren walks around the church with Fr. Francisco, asking questions about the posters on the walls, moving through the sanctuary from one poster to the next. These permanent displays include photographs and descriptions of Catholic priests and nuns as well as members of Las Madres and other Buenos Aires citizens who were disappeared and killed by the state, each with the status of a martyr. Despite its staged quality, Fr. Francisco and Loren's movement replicates the passage that penitents follow whenever they perform the stations of the cross during Lent. The stations traditionally comprise 14 images from the core Christian story of Jesus' condemnation, crucifixion, and resurrection. The images of the martyrs of the dictatorship on the sanctuary walls near the older altar merge the memory of this period with the memory and commemoration of Jesus' final hours. This interpolation serves to shift the remembrance of the dictatorship into the core mythical framework of Christianity. As the interview ensues, Fr. Francisco notes how entwined the work of memory and justice is here within the church and for Argentines as a whole. At one point he

DOI: 10.4324/9781003184195-5

> informs us, "Memory is permanent. It is not possible [to have] a reconciliation for us if there is no public, social recognition of crimes against humanity." We are left lingering with this idea about what the (im)possibility of reconciliation means for this Catholic church in Buenos Aires.

For the past several decades, the prospect of reconciliation in Argentina about events tied to the military dictatorship from 1976 to 1983 has remained tangled in a web of competing memory politics and changing understandings of transitional justice (Lessa, 2013). The term reconciliation suggests a restoration of relations, the rendering congruent of conflicting interpretations, or the mending of a strained or damaged relationship: that some mutual understanding has been attained or a conflict resolved. Framed through a wider secular or political lens, reconciliation might entail all Argentines acknowledging the abuses of the state during the dictatorship, the perpetrators apologizing and accepting consequences for their actions, and victims accepting these apologies as justice served. This has not occurred in Argentina. A number of older Argentines supported the coup and *Proceso* (PRN) in 1976 and many Argentines today, old and young, retain the view that at least some of the government's efforts during that time to combat subversion were warranted.

The term reconciliation also retains particular religious significance. As one of seven sacraments in Catholicism, reconciliation starts with contrition, or sincere penitence and remorse, moves to confession of the sin(s) and penance (considering and taking actions to restore relationships fractured through injuries caused to another), and then absolution where a priest liberates the person from her or his sins. The desired end result is the penitent's restoration to God and to the community. Many Argentines, including Father Francisco of the Santa Cruz Church in Buenos Aires, have argued that reconciliation, in secular or religious form, is not possible without greater societal recognition of human rights crimes committed during the dictatorship. Other Argentines, including Catholic priests, have advocated for the reconciliation of all Argentines to God and to each other in an attempt to focus on the future, moving away from blame and victimhood discourses rooted in the past.

This chapter steps into this tangled web to explore the ways commemorative literacies shaped particular memory mobilizations at the Church of Santa Cruz in March 2016 toward a complicated conception of reconciliation, one that was distinctively Catholic and Argentine. We begin with an historical account of perspectives and practices within the Catholic church in Argentina leading up to and enacted through the dictatorship. We then highlight how the spatial configuration of commemorative literacies at the Church of Santa Cruz situates this parish squarely within the tradition of "Committed Catholicism." In Argentina, this tradition has historically integrated the tenets of Catholicism with political struggles rooted in resistance to repressive or terrorist acts such as those committed by the military at Santa Cruz during the dictatorship.

This sets the stage for an examination of a ritual led by Fr. Francisco on March 23, 2016. This ritual, in which Fr. Francisco invited us to participate alongside his parishioners, mobilized memories of the dictatorship and the more recent past toward what we have deemed to be justice work as reconciliation. During our time at Santa Cruz, we also discerned transnational resonances of this work to justice struggles in South Africa and Vietnam. The chapter concludes with an exploration of a mural situated prominently behind the revised altar space at Santa Cruz. Created by the 1980 Nobel Peace laureate, Adolfo Perez Esquivel, this mural invoked notions of radical reconciliation and what Dr. Martin Luther King, Jr., noted civil rights leader in the United States, called the "beloved community" because "the end is reconciliation; the end is redemption; the end is the creation of the beloved community" (Boesak & DeYoung, 2012).

Catholicism in Argentina during the Dictatorship

The centrality of the Catholic Church to Argentine politics came directly to the forefront during the period of state terror that began officially in March 1976. This vital role took various conflicting forms. Morello (2015) outlines three different categories: 1) anti-secularist, 2) institutional, and 3) committed. First, important elements of the Argentine Church—in particular, priests and bishops in the military vicariate—backed the junta and its use of torture, disappearance, and mass executions, offering moral guidance and religious absolution for the Armed Forces (Bilbao & Lede, 2016; Catoggio, 2016; Mallimaci, 2015; Morello, 2015, pp.12–13; Verbitsky, 1995, 2005). Ideologically, the pro-regime prelates invoked the language of pollution and purification, claiming the military was an instrument of God's justice to cleanse the nation of the idolatrous defilement of secularism and of Marxist atheism. Morello refers to the segment of the Church that performed this work on behalf of the regime as the "anti-secularist" wing because of its reactionary stance against any diminishment of the Church's status and power in social and political spheres. Their vision of Argentina was patriarchal and authoritarian, rooted in an ecclesiastical vision in which Church and State collaborated to instill Catholic morality and Christian unity in the society (Morello, 2015, pp. 12–13).

In addition to the anti-secularist clerics, Morello (2015) describes a second group, the "institutional" Catholics. This group comprised leadership that sought to preserve a political space for the Church free of governmental control. They also sought, however, to retain access to political institutions and leadership in order to influence policies. These individuals operated outside of the military vicariate. They were aware of the policies and actions of the regime and did not openly contest them. Indeed, in some cases, they approved of the coup, viewing it as a necessary evil to restore order. As the terror progressed, however, some became quietly critical. They avoided public censure of the generals while attempting to mitigate the violence by seeking information about the detained and urging moderation.[2]

Finally, a third segment of the Church, what Morello (2015) describes as the "committed Catholics," though less well known, criticized or resisted the regime and became a target of the military repression. This group aligned with the social mission emphasizing solidarity with the poor as articulated in various papal encyclicals beginning with Rerum Novarum and continuing through the Vatican II reforms.[3] Committed Catholics worked on the fringes of Argentine society establishing missions in the impoverished *villas miserias* (urban slums) and participating in openly political formations such as the Movement of Priests for the Third World. There were other Catholics, a small minority of laity and religious within the committed milieu, who argued for a further, radical step: armed struggle to overturn the conditions of repression and inequality in the country. These individuals would help form violent Marxist guerrilla groups including the Montoneros.[4]

At the core of the activities inspired by this "committed" theology were individuals who embraced the notion that individual salvation required social salvation and that to achieve this wider liberation in the context of mounting political violence required a total commitment even to the point of death. The preeminent model of and for this process was the crucified Christ. The process began with the theological and practical formation of the servant—religious or lay—and then continued through Christ-like action in the world. One worked directly to transform the suffering of the poor through charity, teaching, and companionship in the very conditions with which the oppressed contended (Catoggio, 2016, p. 106).

These three doctrinal trajectories—anti-secularist, institutional, committed— sought to bring Argentina in line with their particular and diverging conceptions of Catholic faith. And, all three viewed the state as an important instrument to achieve this goal (Catoggio, 2016; Morello, 2015). Their respective visions of and for the nation overlapped with other sectors—military and right-wing populism, in the case of the anti-secularists; the broad middle spectrum of Argentines trying to navigate between or straddle the divided political terrain in the case of institutional Catholicism; left-wing populism and Marxism in the case of the committed Catholics—but it is critical to grasp that religion was a central orienting frame for their different political interventions. Within this context, the Church of Santa Cruz emerged, in our direct experience of it, as a parish firmly aligned with the committed trajectory.

The Church of Santa Cruz, Committed Catholicism, and Reconciliation

The Church of Santa Cruz is situated near the center of Buenos Aires at the corner of Urquiza and Estados Unidos in San Cristòbal.[5] During the late nineteenth century, hundreds of Irish families migrated to the area. Irish Passionist priests accompanied them and in the 1890s worked with their constituents to build Santa Cruz. The church quickly became the center of the community. Between the 1920s and the 1960s, it expanded its institutional footprint by establishing a school and a community retreat and study space called Casa Nazaret. In the 1960s, the Archdiocese of Buenos Aires declared Santa Cruz a parish.

At the center of Santa Cruz's orientation has been an emphasis on the "theology of the people," which placed the laity at the center in an attempt to discern the presence of God in the wider world.[6] This positioning solidified when lay activists at Santa Cruz revived the church's magazine, *Revista de Santa Cruz*, in 1976, as the period of state terror began. The magazine became a vehicle for deepening ties between the parish and its neighborhood and for debating the social and political problems confronting Argentina at that time. The voicing of such concerns in this way marked Santa Cruz as a site of protest and resistance, a status that strengthened when the parish joined with other churches to issue a public affirmation of the inviolability of life. This statement implicitly criticized the regime's violent campaign against those deemed "subversives." It also repudiated the stance that hierarchs within the national Church had taken in support of the coup and the violent repression. In addition to this public protest, Santa Cruz continued to engage in its mission of outreach in the slums. The regime took notice. On May 2, 1976, just six weeks after the coup, graffiti appeared on Santa Cruz's walls accusing the Passionist priests of ties with Communists, the Montonero guerrillas, and the leftist Ejército Revolucionario del Pueblo (Revolutionary Army of the People, or ERP). Surveillance records that later came to light also revealed that military intelligence attempted to slander a priest at Santa Cruz for engaging in "suspicious" behaviors, including facilitating a cell for the Federación Juvenil Comunista (Communist Youth Federation) and for traveling, in that connection, to Northern Ireland, Spain, Mexico, and Costa Rica (Catoggio, 2016, pp. 127–129). Three months later, in August 1976, a bomb exploded outside of the Casa Nazaret, the parish's community space. Although no one was injured in the blast, the message behind the incident was clear.

Toward the end of 1976, the church also began to provide space for laity who helped to found protest movements like the Madres de la Plaza de Mayo. Some of these individuals formed a prayer and reflection group that planned to issue public statements demanding accountability for the disappeared. By November 1977, the security forces had infiltrated this group, sending an officer to pose as a fellow activist looking for a disappeared relative. On December 8, 1977, multiple Ford Falcons, the vehicle of choice of the regime's secret police, appeared outside the church. Plainclothes security personnel emerged from the cars and then arrested seven members of the group, including one of the two French nuns who had been working in the *villas miserias*. Over the next 48 hours, the other five members would be kidnapped from around Buenos Aires[7]. Five bodies would later appear on the shore approximately 280 miles south of the capital, only for the military to immediately bury the corpses in unmarked graves. In 2003, investigators discovered the graves and disinterred the bodies. After two years, the remains were positively identified as five of the 12 people disappeared from Santa Cruz, four of whom were reburied on church grounds.

In 1978, Santa Cruz publicly commemorated the disappeared in what became an annual vigil. After the return to democracy in 1983, the church extended this practice by holding public commemorations at the site of the bomb blast outside the walls of Casa Nazaret. Alongside these rituals, the church also created permanent memorials to the church's dead and disappeared. Taken together these mechanisms of commemoration marked Santa Cruz as a site of local memorialization within the committed Catholic milieu.

Spatial Reconciliation of Religion and Politics

Commemorative literacies at Santa Cruz intentionally integrate religious faith with core political and human rights struggles. In doing so, these literacies articulate a stance characteristic of committed Catholicism. In the next section, we explore Santa Cruz's sanctuary space, attending to several large permanent displays that commemorate the disappeared and assassinated: Nuestros Profetas, Nuestras Hermanas, Madres de la Plaza, and Familiares/Militantes.

Nuestros Profetas

Within the apse, next to statues of Mary with the baby Jesus and other biblical figures, was a large poster titled, "Nuestros Profetas" [Our Prophets] (see Figure 4.1).

The poster depicted three clerics whom right-wing paramilitary groups and state security services assassinated during the 1970s and 1980s: Archbishop Oscar Romero of El Salvador (1917–1980); Fr. Carlos Mugica (1930–1974) of Argentina; and Bishop Enrique Angelelli (1923–1976) also of Argentina. The "Nuestros Profetas" poster construed the priests as prophets in relation to the biblical ideal type: the martyred pastors spoke fearlessly and prophetically in witness to divine commandments; experienced rejection by their fellow citizens and ultimately execution at the hands of the state; and led lives that exemplified the Christ-like behavior they called the community to embrace. Mugica's assassination, which occurred just two years before the start of the dictatorship, showed that officially sanctioned right-wing paramilitary violence preceded the period of state terror. In a similar fashion, Bishop Angelelli, who was assassinated during the first year of the dictatorship, symbolized the continuing prophetic stance of the committed wing of the church into and through the period of state terror. His prominence as a bishop, moreover, indicated that the committed stance was not marginal but rather reached into the hierarchical center of the Argentine church. His death symbolized the struggle within and for the leadership of the church itself during this period.

Labors of Justice as Reconciliation   99

FIGURE 4.1   Nuestros Profetas

The memory of Bishop Angelelli also transcended the Church. As we documented the sense-making activities at the ex-ESMA facility (next chapter), which had become a museum and site for commemorative installations and archival documentation, we came across an exhibit dedicated to the slain bishop.

This poster (Figure 4.2) featured a caricatured rendering of Angelelli's face and this quotation from one of his poems: "Déjenme que les cuenta lo que me quema por dentro es Amor que se hizo carne con chayas y dolor de pueblo" [Allow me to tell you what burns me within/ the Love that became flesh with people's celebrations and pain].[8] The memorial, and its placement at the ex-ESMA, transformed Angelelli from a moral symbol of committed Catholicism into a representative of broader currents within Argentine society that included many of the human rights groups, non-governmental organizations, poets and artists, and families throughout the nation who remembered their dead and disappeared.

The inclusion of Archbishop Oscar Romero of El Salvador in Figure 4.1 projected a solidarity between the Santa Cruz church as a site of Argentine committed Catholicism, rooted in the theology of the people, and Latin America as a whole and, specifically, the cause of Liberation Theology as it had come to shape left-wing Catholic resistance to dictatorship and to U.S. hegemony in the region.

100 Labors of Justice as Reconciliation

FIGURE 4.2 Angelelli poster at ex-ESMA

Assassinated by right-wing paramilitaries in El Salvador, Romero, who originally held conservative theological views but shifted in his stance and became a human rights defender in response to the slaying of his priests and parishioners (Reese, 2015), had come to symbolize the ideal of courageous prophetic witness against state terror in the region. His image on the wall in Santa Cruz effectively linked his example as a martyr in the cause of liberation and justice to the memory of the Argentine figures of Mugica and Angelelli.

Fr. Francisco reinforced the sense that these three priests pictured in the poster—Mugica, Angelelli, and Romero—transcended the sacred domain to include the wider secular context of Argentina as a nation. He stated, "we feel and remember them as our prophets—[…] in the sense that they mark a way of living, of facing reality, difficulties […] [for all believers] and also non-believers; many in Latin America, and in Argentina, recognize in them a way of living *whether or not they are believers in Jesus*" (emphasis added). This last point underscores why Argentina's secret police sought to describe Mugica and Angelelli as immoral (Catoggio, 2016, pp. 116–129). This act of slander by the police indicated a sensitivity within the regime's security establishment precisely to Fr. Francisco's point that these martyrs (Mugica and Angelelli), in their time, constituted moral and political exemplars for and beyond the Church. Their altruistic embrace of the oppressed and their fearless defiance of state repression not only contrasted sharply with the state's use of torture, disappearance, and murder but also modeled a compelling counter-morality indicating how one should confront injustice and tyranny.

Nuestras hermanas/Madres de la Plaza de Mayo/Familiares Militantes

To the right, across the front of the traditional altar, there was a second apse featuring another set of posters. These displays commemorated six victims: two French nuns, three co-founders of the Mothers of the Plaza de Mayo, and a human rights activist, all of whom were residents in the parish neighborhood or participants in the mission of the church. The two posters occupied the left and right spaces, respectively, alongside a troika of statues depicting Jesus and two female saints.

One poster, to the left of the statues, was titled "Nuestras hermanas [Our Sisters]" and featured the images of the two French nuns, Alice Domon and Léonie Duquet, whose mission had been to support and accompany individuals and families who were experiencing suffering in their lives[9] (see Figure 4.3). They did this work in impoverished areas both within, and on the outskirts of, the city. After the start of the dictatorship in 1976, they shifted their focus to supporting the families of the disappeared. The text directly beneath the title of this poster stated: "The truth will set us free," a biblical reference (John 8:32). The second poster, titled "Madres de la plaza" (Figure 4.4) depicted four women—three of them founding members of the Madres and the fourth a human rights worker. Beneath the poster title ran the declaration, "la impunidad no será eterna" (impunity will not be eternal). This statement related directly to the long-standing demand for formal justice and accountability with respect to the perpetrators of the terror.

In some sectors in Argentina, a deep and abiding anger remained at the perceived failure of the government to dispense justice and to account for the dead and disappeared—a perception that the ascension of the center-right Macri's government only intensified. In the absence of a full accounting, communities such as Santa Cruz have maintained the memory of the disappeared, making the dead present. The "Las Madres" poster rendered alive the memory of the four assassinated women. Text at the bottom of the poster stated that their remains lay in the church's garden and that there were others, whom the church named explicitly, for whom the congregation continued to search. Following this statement was the declaration that the disappeared and dead were "Presente, ahora y siempre" (Present, Now, and Always) and that state terrorism should never again happen in echo of the CONADEP commission's report, "Nunca Màs."

102 Labors of Justice as Reconciliation

FIGURE 4.3   Nuestras hermanas

FIGURE 4.4   Madres de la Plaza

Labors of Justice as Reconciliation   **103**

The church's inclusion of founders and members of Las Madres gestured toward the extension of the religious into the secular political space and, conversely, the presence of the secular within the religious one. The posters of the dead and disappeared, a group of martyrs that included secular and religious figures, conveyed a sense of the Kingdom of God—which Jesus inaugurates through his preaching as described in the Gospel texts—that transcended the Church. Any action that sought justice became, in this sense, expressive of the Kingdom in actuality. This sensibility found expression in the memorialization of the Madres founders. Santa Cruz embraced these founders as secular martyrs.[10] Like all martyrs, in Santa Cruz's interpretive setting, they witnessed—in Greek, μάρτυρας (martyr) means "witness"—to the truth of God's overcoming of injustice in the utopian kingdom to come.

Across from this display, on the other side of an adjacent side altar, was another poster titled, "Familiares/Militantes [Family/Activists]" (Figure 4.5) that commemorated the lives of six disappeared others affiliated with Santa Cruz. Given its fixed spatial arrangement, this poster accorded martyr status to these individuals through the juxtaposition with the adjacent images of "Las Madres" and "Nuestros Profetas" and with the traditional iconic representations,

FIGURE 4.5   Familiares/Militantes

also situated on Santa Cruz's walls, of the crucified Christ and the saints who gave their lives in witness to Christ. Fr. Francisco explained that traditionally every church honored martyrs of local significance. The images of the disappeared parishioners and the assassinated priests held such significance because, as Fr. Francisco implied, the parish remembered them as their own. If the commemorated individuals were not of Santa Cruz directly (e.g., Archbishop Romero, Bishop Angelelli, and Father Mugica), the church nevertheless saw them as symbols that reinforced and extended the meaning of the sacrifice of their own parish members. These symbols formed a nexus of meaning, linking local martyrs to national and regional ones. Through the nuns, they also connected to the wider, global Church.

The symbolic nexus among these various posters evoked the history and mission of the religious order that founded Santa Cruz. "[As an order] we emphasize the suffering that Christ underwent in the crucifixion," Fr. Francisco explained, "his passion." During the military dictatorship of the late 1970s and early 1980s, the church focused on the suffering of the families of the disappeared in their midst. "Anyone living the passion [undergoing great suffering] is our brother," Fr. Francisco explained, "and for that reason the posters of the assassinated and disappeared are examples of those crucified among us and the meaning of our mission."[11]

Reconciliation

The ethos and practices of committed Catholicism at Santa Cruz is part of larger Argentine narratives of memory and transitional justice since the transition to democracy in 1983. Since that moment, shifts in transitional justice policies and accompanying memory narratives have shaped attempts to address the atrocities of the dictatorship (Lessa, 2013). Francesca Lessa identifies three critical junctures to account for these shifts over time. The first juncture, what she calls "Truth and Limited Justice," covers the initial post-dictatorship years from 1983 to 1985 when memory narratives emphasized findings revealed in the CONADEP report and trials and prosecutions of military leaders. Pardons and amnesties for these leaders and the state's attempts to focus on the future rather than relive or litigate the past marks the second juncture (1986–2002), which Lessa discusses under the heading, "Impunity Laws and Pardons: Challenging Oblivion." The third critical juncture, "The Return of Prosecutions and Memory," covers the years 2003–2012, with an emphasis on the derogation of amnesty laws and a return to prosecutions. Robben (2018) also notes this as a time when attention is directed to transnational discourses of human rights.

Competing memory narratives have persisted since the end of the dictatorship in 1983. Lessa contends, however, that a more dominant or representative memory narrative corresponds to each of these three critical junctures and transitional justice phases. A *two-demons* memory narrative characterized the first phase, for example; a *reconciliation* narrative marked the second one; and, a memory narrative centered on *state terrorism, impunity, and justice*, predominated in the third (Lessa, 2013, p. 222).

Moreover, while a *reconciliation* memory narrative (1986–2002) reflected the transitional justice emphasis on impunity laws and pardons at the national level, this narrative began before the dictatorship's end. Notably, the anti-secularist group within the Argentine Catholic Church were early supporters and remained staunch allies of a wide-sweeping view of reconciliation in Argentina, an approach in which all Argentines would be reconciled to God and to each other as the nation moved past narratives and accusations of blame and victimhood toward some type of harmonized future. One striking example of this stance occurred a year before the official end of the dictatorship. On December 19, 1982, Argentine bishops organized a day of National Reconciliation where churches held masses to help Argentines reconcile themselves to God and to restore peace with each other through some type of acknowledgment of shared responsibility for political violence (Robben, 2010, p. 204). This perspective also resonated with large segments of the Argentine population who preferred reconciliation during the transition to democracy in 1984 rather than efforts to unearth all atrocities committed during the dictatorship (Lessa, 2013).

Up to this point in the chapter, we have demonstrated how the Church of Santa Cruz embodied a Committed Catholic ethos as it integrated the justice work of clergy and laity. This work expressed itself through commitments to the poor and resistance to political persecution and injustice. We now turn to a commemorative ritual that reveals how the concept of reconciliation can take on a very different kind of meaning from the one that the anti-secularist wing of the church has promoted.

The March 23rd Vigil

We returned to the Church of Santa Cruz on March 23, two days after our initial meeting with Fr. Francisco. This second visit occurred the evening before the official "Day of Remembrance for Truth and Justice." Fr. Francisco had invited us to attend a special vigil to commemorate lives lost during the period of state terrorism. Even though only a short time had passed since we were in the spaces of Santa Cruz, we were not the same people. Two-and-a-half days of interviews with scholars, artists, and educators, a lengthy visit to the ex-ESMA, and participation in a special commemorative event at the University of Buenos Aires's Ciencias Sociales had enlarged and deepened our perspectives about relationships among memory, truth, and justice.

We arrived at dusk. The sanctuary remained dimly lit as Fr. Francisco fiddled with the projection and sound equipment in front of the Esquivel mural in the reconfigured worship space. A contingent of young adults sat with a young bearded priest in jeans and sandals to the immediate left of the oaken altar table.

106 Labors of Justice as Reconciliation

They were sipping maté, a traditional South American drink, from the priest's gourd. At one point, the priest handed the gourd to a woman and then walked to the pews to the right of the altar to tune a guitar. This priest, we later learned, worked in one of the villas miserias—an instance of the continuation of the social mission of the church and the committed Catholic networks of which it was part.

The worship space also differed from two days prior. Three large handmade banners had been hung in the interim and now served to enclose the worship space. Two of these banners draped down from the balcony behind the pre-Vatican II altar (Figure 4.6). The hand-rendered words on these banners quoted well-known songs expressing a populist sentiment of commitment to land, people, and those who had given their lives for liberty. One set of words, visible on the right side facing the altar, were from the chorus of a song by the contemporary singer Raly Barrionuevo. They proclaimed: "Soy esta tierra / soy esta gente / soy esta memoria / soy esta historia" ("I am this land / I am this people / I am this memory / and I am this story"). The other set of words quoted the chorus of Víctor Heredia's song, "Patria": "Mira mis manos, lleno de hermanos que tu sangre cante en el viento como bandera de libertad" ("Behold my hands, full of brothers, let your blood sing in the wind like a flag of liberty.")

FIGURE 4.6 Banners above pre-Vatican altar

The military regime banned Heredia during the period of state terror. He had allied himself with the Las Madres movement. The presence of these banners gestured to Santa Cruz's position within a broader current of populist nationalism in Argentina. The military crackdown had divided the Church, positioning its committed wing as a segment of the opposition. Rather than undermine or destroy this segment of the Church, the violence perpetrated against it functioned to solidify the connections between committed Catholicism and anti-regime nationalism beyond the institutional Church.

Opposite to these two banners and above the main church entrance hung another handmade sign that read "La ESPERANZA alimenta y se nutre de la MiSERiCORDiA, LA JUSTICiA, Y LA FRATERNIDAD" ("Hope feeds and is nourished by mercy, justice, and brotherhood") (Figure 4.7). The invocation of the themes of mercy and justice resonated with biblical demands to "do justice, love mercy [kindness, goodness], and walk humbly with your God" (Micah 6:8). Most immediately, it echoed the demands for accountability for the disappeared. Hope for a reconciled Argentina entailed justice but also a profound pity in the depths of the heart (mercy)—"misericordia" is a Latin compound that unites the words for "pity" and "heart"—for those who suffer. Rituals of reconciliation seek to awaken this pity and in so doing render an acknowledgment of injustices. Only with such mercy and acknowledgment does fraternity become possible.

FIGURE 4.7 Banner at back of church near main entrance

108　Labors of Justice as Reconciliation

The March 23rd commemoration ritual began with a welcome from Fr. Francisco. Wielding a microphone and pacing across the dais in front of the altar, he outlined the purpose of the ritual and the process to follow. He then introduced us as "new friends from the United States." As we stood in our individual pews, the congregants turned to look at us. The lights dimmed, and we sat down. Someone at a laptop cued a film about the period of state terror. Fr. Francisco then reflected on this history as he called the congregation to the work of remembrance. The young priest began to play his guitar as someone else accompanied him on a hand-held drum. The congregation sang a series of songs, including the ones whose lyrics were on the two large banners hanging from the balcony. Prayers and moments of reflection followed the singing.

These preliminary moments built toward what would be the central event of the ritual: an embodied exercise of direct encounter, remembrance, confession, healing, and reconciliation in the sense of a restoration to a balanced, just order. In a follow-up communication with Fr. Francisco in 2020, he confirmed this ritual was performed each year. At Santa Cruz in 2016 Fr. Francisco explained that we were to choose a partner and process jointly through the sanctuary in a counterclockwise direction. The direction of movement was in the reverse order of the stations of the cross. As we moved together we were to share any thoughts and feelings we might have had about the period of state terror. Fr. Francisco asked us to speak openly and honestly, "heart to heart." The following is Loren's account of his experience.

> *As Father Francisco calls all of us to stand and process, I feel anxious and awkward. I came here as an observer—a role I am comfortable inhabiting from years of practicing ethnographic research—but now I feel the ground shift under me as the ritual and Fr. Francisco demand my participation. Like a shy teenager at a dance, I don't know who to pair with, I don't know what to do. Within a couple of minutes, the young woman who had come with the maté-sipping, guitar-playing priest approaches me. She appears to be the age of the undergraduate students at UBA, perhaps in her early twenties. She smiles and asks if I'll walk with her. I respond that I will. We start to move. She begins speaking rapidly. I am conscious of my height as I stoop to hear her words. We pass in front of the posters of "Las Madres" and "Nuestros Profetas." I struggle to follow her as she speaks but I feel her urgency to connect with me. I understand enough to know that she is expressing strong negative feelings about the U.S., its support for dictatorships in the region. I am anxious to make sure she knows I understand, that I, too, am critical of my government's policies and my country's interventions in the region.*
>
> *I say, "Lo siento por mi país"- that I am sorry for what my country has done. I tell her that I am ashamed. Her strong words have implicated me; and I am anxious to distance myself from blame, to show which side I am on. Suddenly, we have completed the circuit. We return to our seats. Fr. Francisco asks if anyone is willing to share with the whole group what they have discussed. My companion raises her*

hand. *Taking the wireless microphone, she tells the congregation how important it has been for her to have had this chance to express herself to me, a US citizen—to express her anger at the United States. I do not respond but listen silently as Fr. Francisco thanks her for sharing, notes the importance of remembrance of and responsibility for the past, and then asks for contributions from any others willing to share. I have no further conversation or connection with my partner the rest of the evening.*

This embodied negotiation between Loren and partner in this ritual is multilayered and raises questions, for example, about the source and direction of her anger at the United States as well as the nature and substance of Loren's apology. We know Loren's apology stemmed from his sensitivity to the history of U.S. interventions in Latin America as a whole. He had read Eduardo Galeano's *Las Venas Abiertas de América Latina* (*The Open Veins of Latin America*) while studying as a college student in Bogotá, Colombia during the mid-1980s (Galeano, 1997). At the same time, he researched the U.S. role in El Salvador's civil war. After college, he sought work as a volunteer teacher in the region but, instead, went to the Middle East, where he learned about yet another history of U.S. hegemony abroad that had enabled and perpetuated significant injustices, especially for the Palestinian people. So, during the ritual at Santa Cruz, he found himself reacting to his companion with a deep sense of guilt rooted in his awareness of the destructive impact of U.S. policy globally and in Latin America specifically.

These underlying narratives about U.S. hegemony that informed Loren's apology, however, are complicated. The United States had never intervened militarily in Argentina as it did in several Latin American countries during the so-called "Banana Wars" (1898–1934) or later in Grenada (1983) and Haiti (1993–1994, with UN Security Council approval). It also had not intervened covertly as it did in the CIA-sponsored coup in Chile in 1973. At the same time, however, Argentine figures such as General Leopoldo Galtieri, who was convicted and jailed for human rights abuses following the return to democratic rule in 1983, did train alongside other Latin American military leaders in counter-insurgency and torture techniques at the infamous "School of the Americas" (which, at the time that Gualtieri was there in 1949, was located in Panama) (Hilton, 2003). In contrast, the United States has intervened economically in Argentina for decades. As noted in the previous chapter, since the return to democratic governance in 1983, the United States and the U.S.-led World Bank and IMF have played a direct role in Argentina's debt crises, enforcing highly unfavorable terms of repayment and requiring austerity measures that have exacerbated poverty rates, especially during and after the Argentine collapse in 2001.

So, it appears that Loren's partner for the ritual went to the societal memory chest to access a particular script that names the United States as a primary source of trauma, a script that dates back to the dictatorship but emerged more forcefully after the 2001–2002 economic collapse. We do not know if Loren's partner lost family members during the dictatorship and linked this type of loss, and anger expressed during the ritual, to the United States; it is likely, however, that her response stemmed from this more recent 2001–2002 social and economic trauma as she implicated him and the United States in Argentine suffering. For the past two decades, especially after Nestor Kirchner became President in 2003, the terror of the past has been connected with the causal role of U.S. hedge funds in Argentina's economic crisis and with the neo-liberal political and economic shift that President Macri's election seemed to herald. In the eyes of many on the political left, the Macri Administration, for which President Obama expressed support, had departed significantly from the commitment of the previous Kirchner governments to human rights and accountability. As Chapter 3 highlighted, this political and economic shift augured new social injustices by minimizing rights and exacerbating wealth inequalities.

There were, then, at least three trajectories that intersected in the interaction between Loren and his partner in the Santa Cruz ritual: Loren's personal history of engagement with Latin America; the specificity of Argentine history and its relationship to the United States; and the generational location of the young woman. This intersection occurred within a very particular ritual structure whose point of departure was the mobilization of memory of the period of state terror and specifically of the disappeared. The structure of the remembrance, the ritual process that was invoked, intersected with the current moment of Argentine history and politics, a moment in which the United States had come to be seen as a malevolent force. The ritual, however, was not simply an unresolved positioning of binaries in tension. Loren was not simply made to inhabit the role of the American oppressor without resolution. The entire point of the ritual was to share from the heart and seemingly to achieve some type of reconciliation. The communication between Loren and his companion, transacted in his imperfect Spanish, had not been seamless; still, a meaningful exchange did occur. Loren's co-participant clearly felt the exchange to be significant. Fr. Francisco registered the significance, speaking immediately after her about the need to restore a just balance through remembrance of, and responsibility for, the past. This was not a ritual of forgiveness or of absolution; rather, it worked toward acknowledgment and repentance and individual healing in relation to the past.

The past was complicated. The role of the United States was not straightforward even if Loren and his partner and perhaps Fr. Francisco, too, were unaware of, or elided, that fact. Nevertheless, some sort of connection and acknowledgment and catharsis had occurred, however momentary. Our presence perhaps expanded the scope of Fr. Francisco's ritual in new, unanticipated directions. It facilitated a connection between the Argentine past and a regional and international present made distinctly and uniquely palpable by our attendance and participation at the behest of Fr. Francisco.

Labors of Justice as Reconciliation 111

A Reconciled Argentina as the Kingdom of the Poor and the Oppressed

The most immediately visible feature of the worship space was a large painting by Argentina's Nobel Peace Prize laureate, Adolfo Pérez Esquivel (Figure 4.8). The painting, which provided the altar with a palimpsestic backdrop (it stood in front of an older tableau of Jesus being lowered from the cross), offered a panorama of Latin America's history and its multicultural diversity.

In the upper right-hand corner (facing the painting) are the wooden ships of the Spanish Conquista—a reference to colonialism and its continuing impact. In the upper center rise the Andes and also the monumental structures of ancient indigenous societies: Machu Picchu is visible. The middle center shows a large cross behind which stands a mass of brown bodies, perhaps indigenous and mestizo peasants. In the upper left-hand corner, time accelerates to the industrialized present. Power plant cooling towers and factory smokestacks belch fumes into the atmosphere. Tall skyscrapers gesture toward modern megacities in the region but also globally. To us, observers from the United States, the tall towers appear similar to those of the (now destroyed) World Trade Center in New York City, symbols of the global economic order that has imposed regimes of austerity on the developing world but has also helped to create a layer of wealthy Latin

FIGURE 4.8 Esquivel painting

American elite. Reinforcing this interpretation of the buildings as symbols of the inequities of the economic order are the images of slums appearing in the shadow of the gleaming skyscrapers and smoking factories.

The main focus of Esquivel's mural, however, lies in the center toward the bottom foreground. A figure immediately interpretable as Jesus appears as a dark-haired, brown-skinned man in white robes surrounded by children and adults of similar complexion.[12] Women carrying posters of images of other children and a sign saying, "Niños desaparecidos [Disappeared Children]," appear in the group. Fr. Francisco explained that the images referred to the Madres de la Plaza de Mayo, who would stand in Buenos Aires's central square with photographs of their disappeared children in silent protest. Other indigenous figures appear alongside the images of the slain Argentine Bishop Enrique Angelelli, the assassinated Salvadoran Archbishop Oscar Romero, and Fr. Luís Espinal (1932–1980), a Spanish Jesuit priest whose paramilitary forces tortured and killed in Bolivia in response to his human rights advocacy.

Taken together, the feeling conveyed in this tableau is one of warm familiarity. It is the gathered community of martyred saints and the beloved poor prefiguring the "new heaven and new earth" foretold in the biblical books of Isaiah and Revelation. The vision is also deeply political in its reference to the history of colonialism and capitalist exploitation and in its focus on the oppressed, the victimized, and the martyrs, whom it exhumes from the oblivion of secret graves, suppressed archives, and the marginalization of public derogation (as "subversives," e.g.). The vision expresses the "option for the poor and oppressed" that liberation theologians and the activists of the Movement of Priests for the Third World have articulated. It challenges the theology of power that justified the counterinsurgency policies of the military regimes in the Southern Cone during the 1970s and 1980s. In the context of present-day Argentina, it expresses at the local level a continuing insistence on justice and equality—or, in Pope Francis's formulation in *Evangelii Gaudium*, the "hope for the kingdom and 'for the possibility of another world'" (as quoted in Scononne, 2016, p. 134).[13] Indeed, it is at this local level of the people that the Gospel, as the "theology of the people" tradition envisions it, becomes materially inculturated and thus incarnated (in theological terms). In his mural, Esquivel visually expresses this sense of the Kingdom embodied in and through "los oprimidos" (the oppressed) in the figure of the enslaved African, who appears on Jesus' right, hands up and apart, manacles broken. Jesus, "the truth," has set the slaves free. This freedom appears within and indeed instantiates the Kingdom as the overcoming, through the *sensus fidei*, the intimate acquaintance of the poor and oppressed with Christ's suffering, of "evil crystallized in unjust social structures" (Pope Francis, *Evangelii Gaudium*, as quoted in Scononne, 2016, p. 133).

Spatially at Santa Cruz, the posters of priests, nuns, and activists and Esquivel's mural convey a sense of justice as reconciliation. The justice envisioned is far from any notion of cheap grace: those who stand at Jesus's right hand are the martyrs—the 30,000 disappeared, the oppressed indigenous peoples, the African slaves, the impoverished campesinos and inhabitants of the villas miserias, and the nuns, priests, and activists who sacrificed their lives in witness against the violence of the state. Reconciliation flows from remembering these martyrs and victims and placing their example at the center of the new Argentina, indeed, at the center of "the new heaven and earth." While the sacrament of reconciliation typically focuses on an individual's relationship with God, Esquivel's mural embodies a stance of "radical reconciliation" where "the deeply personal does not cancel out the thoroughly systemic" (Boesak & DeYoung, 2012, p. 155). This emphasis on systemic change gets at the roots of inequality and the challenge of creating a more equitable, just society. Esquivel's mural leads us toward what Dr. Martin Luther King, Jr., celebrated U.S. civil rights leader, called the "beloved community" where "the end is reconciliation; the end is redemption; the end is the creation of the beloved community" (1957, n.p.). Extended to its theological extreme, however, this vision of a redeemed nation and humanity encompasses oppressors, too, so long as they confess, repent, and seek the forgiveness of the aggrieved. Loren's vigil encounter with a Santa Cruz parishioner, through his confession and apology for his country's complicity in state terrorism, created an opportunity for one type of forgiveness.

As with the Chapter 3 focus on the UBA sites, the commemorative literacies at the Church of Santa Cruz were *liturgical* and *testimonial*. As liturgies, the appeals to particular shared ideals to comprise "the sacred" or sense of "things set apart" (Durkheim [1912] 1995; Taves, 2009) can be found in the permanent exhibition of photographic posters and murals and other objects commemorating the disappeared in the sanctuary space juxtaposed with images of Christ and the saints with references to Argentina's colonial past. As testimonios, these posters, murals, and objects, along with an embodied ritual process, forged a particular "discourse of solidarity" (Partnoy, 2006) that honored victims of past atrocities and advanced ongoing justice efforts. At Santa Cruz, memory mobilizations of the past were intricately layered, temporally, extending backward to Christ's crucifixion through the 1976 coup and into the present.

Transnational Resonances

Toward the end of our visit at Santa Cruz, Fr. Francisco made a distinction between South Africa's Truth and Reconciliation Commission and what had transpired in Argentina:

> In South Africa, [the Truth and Reconciliation Commission] offered less punishment in exchange for truthful statements. Therefore, we can say that as a result there was a lot more revelation of the crimes. They opted for that kind of justice. For us [in Argentina] we remained so closed and secret, so hidden, everything that was done, the archives, so covered. So, we opted for

> another kind of justice—judging the crimes. But, because so little was actually revealed, very few were equally judged and condemned. And the Church did not actively participate as in South Africa. In South Africa the participation of the bishops, whether Catholics or other Christian confessions, was very important and very good. But in Argentina that theme of reconciliation cannot happen because of the secrecy, which remains very great, surrounding the past.

The differences that Fr. Francisco identified—particularly the idea that reconciliation remained impossible without acknowledgment of crimes committed—spoke both to the specific Argentine reality and, indirectly, to the utopian "Kingdom" envisioned by Esquivel's painting in the reconfigured worship space. The continued silence around human rights abuses extended beyond the military to different elements of civil society, including the Catholic Church. The continuation of "the horror"—Fr. Francisco's term—into the present meant that the period of state terror was not yet a fully completed event. Argentines were still coming to terms with it as contemporary events forced renewed debate. The Church hierarchy, for example, had been complicit in the terror but much still remained hidden about the extent of its role. Only in 2015 did the Vatican decide to open its archives on the period, possibly in response to the controversy that erupted after the election of Pope Francis (the former Archbishop of Buenos Aires, Cardinal Jorge Bergoglio).[14] Fr. Francisco also compared justice efforts in Argentina with the struggles of the Vietnamese people. During his Easter sermon, which took place on March 26, 2016, two days after the March 24 public holiday and march to La Plaza de Mayo, Fr. Francisco made this connection, linking a successful freedom struggle in Vietnam to the ongoing justice efforts in Argentina.

> When Vietnam comes.... the experience of the Vietnamese resistance... they knew what they wanted. Because they wanted to get ahead in their own way. And so they also won a war, with much pain, with a lot of death, but they knew what they wanted: freedom.

Conclusion

Overall, the idea of reconciliation at the Church of Santa Cruz provided a way to partially integrate the past into a coherent narrative through the use of martyrological memory, the prominent display of martyrs to cultivate particular kinds of memory work (Lybarger et al., 2018). Esquivel's painting exemplified this particular type of commemorative literacy with its temporally broad invocation of Spanish colonialism, economic imperialism, and military dictatorship alongside the image of the gathered community of the oppressed and martyred around the risen Jesus. The scene thus contained both historical interpretation and utopian projection: it was both commemorative and prefigurative.

Fr. Francisco drew on a similar duality in our initial interview with him when he described Argentina and the Church as situated in a rowboat, facing the past while moving with every stroke toward an unknown future. Any idea about what that future held was necessarily informed by what had come before—what the passengers of the rowboat could see as they moved away from it. In commemorating the martyrs, the church retrieved and carried forward a particular kind of past and in doing so propelled Argentines—those who engaged Santa Cruz's space of remembrance—into a future imagined through that past. The martyrs embodied the values of the Kingdom of the Saints, persecuted for the sake of justice. Their altruism and suffering modeled the virtues of this ideal community. Santa Cruz and its Passionist priests offered the model to all Argentines as a proleptic goal and as a map to that goal.

The memory work at the Church of Santa Cruz was also intergenerational. For example, Loren's experience during the vigil in which his walking partner expressed her anger at the United States suggested some level of dynamic interplay among the time of state terrorism, Argentina's economic collapse in the early years of the twenty-first century and the contemporary context with Macri in power. The visceral, affective response of Loren's partner as she seemingly moved across time and space also gestured toward what might be called intergenerational "hauntings" (Abraham & Torok, 1994; Cho, 2008; Navaro-Yashin, 2012; To, 2015).

Returning to the idea of the rowboat, the image of movement invoked in this metaphor also resonated with our understanding of Santa Cruz as a dynamic space through which we moved in different ways at different times. At the church, we experienced what Massey describes as space, the multiplicity of intersecting "stories so far" (Massey, 2005). The posters of martyred priests and human rights activists, the banners with song lyrics, the references to a centuries-long history of Latin American violence and exploitation all overlapped in constructing Santa Cruz as a space in that particular moment. At the same time, we brought with us our own memories and narratives that both changed and were changed by the existing stories that defined the space. In both our engagement with the posters and worship space, and in our experience with the vigil, Santa Cruz became dynamic. It elicited responses and reflections within us and with those who engaged us, thus showing how sites of memory are active, moving, and agentive. The permanent installation and ritual forms of worship and remembrance established definite parameters and possibilities for memory to be mobilized. But within these structures, individuals could articulate their own narratives and improvise within the established liturgical forms to generate new syntheses of meaning. The synthesis we experienced during our time at Santa Cruz manifested as an elicitation of justice as reconciliation in the very particular sense instantiated at the church and highlighted one way in which commemorative literacies for justice work manifested during the March 2016 events in Buenos Aires.

Notes

1 Segments of this chapter first appeared in published form in Lybarger et al. (2018).
2 Morello's concept of "institutional Catholicism" points to a grey zone spanning the anti-secularists and the committed. His arguments in this respect are at odds with the reigning historiography of the Argentine Church. This historiography has established how the Church hierarchy, including but also extending beyond the military vicariate, supported the regime. Morello does not dispute this conclusion but argues, in effect and persuasively, that the relation of Church leaders to the junta was not always interpretable as simply resistance or complicity. See Morello (2015, 176–180).
3 Rerum Novarum (1891) responded to the rise of Marxism, atheism, and the trade union movement in Europe by attempting to revive the medieval corporate model of the church, in which different orders of society were seen as contributing to the whole and in which charity was the governing social and economic ethic. In the spirit of this organic social conception, the encyclical simultaneously affirmed the right to property and the right to organize into unions. It also called upon owners to treat workers fairly in a spirit of Christian charity (caritas) and unity. In Argentina, during the 1920s and 1930s, various lay and ecclesiastical groups, such as Catholic Action, which formed in response to Rerum Novarum, sought to chart a third way between Marxism and liberalism. See Taylor (2007) on the Medieval Church's conception of an organic Christian society.
4 The Montoneros formed from the confluence of left-wing student groups, left-wing Peronist cadres, and elements within the "committed" Catholic milieu. The movement called for armed rebellion to overthrow authoritarian regimes and establish a socialist state in Argentina. Declared illegal by Isabel Perón and harassed by the Anti-Communist Alliance, the Montoneros ultimately succumbed to defeat in 1979 following sustained violent repression during the first three years of the military dictatorship.
5 Details of the following history derive, in part, from Taurozzi (n.d.).
6 The "theology of the people" was a uniquely Argentine development. It had roots in the social teaching of the papal encyclical, Rerum Novarum (1891) and the early social initiatives that grew from this papal statement (Catoggio, 2016, pp. 26–27). It acquired definite form in the aftermath of the Second Vatican Council. Argentine bishops who participated in Vatican II returned to establish the Episcopal Commission for Pastoral Practice (COEPAL) in a bid to initiate a national strategy for pastoral care. Participants in COEPAL also created a range of centers focused on social problems, following the teachings of Vatican II. Priests connected with this emerging movement extended their mission work into the villas miserias. The "theology of the people" emphasized the laity, and especially the poor, as carriers of an embodied, inculturated Gospel. This focus provided the starting point for a vision of a "people of God" as a unified yet internally diverse whole. Injustice was a betrayal of the unity of the people of God and in that respect, it called for the faithful to engage in a non-violent but determined effort to establish the ethos of charity and love. The poor served as the theological starting point because of their perceived proximity to and capacity for understanding the suffering that Christ endured. In this sense, the "theology of the people" hearkened to the medieval notion of the poor as providing the occasion, for other social orders (nobility, e.g.), to gain salvation through the giving of charity. The poor signified the presence of Christ; charity toward them signaled a response to Christ and thus served as a means to grace. Proponents of the "theology of the people" were in conversation with the regional liberation theology trends, especially at the founding conference in Medellín, Colombia in 1968, where Latin American bishops affirmed the church's "preferential option for the poor." The "theology of the people" departed from liberation theology, at least in the initial phases of these two movements, in its critique of Marxism and in its prioritizing of culture—principally through

the notion of the poor as carriers of an inculturated (and unadulterated) Christian social ethos—over economics. For more, see Scononne (2016), Catoggio (2016), and Ivereigh (1995).
7 The twelve *desaparecidos* associated with the Church of Santa Cruz are: María Eugenia Ponce de Bianco, Esther Ballestrino de Careaga, and Azucena Villaflor (all members of the Madres de la Plaza de Mayo); Ángela Auad, Raquel Bullit, Eduardo Gabriel Horane, José Julio Fondevilla, Patricia Cristina Oviedo, Horacio Aníbal Elbert, and Remo Berardo (human rights activists); and Léonie Duquet and Alice Domon (French nuns working in the villas miserias of Gran Buenos Aires).
8 The poem, titled, "El hombre proyecto de pueblo," can be read and listened to here: https://www.ivoox.com/hombre-proyecto-de-pueblo-enrique-angelelli-audios-mp3_r6_3419139_1.html.
9 Interview, Fr. Francisco, 21 March 2016.
10 The term "secular" is complex. In a Catholic context, it refers to anyone or any space separate from the formal religious order—that is, parish priests and laity as well as the parish and wider political and social spheres not directly encompassed within a monastic context. Since the European Enlightenment, and especially with the rise of the modern social sciences, the term refers to anything which is not religious or which is made nonreligious (secularized). The literature on "the secular," "secularism," "secularization," and "secularity" is immense. See Taylor (2007) for a recent comprehensive discussion.
11 Fr. Francisco went on to explain that the historical mission of the Passionists included advocating for truth and justice and "the defense of human rights." The remains of five of "the crucified" (in Fr. Francisco's terms) whom the church honors in the posters are also interred on the church grounds. Their graves function as a type of reliquary. Their presence endows Santa Cruz with a distinct status: the church participates in the honor of these martyrs even as it creates this honored status through its martyrial commemorative process. On March 24 every year the church sanctifies these dead in a mass of commemoration that entails standing behind the grave markers to proclaim, "Presente! Ahora y siempre!" [Present! Now and always!].
12 This image constituted a reclamation of the memory of Jesus of Nazareth, who was likely a darkly complected, poor, and oppressed Jew living during the Roman Empire. As Christianity became integrated within European societies, the image of Jesus began to reflect a "white" phenotype: as in other cultural contexts, Jesus served as a mirror of the racial self-perception of the society in which Christianity had become embedded. In the colonial period, the white Jesus became associated with European domination: "A white European colonial image of Jesus was constructed, owned, and manipulated by empires for domination" (Boesak & DeYoung 2012, 49). For a wide-ranging and fascinating discussion of the inculturation of Jesus' image across diverse societies, see Pelikan ([1985] 1999).
13 Scononne argues that Francis's doctrinal positions directly reflect the emphases of the "theology of the people."
14 For more on these matters, see Verbitsky (2005); Anderson (2013); Hernandez (2013); Rebossio (2013); "Vatican to open Argentina's 'Dirty War' archives" (2016); "Pérez Esquivel: 'El Papa no tenía vínculos con la dictadura'" (2013). Note that Verbitsky has been accused of collaborating with the military himself during the terror. See the investigative articles at http://www.plazademayo.com/?s=Verbitsky.

References

Abraham N. & Torok, M. (1994). *The shell and the kernel*. University of Chicago Press.
Anderson, J.L. (2013, March 14). Pope Francis and the dirty war. *The New Yorker*. http://www.newyorker.com/news/daily-comment/pope-francis-and-the-dirty-war

Bilbao, L. & Lede, A. (2016). *Profeta del genocidio: El vicariato castrense y los diarios del obispo Bonamín en la última dictadura*. Penguin Random House Grupo Editorial, S.A.

Boesak, A.A. & DeYoung, C.P. (2012). *Radical reconciliation: Beyond political pietism and Christian quietism*. Orbis Books.

Catoggio, M.A. (2016). *Los desaparecidos de la iglesia: El clero contestatario frente a la dictadura*. Siglo Veintiuno Editores.

Cho, G. (2008). *Haunting the Korean diaspora: Shame, secrecy and the forgotten war*. University of Minnesota Press.

Galeano, E. (1997). *Open veins of Latin America: Five centuries of the pillage of a continent*. Monthly Review Press.

Hernandez, V. (2013, March 15). Argentina 'dirty war' accusations haunt Pope Francis. *BBC News*. http://www.bbc.com/news/world-europe-21794798

Hilton, I. (2003, January 12). General Leopoldo Gualtieri. *The Guardian*. https://www.theguardian.com/news/2003/jan/13/guardianobituaries.argentina

Ivereigh, A. (1995). *Catholicism and politics in Argentina, 1810–1960*. St. Martin's Press.

King Jr., M.L. (1957, January 1). *Facing the Challenge of a New Age. Address Delivered at NAACP Emancipation Day Rally*.

Lessa, F. (2013). *Memory and transitional justice in Argentina and Uruguay: Against impunity*. Palgrave Macmillan.

Lybarger, L.D., Damico, J.S., & Brudney, E. (2018). Religion and the commemoration of the disappeared in Argentina 40 years after the dictatorship: A study of martyrological memory at the Church of Santa Cruz. *Journal of Religion and Society, 20*. https://dspace2.creighton.edu/xmlui/bitstream/handle/10504/116848/2018-15.pdf

Mallimaci, F. (2015). *El mito de la Argentina laica: Catolicismo, política y estado*. Capital Intelectual.

Massey, D.B. (2005). *For space*. SAGE.

Morello, G.S.J. (2015). *The Catholic church and Argentina's dirty war*. Oxford University Press.

Navaro-Yashin, Y. (2012). *The make-believe space: Affective geography in a postwar polity*. Duke University Press.

Partnoy, A. (2006). Cuando vienen matando: On prepositional shifts and the struggle of testimonial subjects for agency. *PMLA, 121*(5), 1665–1669.

Pelikan, J. ([1985]; 1999). *Jesus through the centuries: His place in the history of culture*. Yale University Press.

Pérez Esquivel: "El Papa no tenía vínculos con la dictadura". (2013, March 14). *BBC News*. https://www.bbc.com/mundo/ultimas_noticias/2013/03/130314_ultnot_perez_esquivel_papa

Rebossio, A. (2013, March s). La sombra de la dictadura argentina alcanza al papa Francisco. *El Pais*. https://elpais.com/internacional/2013/03/14/actualidad/1363224768_851250.html

Reese, T. (2015, February 6). Oscar Romero, martyr to the faith. *National Catholic Reporter*. https://www.ncronline.org/blogs/faith-and-justice/oscar-romero-martyr-faith

Robben, A.C.G.M. (2018). *Argentina betrayed: Memory, mourning, and accountability*. University of Pennsylvania Press.

Robben, A. (2010). Testimonies, truths, and transitions of justice in Argentina and Chile. In A.L. Hinton (Ed.), *Transitional justice: Global mechanisms and local realities after genocide and mass violence* (pp. 179–205). Rutgers University Press.

Scononne, J.C. (2016). Pope Francis and the theology of the people. *Theological Studies, 77*(1), 118–135.

Taurozzi, S. (n.d.). *La parroquia Santa Cruz y el ejercicio de reconstrucción de la memoria: 1961–2012. Ciencias Sociales*. Universidad de Buenos Aires.

Taylor, C. (2007). *A secular age*. Belknap Press of Harvard University Press.

To, N. (2015). Diasporic montage and critical autoethnography: Mediated visions of intergenerational memory and the affective transmission of trauma. In Britta TImm Knudsen & Carsten Stage (Eds) *Affective Methodologies: Developing Cultural Strategies for the Study of Affect* (pp. 69–96). Palgrave Macmillan.

Vatican to open Argentina's 'dirty war' archives. (2016, October 25). *BBC News*.

Verbitsky, H. (1995). *El vuelo*. Planeta.

Verbitsky, H. (2005). *El silencio: De Paulo VI a Bergoglio: Las relaciones secretas de la iglesia con la ESMA*. Sudamericana.

5
LABORS OF JUSTICE AS RECOVERY

Individual, Societal, and Spatial Modes of Meaning-Making

We want to feel their presence but in reality they aren't here.
But it is something about them that leaves a shadow, something that is a part of us.

—Nico Arrúe (March 22, 2016)

It is mid-afternoon on Tuesday, March 22, 2016, when we leave one of the buildings of the ex-ESMA and step out into the bright sunshine. Earlier that morning, we learned about the human rights project called "Memoria Abierta" (Open Memory), which includes a repository of 900 testimonies of victims from the dictatorship and of social and political activists of the 1960s and 1970s. Through this project, viewers are confronted with testimonios and deeply personal accounts about what it meant to have a missing or disappeared family member. Memoria Abierta is one project among many stationed at the ex-ESMA. Following our meeting, we proceeded to tour the space of the ex-ESMA itself, experiencing a series of evocative exhibits making claims about memory, truth, and justice.

We now move across the open courtyard to a small building called La Casa de Nuestros Hijos (The House of our Children). As we enter the building, Paul, our filmmaker, prepares the camera for an interview with Nico Arrúe, an artist who created an installation called "Presencias" (Presences).[1] *Our time in Buenos Aires has been marked by ideas of presence and absence, and they rang out the night before at the University of Buenos Aires' Facultad de Ciencias Sociales (CS) in a moving memorial service to commemorate the students and faculty who were disappeared from that university space. The chant, "Presente ahora y siempre" (Present, now, and always) from the night before at CS led by one of the Madres reverberated in our ears, and we were eager to see how Nico would explore the theme of presence(s).*

DOI: 10.4324/9781003184195-6

> Liliana, core member of our research team and knowing guide, is Nico's cousin, and the two embrace upon seeing each other. Nico and his wife greet the rest of us with a warm smile, handshakes, and hugs. We feel welcomed into the space of this relatively small one-story building. As we enter, Nico's art installation is to our left and there are several paintings on the wall in front of us and to our right. Another open room sits to the right with more paintings and artwork. A mostly unadorned corridor is off to the left leading to offices and restrooms. Nico is ready to begin our interview and guide us through his art installation, a provocative exploration of trauma and loss and what it might mean to recover the life and memory of his father, who was disappeared, a father he never met.

Introduction

This chapter is about the relationship between justice labor and processes of recovery in the spaces of the ex-ESMA (*Escuela Superior de Mecánica de la Armada*), a former naval mechanics' school and detention center, and currently one of Argentina's most prominent "memory spaces" (*espacios de memoria*).[2] Recovery connotes recuperation or improvement. An economy recovers from a recession, for example, a patient recovers from an illness. Recovery can also refer to retrieval or reclamation of something lost or stolen. We emphasize justice work as a process of recovery to stress an unfolding set of events and experiences rather than a destination or a definitive arrival point. Meaning-making amidst a complex array of texts in the spaces of the ex-ESMA, especially through our perspectives as U.S. citizens, was, and continues to be, ongoing and emergent.

Within the ex-ESMA, meaning-making occurs in complicated patterns that complement and exist in tension with each other. Our visit helped us discern three interwoven layers of justice work as recovery. The first is an *individual layer*, where we examine Nico's attempt to recover a relationship with his father through his art installation, "Presencias." We then build on Nico's claim that his account "was not just a personal story but a national story as well" to explore a *societal layer* of justice work as recovery. Here, we connect Nico's account and experience with broader collective struggles around human rights in Argentina. Specifically, we draw on interviews conducted with Alejandra Oberti, Director of the Oral Archive and the Program in Oral History for *Memoria Abierta*, housed within the ex-ESMA, to explore ongoing efforts to recover individual accounts of trauma and violence and to stitch these stories into a collective cloth. A third and final *spatial layer* of justice work as recovery provides a deeper understanding of how the ex-ESMA transitioned from naval base and clandestine detention center to memory space and headquarters for a range of human rights organizations. Tracing this evolutionary process highlights the nearly two-decade debate over what the ultimate purpose of the site should be. This manifestation of justice work as recovery is closely tied to ideas about reclamation, as people and organizations have attempted to reclaim and repurpose the space of the ex-ESMA to align with their own social and political goals. In the conclusion, we return to Nico's "Presencias" to explore how this spatial layer helps explain the fluid relationship between individual and collective layers of recovery.

The imbrication of these layers of justice work and recovery (individual, collective, spatial) make the ex-ESMA an especially interesting case study for examining commemorative literacies and memory mobilizations. Our time at the ex-ESMA was largely defined by our interactions with Nico, but we also moved through the site itself and came into contact with other individuals, groups, and physical markers that all spoke to the naval base's difficult history. Returning to historian Steve Stern's metaphor of a societal memory chest, the ex-ESMA was an important section within the "album" that represents "memory as persecution and awakening," in which memory is marshalled to summon the repressive tactics of the junta as well as spur a subsequent social awakening against these draconian forces (Stern, 2004). The ex-ESMA itself, its buildings, and its settings constitute a set of texts ("photographs") within this album to be analyzed as such.

Historical and Political Context

To situate Nico's exhibit at the ex-ESMA within the broader framework of justice work and recovery in Argentina requires additional historical context. In 1924, the city of Buenos Aires leased a parcel of land along the Río de la Plata to the Argentine Navy for the construction of a technical and mechanical school for recruits. Within a few years, the first buildings had been completed and the school began admitting students. The following decades saw the ESMA expand until it covered 17 hectares on what became the Avenida del Libertador, in the neighborhood of Núñez.[3] The total number of buildings eventually reached 34, including barracks, housing for senior and junior officers, classrooms, a bakery, workshops, and a fire station, among various others. Throughout much of the twentieth century, including the 1970s and 1980s, several thousand naval recruits lived on the premises, usually for periods of one to three years, depending on their specialization. On completing their studies, most students were able to choose between either continuing with their military service or graduating and pursuing employment in the private sector. Until the 1970s, there is little to suggest that the ESMA differed markedly from other military academies around the country.

This would change, however, during the final months of Isabel Perón's presidency. The radicalization of Argentine society in the late 1960s produced a climate of unprecedented political violence. Kidnappings and bombings by armed leftist groups were answered with campaigns of extralegal terror coordinated by right-wing members of the state's security forces. It was during this period that the practice of disappearing people became commonplace. Because of the lack of physical remains, together with the general unwillingness of most of those involved to testify to their actions, it has been difficult to establish with certainty when the first clandestine detention centers (*centros clandestinos de detención* or CCDs) began operating. However, from 1976, the ESMA was the most prominent of the final destinations for the disappeared.

The counterinsurgency strategies developed both domestically and as part of the continent-wide Operation Condor found their full expression during the Proceso de Reorganización Nacional (PRN). Starting immediately after the coup, when Argentines classified as political enemies were rounded up by the military in the middle of the night, the ESMA rapidly became the country's largest CCD. Between March 24, 1976 and the return of democracy in December 1983, approximately 5,000 civilians were imprisoned in the school at various points. For most, once they had been physically abducted by the security forces, they lost not only their freedom but also their legal status as citizens. The ESMA became a liminal space, outside the dictates of even the superficial legal structures overseen by the Armed Forces—a place where the writ of habeas corpus simply did not apply.[4] Of the approximately 5,000 people who passed through the ESMA, it is estimated that around 200 survived (Feld, 2008, p. 82). Much of what we know about the internal functioning of the detention center comes from firsthand accounts of survivors, together with a very limited number of testimonies from participants in the repressive apparatus.[5] These reports have helped construct a limited picture of what the daily routine within the school looked like.

Among the various buildings that constitute the ESMA, one functioned as the primary site for interrogation, imprisonment, and torture. At any given moment in the attic of the *Casino de Oficiales* (Officers' Quarters), dozens of men and women lived under the control of the members of the "Grupo de Tareas 3.3.2," which operated from the school. The attic was called "La Capucha" ("the Hood"), referring both to its location on the top floor of the building and also to the fact that prisoners were blindfolded or hooded at all times while there. Throughout the day, people were escorted by soldiers down to the basement to face brutal torture, sometimes for the purposes of extracting information, sometimes not. A modified cattle prod (*la picana*) was a favorite tool of interrogators in these situations. Sexual violence against women was common, and women who gave birth while in captivity frequently had their newborn children taken from them and given to the families of soldiers or sympathizers to be raised. The practice of disappearing suspected "subversives" almost immediately expanded to the kidnapping of anyone with even tenuous connections to leftist politics, as well as repression for profit. Theft occurred on a massive scale as the military ransacked the houses of prisoners, and those who owned property were often coerced into signing it over to the Armed Forces (or their signatures were forged, which produced the same result) (Hauser, 2007; Relea, 1998).

In addition to first-person accounts, photographs have been critical to the reconstruction of what occurred within the walls of the ESMA (Andermann, 2012; Feld, 2012). It was in the basement of the Casino de Oficiales that the military staged the infamous photo of two French nuns, Alice Domon and Léonie Duquet (discussed in relation to the Church of Santa Cruz in Chapter 4), in front of a flag bearing the insignia of the Montoneros. The photograph was used in an attempt to convince the world that leftist guerrillas had taken them. The kidnapping of the nuns and the clumsy cover-up sparked an international outcry, bringing the world's attention to human rights abuses in Argentina. Two years later, in 1979, the Armed Forces kidnapped Víctor Basterra and brought him to the ESMA, where he was assigned to a group charged with manufacturing false documents for the state security forces. His duties included photographing the prisoners who arrived at the school. Basterra was among the fortunate few who received his release, and when he left he managed to smuggle out dozens of negatives of these photos, which have helped provide some record of the people disappeared from the ESMA.[6] Thus, photography and testimony have combined to partially illuminate the day-to-day repressive practices at the school during the 1976–1983 period.

The return of democracy at the end of 1983 under President Raúl Alfonsín restored the rule of law but did not necessarily bring about a meaningful transformation of the relationship between civil society and the Armed Forces. The inability to successfully pursue and punish those responsible for the repression was epitomized by the decision of Carlos Menem, Alfonsín's successor, to issue blanket pardons for even those few who had been convicted of crimes in the mid-1980s. Further proof can be found in the fact that after 1983, while the detention center no longer operated, the ESMA itself continued to function as a school for naval recruits. For the next 15 years, the legacy of violence carried out by the dictatorship remained officially unacknowledged but known to all. In 1998, the Navy moved the school several hundred miles down the coast, near the city of Bahía Blanca. Menem planned to demolish the buildings of the now ex-ESMA and replace them with a public park symbolizing "national unity."

However, his proposal generated a fierce backlash. As president, Menem consistently pursued a politics of "national unity" (exemplified by his pardoning of the members of the ruling junta), and his idea to raze the school and replace it with open green space reflected this approach. The result, though, was a fierce and concerted pushback against the project by social movements and human rights organizations in Argentina. Family members of two *desaparecidos* filed an injunction with the federal judiciary, which they won, and used the occasion to demand that ownership of the site be transferred from the Navy back to the City of Buenos Aires. Several years passed before the Armed Forces formally ceded the site, but the argument drawing on the experiences of the victims and the needs of the collective had laid the groundwork for a dramatic next step in Argentina's struggle to come to terms with its past.

The third section of this chapter will explore the transformation of this CCD into a memory space more fully, but here it is enough to note that the transition began in earnest with the election of Néstor Kirchner in 2003. Between them, Néstor and his wife Cristina held the presidency from 2003 until 2015 and made human rights a pillar of their political agenda. The ex-ESMA, rechristened the

Space for Memory and for the Promotion and Defense of Human Rights (*Espacio para la Memoria y para la Promoción y Defensa de los Derechos Humanos*) in 2004, formally opened in 2007. Since that date, more than a dozen prominent human rights organizations have established their headquarters on the site, and the *Casino de Oficiales* has become a museum, with visitors able to tour the spaces where the military tortured and murdered thousands of Argentines during the *Proceso*. In addition, numerous exhibit halls and art spaces have been created that regularly host installations and performances, which provide not only "repositories, reflections, and expressions of the force of the past in the present" but also serve as "productive sites of social meaning where societies deal with, contest, struggle over, represent, and continue their journey through rupture" (Gómez-Barris, 2009, pp. 8–9). It was in one of these spaces that we encountered Nico Arrúe's "Presencias."

Justice, Recovery, and the Individual: Nico Arrúe's Presencias

Conjuring the Disappeared

"The shadows were telling me about the disappeared."

– Nico

Nico's installation consisted of a series of white screens on which grey shadow images of individual forms, either alone or in groupings, were projected, appearing and disappearing intermittently. These images included: a man supporting a child taking a step, a woman holding a child, a child alone on a swing, a man and woman each holding a child, a man and woman embracing, and a pregnant woman looking down toward her midsection. A soundtrack of voices—children at play, a baby cooing—accompanied the projections.

Nico guided us from one panel to another, explaining the shadow images as they appeared and then moving to the next panel as each faded. The silhouettes that emerged on the first panel were of a man, the taller figure, and a woman, who was facing him (Figure 5.1). The man cradled a baby in his arms; the woman held a toddler. "This is a photograph of my grandfather and my grandmother and my sister (pointing to the toddler) and my brother (pointing to the infant)—my sister, Carola, and my brother, Marcos […] This is the idea of the photo." In the image, light seemed to emanate from the lower right-hand corner, casting the woman in a sharp profile while the outlines of the man and the infant, shadowed by the woman and the toddler, were less distinct. The sound of a very young child singing a nursery rhyme played on a loop. The effect was to create a sensation of a separate world occurring in parallel to the one we inhabited as observers. Visually, the windows into this world were the shadow images—featureless stills, frozen except in the moments of their appearing and disappearing from the screens. The loops of sound opened an imaginative space of movement and connection, rendering the still images sonically fluid but also intensifying their elusiveness.

126 Labors of Justice as Recovery

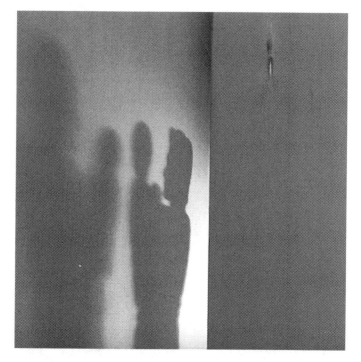

FIGURE 5.1 Grandparents and siblings

Nico pointed to the groupings of grandparents and siblings and smiled, commenting on how the image was from the time of their youth. The image then suddenly disappeared.

Nico then walked us to the right toward panels where other images had appeared. The first panel showed two figures, a man and a woman embracing (Figure 5.2). Their fusion created a single silhouette. As in the first image, a beam of light appeared to shine from the left side of the screen, bringing the man's rounded back into sharp definition and softening the outline of the woman, nestling into her lover's chest. Nico explained:

> The first image that appears is… to be honest… I found an old picture of my father and my mother where they are in Mar del Plata, standing on a rock looking out onto the ocean and they are both very young, before they had children. Around that time they were starting their family and had certain dreams, or certain things they expected out of life and what they wanted to do, at least that's what it represents to me.

This melded image of a couple's love before children then faded, leaving only the second image, a shadow-still representing a boy standing in front of, or sitting on, a swing, his arms held out at the shoulders to grasp the chains on either side.

Labors of Justice as Recovery **127**

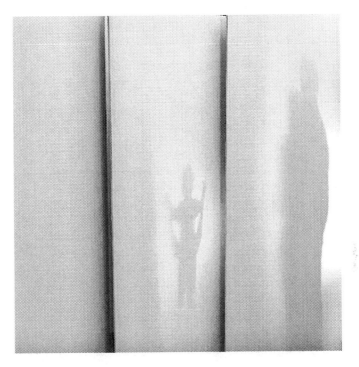

FIGURE 5.2 Parents by the sea; child on a swing

If we imagined the child to be sitting, the swing appeared to be moving toward us; if standing, then it seemed to remain still.

Nico paused, waiting. New images appeared on the screens on the other side to the right of the child on the swing. These images showed the silhouette of a woman holding a toddler, her hair falling to her shoulders, the hem of her skirt visible toward the bottom of the panel (Figure 5.3). Next to this image were two other silhouettes of a child seeming to climb a stair and a man standing behind, holding him. In the first image, a light shone softly from the left side of the panel, bringing the child's figure into relief and softening that of the woman. In the second image, the child, his outline sharply defined, appeared to step into the bright light. The figure of the man appeared blurred.

As Nico explained, "Now, when everything starts to come together…for example, here, it's as if all my family were here, as if my mother, my father, my sister, and my brother, and me…like the family is reunited again." The sound of a baby making babbling sounds played on a loop in the background. Nico explained that this sound was actually from recordings of his own son, Santi, when he was young. The memory of the use of his child's voice to evoke something he lost in his own childhood brought a smile to his face. Nico paused again,

FIGURE 5.3 Father, child on step; mother, child; child on swing

waiting as the images disappeared and a new one appeared showing the silhouette of a pregnant woman, her hands clasped above her belly (Figure 5.4). "And now the image of my mother when she was pregnant," Nico commented as he pointed to the shadows, "is going to combine with the image of my grandparents, who were left with my brother and sister."

As the shadowed images of these individual forms and groupings continued to appear, disappear, and reappear in a loop, our own emotional responses intensified. For James, seeing the shadow of a child on the swing evoked a stabbing sense of sadness and loss, and he chose to briefly step out of the space before re-engaging Nico's work. And our filmmaker, Paul, stopped filming and stepped outside the building to regain his composure.

Universalizing the Individual

As our interview with Nico proceeded, the conversation helped illuminate the context of "Presencias" and offered us new interpretative possibilities. Nico was born in captivity in 1975, one year prior to the coup. (As explained in previous chapters, instances of state violence preceded the dictatorship.) Argentine

FIGURE 5.4 Pregnant woman

security forces had detained and imprisoned his mother but, according to Nico, she "convinced them to deliver me to her family." The significance of the image in Figure 5.4 emerges, in light of Nico's story, in a new way: the woman cradles the child in her womb in the isolation of a narrow chamber indicated by the tight parameters of the screen. Naked and vulnerable, she peers down toward the light, seeming to direct her gaze toward its source, a window in the early morning perhaps or an open door leading to a hallway.

Nico's mother would remain in prison for another five years. During that period, Nico stated, his father "was kidnapped and murdered." When his mother was released, she was able to return to her children and her parents. Reflecting on this exceptional circumstance—few of those arrested were ever released—Nico explained: "My mother's family did not have a history of militancy [leftist political activism]. In reality, they did not educate me with the same values that my father would have had, because he was the one who would participate [in activism] [...] Everything to do with my father was something that wasn't spoken of often and it wasn't something I could speak about with my friends in general [...] because it was in its own environment; [the reality of my father] was partially covered." The regime's security forces had executed his father; his family obscured the memory of his father.

When Nico was in his mid-20s, he began to question this silence about his father. He was married by then and he and his wife had welcomed their first child, a boy. The experience of becoming a father caused him to think about the absence of his own father. He embarked on a "long process" of questioning and investigating, "a process where I came to understand that this family story [...] in reality was not just a personal family story but a national story." In part, Nico's exhibit reflected his attempt to put his own experience in conversation with society at large—to highlight, through his own life, the legacies of the dictatorship in Argentina more generally. Returning to Stern's metaphor of a societal memory chest, Nico could access and even contribute to the albums, scripts, and related lore connecting with stories of the disappeared in Argentina. Yet, it is important to note that Nico's story was exceptional in certain ways. Though he was not unique in being born in captivity, the number of children who shared that experience was, according to the best estimates, in the hundreds, making them a relatively small number (at least compared to the tens of thousands of adult victims). Further, Nico was born in 1975, before the coup that installed the *Proceso*. Abductions, assassinations, and arbitrary imprisonment occurred under the government of Isabel Perón, but their relationship to the more systematic use of state terror after March 24 is complex, and remains largely unexplored. Finally, unlike many children born in captivity, Nico was not given over to be raised by *militares* or sympathizers, but rather was returned to his grandparents—and ultimately, miraculously, his mother came back to their lives, as well. In these concrete ways, his story did not track with the collective narrative about repression and the Armed Forces.

Nico commented on the disjuncture between these narratives. Referring to the National Day of Memory for Truth and Justice (Día Nacional de la Memoria por la Verdad y la Justicia) on March 24 that commemorated the anniversary of the coup d'état, he explained: "Memory is not one singular truth about something that happened; rather, it is very subjective [...] There are many distinct stories from many people that get intermingled and we all end up participating and constructing that collective memory." In contrast with the built forms surrounding him and within which he had created his exhibit at the ex-ESMA—architectural structures from the military's occupation of this site and which the groups now inhabiting them wished to preserve—Nico emphasized the fluidity and discontinuity of memory. Whatever "collective memory" was, it was neither monolithic nor unchanging.

Moreover, in Argentina, and spotlighted at the ex-ESMA, there exists a paradox of absence. How, Nico wondered, was it possible to render an absence present. The families of the disappeared claimed the disappeared as "presente, ahora y siempre [present, now and always]." This insistence was the beating heart of the March 24th commemorations and multiple other remembrances of the period of state terror that occurred within local communities and families. And, yet, the problem of remembering an absence—in Nico's case, a nearly complete absence—remained. His solution came to him when he encountered "shadow sculptures" while looking at an artistic display one day:

> About the installation, I came across shadow sculptures one day while looking at art. The sculptures spoke to me: the shadows represented those who disappeared. The shadow of a person implies the presence of that person; it implies there is a person there, and those who were disappeared have that [implication, i.e.]. We want to feel their presence but in reality they aren't here. But it is something about them that leaves a shadow, something that is a part of us. So we can begin to talk to this shadow and reconstruct stories and that is how my installation came to be. What I wanted was to answer the absence with presence. This is to say, we make these people present again with the things we do and live for. With this we can speak to the things that I wasn't able to do with my father that any normal kid in the world was able to do. But now I am able to do it with my own children and I can help others to have better experiences with their children, and that in some way closes the circle.

Shadows haunt. When loved ones disappear—or are disappeared—they leave behind a residual mark, like a shadow that one casts in daylight or in a full moon. For those who were violently disappeared, as in Argentina, there is also a remainder, an implied "presence of that person" even for those children who were ripped from their mothers as babies or very young children. For these individuals, this remainder resides within the photographs handed down within families. But the relation—fractured at the very inception of life—must be conjured ex nihilo (from the void) in a manner similar to the biblical account of the creation of the world. Nico's installation demonstrated the difficulty of this act of conjuring. What appears are shadows. One can speak to these shadows that haunt survivors like Nico in a manner similar to how participants in a Haitian possession performance speak to the ancient ancestral spirits that "ride" the priest or priestess. Families tell stories about the spirits; they are, in fact, a part of the extended community: the dead reside with the living in this way (Brown, 1991). Nico conjures the dead in his own way as shadows that are the implications of family photographs and family stories. And as he and others speak to the shadows they extend and elaborate the narratives. Nico imagines being held by his mother, feeling her caress and hearing her whisper soothingly in his ear. He feels the reassuring grip of his father's hand as he steps into the light in front of him. And these imaginings then become stories that reconstruct a normal life that never occurred. As one encounters the shadows, the looped sounds of children at play lead the mind's eye into this space of normal life. And then, in an instant, the image and the sound cease.

Nico's choice to use shadows in his work calls to mind the work of Diana Taylor (1997) and her exploration of the "unmaking and remaking of the human body" in and through representations of the disappeared. She writes, "decomposition involves the disappearance, torture, and murder of the victims; the remaking or recomposition involves attempts made by oppositional forces (from human rights advocates to the Madres to artists to scholars) to make these disappeared bodies visible again to the national and international community" (pp. 150–151). To some degree, shadow installations like Nico's might be best understood as existing in a space between decomposition and recomposition. That is, Nico chose not to use actual photographs of his parents; rather he created shadows from these photographic images.

As part of his *Presencias* project, Nico had also written a poem, which was posted near the entrance to the installation. We asked Nico to share the poem which he read to us:

Presencias	Presences
Un paseo a la plaza	A walk to the square
educar a tu hijo	educate your son
salir de vacaciones	go on vacation
patear un rato en el patio	kick a while in the yard
Lo que pudo haber sido	What could have been
lo que vuelve en sueños	what comes back in dreams
de ningún lado	from nowhere
de mi	from me
Volver del trabajo	To come back from work
conversar hasta tarde	to talk until late
aprender a vivir	to learn to live
tener tiempo de morir	to have time to die
Mirar hacia atrás	To look back
festejar aciertos	to celebrate success
remendar errores	to mend errors
otra vez: cambiar el mundo	again: to change the world
desde tu casa	from your house
con amigos	with friends
en pareja	in couple
en comunidad	in community
Planear un viaje	To plan a trip
cambiar de trabajo	to change job
hacer un regalo	to give a gift
reirse de nada	to laugh at nothing
Enseñar	To teach
eso que te hace único	that which makes you unique
sentar posición	to take a position
dar el ejemplo	to give the example
Escribir algo	To write something
y que no lo quemen	and not have them burn it
tener un hijo	To have a child
y que no lo roben	and not have them steal him

Poder elegir	To be able to choose
cómo, con quién, y cuándo	how, with whom, and when
Volver a equivocarse	To make mistakes again
una y otra y otra vez	Over and over and over again
Tocar la guitarra	To play the guitar
tomarse el tren	to take the train
saludar a cualquiera	to say hello to anyone
defender una idea	to defend an idea
Cosas que pudieran ser	The things that could have been
pero sólo en sueños	but only in dreams
De todos lados, de nosotros	From everywhere, from us
Como sombras sin figuras	Like shadows without figures

The poem amplifies key themes of Nico's art installation. There is profound loss when someone is denied life. Nico addresses missed opportunities to engage in daily life events and experiences (walking in the square, playing a guitar, saying hello to someone) along with articulating more general or philosophical preoccupations (for example, phrases like "things that could have been"). In the last stanza, Nico also seems to move from an individual focus, with the narration suggesting a single person, to something more collective with the phrase "from everywhere, from us," which complements one of his key points that his story "was not just a personal story but a national story as well." In the final line of the poem, Nico suggests that what we are left with in our own presumably collective presences is but dreams and shadows.

Historian Steve Stern captures this tension between individual and collective memory building about traumatic events, noting that these memory struggles "create a symbolic process that blurs the line between the social and the personal—creating a two-way street of influence and testimony" (Stern, 2010, p. 11). He continues:

> When the cultural echo effect happens, mysterious vanishing of "my" son is no longer a story of personal misfortune or accident that floats loosely, disconnected from a larger meaning [...]. The question asked when I bear the photo of my son at a demonstration is phrased in the plural: Where are they? donde estan? My personal experience has acquired value as a cultural symbol or emblem, but conversely, what matters most when remembering my son is shaped by a wider social struggle about memory.
>
> (p. 11)

The "What could have been..."

Nico's "Presencias" embodied how personal history can connect with narratives surrounding broader collective trauma. The exhibit had grown out of the artist's unique experiences and focused on the struggle to come to terms with the loss of something that never was. At the same time, the meanings of the installation expanded beyond the specifics of Nico's life to encompass the pain and suffering of all Argentines who had lost family members—and especially of those children born in captivity whose parents were likely never part of their lives. Locating the project in the space of the ex-ESMA implicitly aligned Nico's intervention with the political stances of groups like the Madres de la Plaza de Mayo and HIJOS,[7] which during the past two decades have fought to shed light on the practice of abducting children during the dictatorship. This intervention highlighted an ambivalence and ambiguity about memorialization that turned on the tension between the preservation of structures and the practices of representation and narration. Nico expressed this tension in his interview with us reflecting on the reasons behind his installation:

> I am an architect and in the last 10 years there have been many courses in architecture in which they began restoring these buildings [connected with the dictatorship, such as those at the ex-ESMA]. I participated in these and I always found myself thinking that all of these buildings form a part in the repressive apparatus of the dictatorship. They are catalogued as historical monuments, not as celebratory ones. Instead they are seen as something untouchable in nature. So there is very little that a person, as an architect, can do to intervene in buildings like these. Because it is a historic monument you cannot touch it. We must conserve a lot of things and cannot interpret it in another form. I needed to express myself in some other form that was a bit more powerful and really had a cause. So in my search this [space and installation] became the centerpiece that I found.

In this discovery of an exhibition space at the ex-ESMA, Nico's personal experience of loss and search for connection and meaning converged with the familial politics of the Madres. The Madres had been one of the few movements capable of public protest against the regime. As mothers and grandmothers who weekly stood in silence with posters bearing the images of their disappeared children, the group powerfully contested the dictatorship's claim to be defending Argentina against atheists and Communists who threatened its institutions, especially religion and the family. The images of the children constituted a damning indictment of the regime, exposing the yawning gap between its rhetoric of traditional order and its violent attack on a main pillar (the family) of that order. The protests were a refusal to acquiesce in the attack. As the slogan insisted, the disappeared were, for the vigil-keepers, the Madres, "presente ahora y siempre." This rendering present of the disappeared wrested the politics of the family from the regime's control, effectively transmuting the inherent conservative symbolism of the regime's politics into an unrelenting demand for democratic accountability. It simultaneously introduced the discursive possibility of the "what might have been" ("lo que pudo haber sido") that undergirded Nico's art.

Nico's creative act of imagining a past that never transpired, an act of making present an absence in a manner similar to the Madres' slogan of "presente ahora y siempre," was only one such effort of recovery. Other groups that had situated themselves at the ex-ESMA focused on the documentation of the disappeared. Their efforts were archival, concerned with establishing files, tracking down details of individual trajectories through the interrogation and torture chambers that now served as museum and exhibition spaces. Memory as recovery in this instance became an empirical matter, entailing the careful uncovering, much like at an archeological site, of the layers of the disappeared past.

Justice Work as Collective Recovery: Memoria Abierta

On the morning of Tuesday, March 22, before viewing Nico's installation, we traveled to the ex-ESMA by taxi for an appointment with Dr. Alejandra Oberti, a sociologist at the University of Buenos Aires and the coordinator of the Oral Archive of the Memoria Abierta (Open Memory) organization. A few weeks earlier, we reached out to her through a mutual contact, and Dr. Oberti graciously accepted our invitation for an interview to discuss her work at Memoria Abierta. Dr. Oberti informed us that Memoria Abierta was an alliance of seven human rights organizations with diverse yet complementary programs and commitments. Their activities included the reconstruction of an archive of human rights organizations and of human rights leaders; a program aimed at further identifying where clandestine detention centers were located and better understanding how they operated; and the archive program that Oberti herself directed, which included a repository of 900 testimonies of victims from the dictatorship and of social and political activists of the 1960s and 1970s. A primary goal of this archive, which began in 2001 and has since become available as a searchable online database, was for viewers to learn about the human rights movement, including deeply personal, subjective experiences about what it meant to have a missing family member.

The archive collection was broad: it documented the lives of politicians, union leaders, and activists from student, social, and Christian movements and included a collection of interviews with human rights lawyers and people who worked at the United Nations or other international organizations, (e.g., journalists, ambassadors) involved in some way with the defense of human rights in Argentina. Oberti described the method and significance of these diverse interviews:

> Each of these interviews tells a little about the history of life in relation to these issues. They are extensive interviews, filmed. All have a relatively similar format, uniform to some extent. We asked about the life of the people, about what that militancy was like. So they are very useful materials to reconstruct the social and political life of Argentina in the second half of the 20th century.

The history of gender repression and violence were also central to the work of Memoria Abierta as cases of sexual brutality, forced abortions, and child theft were documented.

In its emphasis on documentation, the work of Memoria Abierta departed from the conjurings of Nico's artistic renderings. Where for Nico the disappeared constituted an absence whose relation to those surviving into the present had to be imagined (and reimagined), for Oberti and her archivists the past remained an obscured empirical fact that had to be recovered through documentation. This distinction between imagined and verifiable fact was not entirely categorical as Nico, too, relied on a documented past: his installation utilized family photographs and stories. But, his work filled the absences with fictionalized moments: a looped recording conveying sounds of children playing; a poem envisioning lost moments of intimacy. Memoria Abierta, by contrast, focused resolutely on the recovery of the empirical. This recovery, in Oberti's understanding, was nothing less than the recuperation (*la recuperación*) of the individual in relation to society. This recuperation occurred in two forms: as archive and as networked space.

Archive and Recuperation

In describing the focus of Memoria Abierta, Oberti stated the organization worked "for and on behalf of the memory of the dictatorship." The building of this archive of the period of the dictatorship, Oberti said, was essential to the process of social memory and justice. The materials allowed for a reconstruction of Argentina's past during the twentieth century:

> The archives are fundamental to the entire process of justice because it is where one can find verification of what occurred. At the same time, however, it is fundamental also to memory processes because they are material elements that permit memory to condense, continue forward, and generate discussions. For that reason, we are very focused on thinking through standards of conservation and access and of forms of expertise in the archives that document the veracity of these documents.

Oberti's description of the archive as the site of "verification of what occurred" and as the source of "material elements" that allowed memory to form, advance, and provoke discussion conveyed the sense of the past as palpable and factual. It was similar in that sense to an archaeological site containing artifacts that the researcher recovered through a painstaking attention to preservation and verification. The past persisted in these material forms; the task was to retrieve and carefully conserve these artifacts. Implied in this conception was that memory was not mere construction. For it to "condense" it had to anchor itself in the record of what actually and verifiably was. In situations in which an active attempt was made to destroy this record, to disappear it, there arose the necessity to recuperate, to retrieve and resuscitate, the suppressed elements and in doing so to reconstitute the empirical, factual baseline. This baseline presumably would serve to correct and prevent false constructions of the past among both the victims and the perpetrators of the suppression. It also would provide a foundation for formal criminal investigation. Justice and memory worked together to "recuperate" the individual as well as the nation.

Networks of Repression/Networks of Memory

Connected to the notion of archive was Oberti's concept of networks of repression as networks of memory. She spoke, in this regard, of "the reconstruction of territorial memory ... that is to say, where clandestine sites of detention were situated, where they came from, how these repressive circuits functioned." Implied in this focus was a concern to triangulate the oral and written records with the spatial remnants—the interrogation, detention, and torture centers. These spaces presumably would serve to confirm the veracity of the retrieved oral accounts. But they also would become sites of "stories so far" (Massey, 2005, p. 9): within their triangulated frame, individuals presumably might fill in their own narratives, intersecting them with the stories of others. Oberti implied such a possibility in her comments on the continental reach of this effort to trace the repressive networks.

As one example of transnational resonances of commemorative literacies at the ex-ESMA, Memoria Abierta's programs linked to human rights organizations across Latin America. The project headquartered two networks: the "Red de Sitios de Memoria Latinoamericanos y Caribeños" (Network of Latin American and Caribbean Sites of Memory) and La Coalición Internacional de Sitios de Conciencia (International Coalition of Sites of Awareness).[8] Dictatorship and disappearances marked the histories of the participating countries. Creating formal networks enabled documentarians to place the Argentine experience in a comparative and linked causal perspective:

> We are also very focused on what we call the regional work, which is to work with people from many countries in Latin America, from Mexico to Argentina, let's say the whole continent. Memoria Abierta manages a network of memory sites across Guatemala, the Dominican Republic, El Salvador, México, Colombia, Perú, Chile, Brasil. Argentina, Paraguay, Uruguay and I'm sure I'm forgetting some more, the Dominican Republic, or almost all of Latin America, all the countries of Latin America. And what we do is to think through networks of contacts. We have an annual meeting. We think about the continent, think about the memory processes in the continent, the different temporalities, the different actors of the processes, both of the repressive processes as of the memory processes. So this work in networks throughout Latin America seems to me to be a very

important focus of work and it is what allows us to think of repressive processes as memory processes, not as an isolated event that happens in a country, which has a particularity, that, of course, each country has its particularity, but as more global processes, at least for our continent. I think those are the two important aspects.

Thinking about "repressive processes as memory processes" across multiple sites regionally provided a broad empirical frame that rendered Argentina's experience comprehensible as a shared phenomenon with common historical and political characteristics. Argentina was not unique; it was not an aberration easily explainable with reference to an Argentine pathology. Rather, it was part of a larger transnational process that had shaped Latin America as a whole. Although Oberti did not discuss the dimensions of this process, her reference to the shared regional experience implied the history of U.S. Cold War interventions, especially through clandestine programs like Operation Condor and the School of the Americas.

Memory as Conjugated in Present Tense

Although focused on empirical retrieval of the past, Oberti's conception of memory as archive and as networked site of repression intersected with memory recovery work, like Nico's, which entailed an imaginative reconstruction. During our interview, she spoke of memory work as "conjugated in the present tense," by which she meant an unending process of reflecting on the past in relation to the current moment and the anticipated future:

> We often talk about the memory process in order to think about, well, I will repeat a phrase by Elizabeth Jelin, which I have found to be very useful lately, which is that, 'memory is conjugated in the present tense; the time of memory is the present tense.' The challenge imposed by our time makes us remember and look at the past in very different ways. There are lines of continuity. There are continuities. That is, it is conjugated in the present tense but it is the past as well. It is the past. It is the future. I mean, it has this peculiarity. Perhaps the strongest continuity lines are the need for memory to serve, it is said, not to repeat. I think I like to think of a memory that helps us think about what happened to us, what happened and why it happened, and how to build a fairer, freer future, et cetera. But we speak of processes, precisely, because that is why it is conjugated in the present time. It is the present: there is an immense variety of situations, of moments, of relationships between actors that are changing. In the Argentine case, we could trace a history of the entire memory process from the end of the dictatorship until now and you would find great changes in who the central actors are, which the most relevant issues are. So this permanent reconfiguration makes it seem to me that the word process is very appropriate.

Memory is permanently reconfigured in the process of retrieval, documentation, compilation, and interpretation. The creation of an archive was a first, necessary step. Ultimately, however, the work of memory was the effort to discern not only what occurred but why it had occurred in the way that it did. This matter of why—and why in this particular way—was crucial to a second question: "how to build a fairer, freer future." The work of memory was thus imaginative and constructive in a future-oriented sense. Argentina has had to make use of the documented past to conceive and create a more just society. In this sense, memory as archive intersected with memory as Nico practiced it in his installation. Drawing on an archive of images and retrieved stories, Nico imaginatively conjured a lost childhood with his disappeared father even as he became a father himself: retrieving those who had disappeared allowed for the reintegration—for the reestablishment of the continuity—of families as new generations formed in the present and created families of their own on the other side of the violent rupture.

Justice and the Recovery of Space: the ex-ESMA

Thus far, we have shown how the concept of recovery functions at both the individual and collective level within the ex-ESMA. In concert with these processes, we also identified a third level of recovery related to Argentina's efforts to cope with the traumas it endured during the 1970s and 1980s. Recovery can also imply a reclamation—in this case, the reclamation of a physical space. The second half of the twentieth century has produced numerous occasions to examine the moral, ethical, and political stakes of transforming sites of violence and suffering into memorials and museums. From concentration camps across Central and Eastern Europe, to the streets of Northern Ireland, to Robben Island off the coast of Cape Town, to the infamous "killing fields" of Cambodia, physical spaces that witnessed human misery on a terrible scale have become disputed terrain, their meanings and legacies constantly debated and remade (Duffy, 2001; Ledgerwood, 1997; Marcuse, 2001; Milton et al., 2011; Shackley, 2001). Although the contexts differ, these debates share a central concern: the intertwined questions of how to remember and how to recover.

Recovery as Reclamation

On March 24, 2004, Argentine President Néstor Kirchner marked the 28th anniversary of the onset of the PRN with the inauguration of a new space dedicated to recognizing, preserving, and publicizing the memory/memories of the violence carried out by the military regime against its citizens. The choice of location spoke to the significance of the project that the Kirchner government had decided to pursue. Since it began operating as a CCD in the mid-1970s, the ex-ESMA had been the country's most recognizable symbol of state terrorism.

Testimonies and first-person accounts from survivors of state terrorism who had passed through the school began appearing during the dictatorship itself, formed an integral part of the work of the CONADEP in the mid-1980s which became *Nunca Más* (1984), and by the 2000s, had assumed a position of preeminence in discussions over the legacy of the PRN and the responsibilities of various sectors of Argentine society. Kirchner's decision to locate the *Espacio para la Memoria* (Space for Memory) at the ex-ESMA placed it at the center of the debates over memory and memory construction in Argentina.

Menem's proposal to bulldoze the school in 1998 sparked a handful of Argentines to fight to preserve it, and their efforts were eventually upheld by a federal court. As explained in Chapter 2, the late 1990s and early 2000s were a moment of transition as discourses around remembrance and human rights evolved and gained momentum. When, in 2007, Néstor inaugurated the new site, thousands of people gathered to hear him speak. The Kirchners' project became a symbol of the government's rejection of the conciliatory attitude of the Menem years. Yet this endeavor was far from uncomplicated. First, a considerable sector of the population responded negatively to the growing prominence of human rights discourse in Argentina. This included not only upper- and upper-middle-class conservatives who remembered the period of the dictatorship with something approaching nostalgia, but also those who were critical of the politicization of human rights, as the Kirchners used the issue to build their base and win popular support. Put another way, we can understand the Kirchners as accessing what Stern (2004) calls an emblematic memory of "persecution and awakening" from the societal memory chest. This emblematic memory invokes the coup and time of state repression with increased awareness of the regime and possibilities for resistance. This differs markedly from emblematic memories of "memory as salvation" (the regime was saving the country from radical subversives) or "memory as a closed box," which seals off the past and prohibits further reflection (Stern, 2004). Second, even within the current of actors and groups that backed this state-sponsored effort to confront the legacies of the PRN, marked divisions existed. These would become clearly visible during the heated debate over what to do with the ex-ESMA.

In the wake of Néstor Kirchner's 2004 announcement, debates over how to cope with and make sense of the horrors of the recent past—which had been simmering just below the surface—exploded into public. Somewhat ironically, the dual logic that had influenced the court to rule for the preservation of the ex-ESMA in 1998, emphasizing the former school's status as both proof and patrimony, now provided the battle lines for the fight over what this new site should be. Questions related to the (re)construction of memory; the various and competing narratives of the period of State terrorism; and the orientation and purpose(s) of the new "museum" space itself provoked fierce polemics (Andermann, 2012; di Paolantonio, 2008; Feld, 2017; Pastoriza, 2005). Survivors, families of the disappeared, human rights organizations, researchers and academics—over the previous 20 years, these groups had created different stories to explain this past, drawing for the most part from the same historical record, but placing their emphases on different themes.

The debate over what form the ex-ESMA should take broke down along three broad axes. The first advocated a preservationist approach, in which the buildings and spaces would be kept exactly as they were left when the Navy abandoned the building in the 1990s. Underpinning this attitude was the significance of the site's testimonial value, whereby "the entire site is taken as unalterable heritage" (Andermann, 2012, p. 85). Others argued that maintaining the site as simply a monument to death and suffering failed to offer a path forward, and that in order for Argentina to progress, the school's meanings had to be transformed. They envisioned a combination of performative spaces and political operations, advocating human rights and justice, that could occupy the buildings of the ex-ESMA, thereby reclaiming them from the military, and for the "people." Somewhere between these poles, a third option proposed a middle road, with a museum space that would "contextualiz[e] and arrang[e] the site's material evidence in ways that allow it to serve certain pedagogic functions" without completely eliminating its testimonial weight (Andermann, 2012). This idea eventually received a majority of support from the various governmental, non-governmental, and human rights organizations involved in the project during the first decade of the 2000s.

As in the 1998 judgment, the debates of the 2000s turned on this three-part dynamic. Although under Menem the meanings that would come to be associated with the ex-ESMA during the Kirchner period had not yet been established, the plaintiffs nonetheless advanced similar arguments. Their case emphasized both the evidentiary and patrimonial value of the ex-ESMA—not only was it proof of crimes committed, it was a physical commemoration of a critical episode in the nation's history (Feld, 2017). The preservation of the site itself was vital to both aspects of their claim. For the ex-ESMA, these two features of reclamation—as both a memorial to human suffering and as a physical location to be occupied and "retaken"—are central to any effort to understand its evolution as a memory space and the oftentimes fierce polemics that have accompanied that development.

Reclamation and the Control of Space

The controversy over how best to utilize the space of the ex-ESMA might appear largely academic, yet the vehemence of the debate and the passion that it inspired would seem to belie that idea. Throughout the mid-2000s, the questions that repeatedly arose centered on the issue of future generations (Brodsky, 2005; di Paolantonio, 2008). How would this place be remembered and what purpose could it serve? Its transformation into a "memory space"—a term that recalls Pierre Nora's "lieux de memoire"—spoke to the memorial aspect of the work that the space itself was tasked with doing.[9] The process of memorialization vested the structures and grounds of the ex-ESMA with new meanings through the simple act of preservation, by opening the space to visitors, and by physically transforming the buildings themselves. Since 2007, these buildings and the territory they sit on have been integral parts of shaping the experience of the ex-ESMA and have facilitated visitors' interactions with the various meanings in play at the site. While the official name of the ex-ESMA, the "Space for Memory and the Promotion and Defense of Human Rights," unmistakably speaks to a mission whose objectives extend beyond commemoration, the fact that its title is commonly shortened to "Espacio por la memoria" ("Space for Memory") should also not be dismissed.

This repurposing has been accompanied by a conscious and deliberate assertion of ownership over the space itself, most notably in the relocation of the headquarters of numerous human rights' groups to the ex-ESMA, including one branch of the Madres de la Plaza de Mayo; the Abuelas de la Plaza de Mayo, HIJOS (Hijos e Hijas por la Identidad y la Justicia contra el Olvido y Silencio); the Permanent Assembly of Human Rights; the Families of the Desaparecidos-Detenidos por Razones Políticas; and the Center for Legal and Social Studies (CELS), among others. The reclamation of the physical space of the ex-ESMA by these organizations—the fact that their work now takes place in buildings that were formerly the property of the very men responsible for committing the violence that they now attempt to work through—suggests the importance of this aspect of recovery.

Reclamation here functions as an assertion of power, by taking that which once belonged to an enemy and repurposing it for one's own benefit. In this case, that benefit is closely related to confronting and mitigating the harm caused by the dictatorship, where possible, and pursuing justice where it is not. With respect to the ex-ESMA, artist and author Marcel Brodsky has argued that it is not enough to simply leave the space as it was found—something must be done to illuminate its multiple and even contradictory meanings. For Brodsky, that project involves art, which can "open an interpretative space" for critical questioning of the past and its relationship to the present, as opposed to simply "presenting the horrors that happened there" (di Paolantonio, 2008, pp. 36–37). Indeed, it was in one of these spaces that we encountered Nico's "Presencias." In both cases, the political and the artistic, the reclamation of the space brings the past into conversation with the present in the manner that Oberti referred to as conjugation in the present tense. It is deemed necessary precisely because of the impact that it might have on future generations.

Challenges of Reclaiming the ex-ESMA

Despite some shared sense of purpose between those involved, the project of reclamation has not been simple. If the idea of reclamation is accompanied by notions of ownership and property, debates over how this control is established and maintained remain unresolved. As described above, the preservation of the site brought with it a series of challenges and forced various actors to wrestle with how they envisioned the ex-ESMA: as commemorative, demonstrative, educational, or some combination of all three. Although it marked the opening of the space, the dedication of the "Espacio por la memoria" did not put an end to these disagreements. Since the mid-2000s, questions about what the "proper use" of the space entails, who has a right to be represented within the space, and what should be the relationship of this space to the rest of society have all complicated the notion of "recovery as reclamation" that was initially present in Néstor's 2004 dedication.

The tensions within Argentine society related to the legacies of the dictatorship remain highly visible.[10] Two specific episodes at the ex-ESMA after 2012 brought these tensions into sharp relief. The first occurred in December 2012 when Cristina Kirchner's then-Minister of Justice Julio Alak chose to hold an *asado* (cookout) as the annual end-of-the-year gathering at the ex-ESMA, with as many as 1,000 people in attendance (Sosa, 2016, p. 124). The scandal that broke in early 2013 revolved around not only people's objections to the Ministry holding a festive event in a space marked by torture and death, but also to the idea of an *asado*, given that during the dictatorship, the military personnel that ran the detention center at the ESMA used the term "asado" as a euphemism for the cremation of the bodies of those killed during torture or subsequently executed. Many argued that, at the very least, Alak had displayed extremely poor taste. Others, however, rallied to his defense with arguments about the repurposing of the space. They echoed, in some ways, comments made by Hebe de Bonafini, a leader of the Madres, who for years had held cooking classes at the ex-ESMA because she rejected the idea that buildings should be "a mere landscape of horror" (Sosa, 2016, p. 137). Although the context and the optics differed, at the heart of the *asado* controversy was a familiar question: was the primary goal of the ex-ESMA commemoration and preservation? Or education and transformation?

The second incident was the construction of an entirely new edifice on the grounds of the ex-ESMA, the Museo de las Malvinas, which opened at the end of 2014. This project marked a significant change from the policy of preservation and non-intervention that had guided the development of the space in the years following Néstor's 2004 declaration. The museum occupies an objectively enormous building beside a reflecting pool in the shape of the Malvinas islands. As then-President Cristina Kirchner explained at its inauguration, the museum serves two purposes: to honor the Argentine soldiers who died in the 1982 war and to promote the country's claim to sovereignty over the islands. Beyond the assertion of ownership that such a project explicitly entailed (the right of the government to alter the property itself in accordance with its aims), the Museo de las Malvinas raised another polemic. In placing the museum on the terrain of the ex-ESMA, the Kirchner administration drew an implicit (or perhaps not-so-implicit) equivalency between the victims of state terror and the casualties of the Malvinas War. This new narrative, reinforced by the mutual proximity of the monuments to both sets of dead, painted them all with the same brush: that they were all victims of the Proceso. This, in turn, has raised questions about the very meaning of "victimhood," and where and how it can (or should) be properly applied.

The ex-ESMA has not remained static over the past two decades. From an initial approach that stressed conserving as much of the site as possible, a new attitude stressing the performative and educative possibilities of the space has become predominant. In 2015, the Kirchner government unveiled a redesigned Casino de Oficiales. In place of the austere and stark emptiness that had previously characterized the building, it now featured multiple multimedia exhibits, interactive panels, carefully curated installations, and a dramatic entranceway of glass with the faces of those who passed through the school etched onto it. While some sectors of Argentina's diverse human rights landscape celebrated the changes, others considered them disrespectful and inappropriate, and condemned the alteration of the space where thousands had been tortured and murdered (Sosa, 2016, pp. 129–130). The polemic over the central objective of the ex-ESMA remains an open debate, and the physical properties of the site itself are active players in this process. As the buildings and the grounds change, so do the meanings associated with recovery and reclamation. The agentive quality of the space continues to influence the conversation around human rights and justice work into the present. In this sense, we see this space of the ex-ESMA as dynamic, constantly reconstituting and shifting through the intersection of multiple narrative trajectories embodied in diverse interventions (e.g., human rights archiving, artistic performances and installations, cookouts, creation of new museum spaces, and so on) (Massey, 2005).

Conclusions

The role of the ex-ESMA as a space becomes clearer when we reread Nico's art installation, "Presencias," in light of the different levels of recovery outlined above. The exhibit is deeply personal: the images are all of his family members, the sounds are recordings of his own son, the story it tells is unique. Yet, as Nico himself commented, his story was also a national story. "Presencias" involved intertwined objectives. It was the culmination of his own search for answers, and at the same time his contribution to a broader conversation around the traumas (individual and collective) inflicted by the most recent dictatorship.

The project's location in an exhibit hall in the ex-ESMA facilitated this duality of purpose. By presenting his work in this space, already loaded with a host of competing and complementary meanings, Nico's art turned the site to his advantage. Beginning in the 1980s with the emergence of the testimonial genre and the publication of the *Nunca Más* Report, the ex-ESMA became perhaps the most prominent physical symbol of state repression. The politics of the three Kirchner administrations deliberately reinforced this association, converting the naval base into a "space of memory" that functioned on a national scale. The school represented all of the excesses of the state's security forces—from the emergence of right-wing death squads in 1974 through the systematic disappearance and murder of civilians into the 1980s.

While Nico's experience of being born in captivity prior to the 1976 coup distinguishes him from the tens of thousands of victims arrested, tortured, and killed during the PRN, the space of the ex-ESMA permitted a sort of transmutation of scale. "Presencias," telling the story of a single individual and his family, could amplify within the chamber of the ex-ESMA, finding echoes in the more diverse experiences of individuals and families throughout the country and over nearly a decade of intense political violence. If on the first level, Nico's art exhibit functioned as a text rich with interpretative possibility, on a second level the space in which Nico had installed his project brought with it its own symbolic, moral, and societal weight. The viewer thus not only confronted the particulars of Nico's experience, but because of the setting also reinterpreted that history through the lens of collective suffering that the ex-ESMA represents. Indeed, it was in large part the space itself that permitted the transmutation of individual recovery into collective recovery by allowing individual trauma to be subsumed into collective trauma.

Historian Steve Stern (2010) contends that struggles over memory in which significant numbers of people have been affected "create a symbolic process that blurs the line between the social and the personal—creating a two-way street of influence and testimony" (p. 11). Stern continues with Chile as a focal country:

> When the cultural echo effect happens, mysterious vanishing of "my" son is no longer a story of personal misfortune or accident that floats loosely, disconnected from a larger meaning. It is the story of Chile: the reality of a state terror that inflicted devastating rupture on thousands of families transformed into subhuman enemies. The question asked when I bear the photo of my son at a demonstration is phrased in the plural: Where are they? donde estan? My personal experience has acquired value as a cultural symbol or emblem, but conversely, what matters most when remembering my son is shaped by a wider social struggle about memory.
>
> (p. 11)

As this chapter has shown, these labors of justice as recovery—at the individual, collective, and spatial levels—overlapped and intersected across space and time in ways that were undeniably intergenerational. Indeed, implicit in our understanding of recovery is a relationship of the past with the present and the future, the idea that things might be better in the future than they were in the past. As Hite (2012) has argued, this relationship across a multigenerational chronology demands that memory be read and analyzed as an intergenerational phenomenon, as a critical element of the interplay between past, present, and future. Nico's installation and Alejandra Oberti's archival efforts constitute mechanisms of memory transmission across generations. Nico's use of old family photos simultaneously reached into the past and projected forward onto his son and their future relationship; Alejandra Oberti's engagement with the concept of the archive evidences a desire to make these experiences accessible to future generations; and the debate over how to preserve the physical structures and territories of the ex-ESMA hinged on the question of how people would use the space in the future. The ex-ESMA, with its ever-present emphasis on how things should be in the future Argentina, offers a space for considering how this intergenerational memory works and also points to broader implications of the relationship between memory and justice work, which we explore in the next chapter.

Notes

1 Footage from this interview is included in a video called "Argentina: Days of Memory" which is accessible here: https://vimeo.com/285268494/d832f08f1b
2 The term "memory space," or *espacio de memoria*, has particular valances that distinguish it from either a memorial or a museum. These will be unpacked more fully as the chapter proceeds.
3 Recognizing the significance of names and periodization, throughout this chapter we will only use "ex-ESMA" to describe the site *after* 1998. Any references to the site during the period prior to 1998, including the years of the most recent dictatorship, will use the name "ESMA."
4 In fact, habeas corpus had been formally suspended in November 1975, under the government of María Estela Martínez de Perón, some 12 months after she declared a national state of siege, nominally in response to increased guerrilla violence in Tucumán.
5 The primary source of these accounts from victims has been the *Nunca Más* Report (1984). In the 1990s, two members of the military famously testified to having participated in the torture, disappearance, and murder of various civilians: Alfredo Astiz, who was directly involved in the disappearances at the Church of Santa Cruz (Cerruti, 1998); and Adolfo Scilingo, a naval officer who confessed in a series of interviews with journalist Horacio Verbitsky (Verbitsky, 1995).
6 Years later, those photos would be displayed in an exhibit within the Espacio para la Memoria, in a fraught return of the victims to the very space where they were tortured and from which they were disappeared. For a more thorough engagement with this question see Andermann (2012).
7 HIJOS is an acronym for Hijos por la Identidad y la Justicia contra el Olvido y el Silencio (*Children for Identity and Justice Against Forgetting and Silence*). Founded in Argentina in 1995, it has sought to represent children of people who were murdered, disappeared, or exiled during the period of state terror.
8 "Conciencia" in Spanish translates as both "consciousness" (as in awareness) and "conscience" (as in feelings of guilt or accountability). In this context, we believe that the former meaning is closer to what is intended in the name of the organization.
9 The concept of the "lieux de memoire" was popularized by Nora and used in his analyses of both the spatial aspects of collective memory practices and the differences between memory and history (Nora, 1989).

10 For example, in 2016, a schoolteacher in the neighborhood of La Boca was dismissed for showing her elementary school class a YouTube video that claimed the PRN had been justified in its use of force; accused the victims of terrorism; and criticized the Kirchners of profiting off of human rights. See Polémica por un video pro-dictadura en un acto escolar en La Boca (2018).

References

Agosin, M. (1998). *An absence of shadows* (C. Kostopulos-Cooperman, C. Franzen, & M.C. Berg, Trans.). White Pine Press.
Andermann, J. (2012). Returning to the site of horror: On the reclaiming of clandestine concentration camps in Argentina. *Theory, Culture & Society, 29*(1), 76–98.
Brodsky, M. (2005). *Memoria en construcción: El debate sobre la ESMA*. La Marca Editora.
Brown, K.M. (1991; 2001). *Mama Lola: A vodou priestess in Brooklyn*. University of California Press.
Cerruti, G. (1998). *A dirty warrior in repose* (M. Miletich, Trans.). Harper's Magazine.
di Paolantonio, M. (2008). A site of struggle, a Site of conflicting pedagogical proposals: The debates over suitable commemorative form and content for ESMA. *Journal of the Canadian Association for Curriculum Studies, 6*(2), 25–42.
Duffy, T. (2001). Museums of "Human Suffering" and the struggle for human rights. *Museums, 53*(1), 10–16.
Feld, C. (2008). ESMA, hora cero: Las noticias sobre la Escuela de Mecánica de la Armada en la prensa de la transición. *Sociohistórica: Cuadernos del CISH, 23–24*, 81–103.
Feld, C. (2012). Image and disappearance in Argentina: Reflections on a photo taken in the basement of ESMA. *Journal of Latin American Cultural Studies, 21*(2), 313–341.
Feld, C. (2017). Preservar, recuperar, ocupar. Controversias memoriales en torno a la ex-ESMA (1998–2013). *Revista Colombiana de Sociología, 40*(1), 101–131.
Gómez-Barris, M. (2009). *Where memory dwells: Culture and state violence in Chile*. Univ of California Press.
Hauser, I. (2007, March 26). *Cómo se enriquecieron los represores*. Página/12.
Hite, K. (2012). *Politics and the art of commemoration: Memorials to struggle in Latin America and Spain*. Routledge.
Ledgerwood, J. (1997). The Cambodian Tuol Sleng Museum of Genocidal Crimes: National narrative. *Museum Anthropology, 21*(1), 82–98.
Marcuse, H. (2001). *Legacies of Dachau: The Uses and abuses of a concentration camp, 1933–2001*. Cambridge University Press.
Massey, D.B. (2005). *For space*. SAGE.
Milton, C., Lehrer, E., & Patterson, M.E. (Eds.). (2011). *Curating difficult knowledge: Violent pasts in public places*. Palgrave Macmillan.
Nora, P. (1989). Between Memory and History: Les Lieux de Mémoire. *Representations, 26*, 7–24.
Nunca más: Informe final de la Comisión Nacional sobre la Desaparición de Personas. (1984). Eudeba.
Pastoriza, L. (2005). La memoria como política pública: Los ejes de la discusión. In M. Brodsky (Ed.), *Memoria en construcción: El debate sobre la ESMA*. La Marca Editora.
Polémica por un video pro-dictadura en un acto escolar en La Boca. (2018, March 28). *Notas: Periodismo Popular*. https://notasperiodismopopular.com.ar/2017/03/28/polemica-por-un-video-pro-dictadura-en-un-acto-escolar-en-la-boca/.

Relea, F. (1998, February 1). La dictadura argentina robó miles de millones a torturados y desaparecidos. *El País*.

Shackley, M. (2001). Potential futures for Robben Island: Shrine, museum, or theme park? *International Journal of Heritage Studies, 7*(4), 355–363.

Sosa, C. (2016). Food, conviviality, and the work of mourning. The asado scandal at Argentina's ex-ESMA. *Journal of Latin American Cultural Studies, 25*(1), 1–24.

Stern, S.J. (2004). *Remembering Pinochet's Chile: On the eve of London, 1998*. Duke University Press.

Stern, S.J. (2010). *Reckoning with Pinochet: The memory question in democratic Chile, 1989–2006*. Duke University Press.

Taylor, D. (1997). *Disappearing acts: Spectacles of gender and nationalism in Argentina's "dirty war"*. Duke University Press.

Verbitsky, H. (1995). *El vuelo*. Planeta.

6
COMMEMORATIVE LITERACIES AND LABORS OF JUSTICE IN BUENOS AIRES AND BEYOND

There are people who just row and look for winning a race, while rowing. They do not care about the past. What matters is to go forward and win all… Others know that sometimes they are in a boat with the current against them and they are facing back so those behind show us where we go, because we do not see the future. But the past guides us forward.
—Fr. Francisco, Easter Mass, March 26, 2016

It is March 24, 2016. We are in downtown Buenos Aires, having marched with tens of thousands of people to La Plaza de Mayo. Many are holding signs, standing behind banners. It is an intergenerational affair with children, parents, and grandparents assembled together for this Day of Remembrance for Truth and Justice (Día de la Memoria por la Verdad y la Justicia), *an official public holiday since 2006. They are here to commemorate the victims of state repression and violence during the most recent military dictatorship and to voice present-day concerns about the status and the future of Argentina.*

Almost everyone we met this week is here in La Plaza. Students and faculty from the University of Buenos Aires (UBA) sites—Ciencias Sociales and Filosofía y Letras (FILO)—are here. Fr. Francisco and the families and parishioners from the Church of Santa Cruz are here. The artist, Nico Arrúe, is here, too, with his wife and children to commemorate the disappearance of his father.

We come across a group of demonstrators holding images of students from a teacher training school who disappeared two years earlier in Ayotzinapa, Mexico.[1] *As we walk past, one of us asks what brought them the great distance from southern Mexico to Buenos Aires. A few offer an overlapping response, "Nuestra*

DOI: 10.4324/9781003184195-7

> *historia es parte de la historia aquí" (Our story is part of the story here)*, a shared story *"de todas las personas desaparecidas" (of all disappeared people)*. They are here to be in solidarity with people who have experienced similar violence, similar horrors.
>
> In general, the tone of the march and activities at La Plaza is not overly solemn or somber. Amidst numerous chants and cheering, there is singing and dancing, celebrations of life.

As invited guests into three sites in Buenos Aires (UBA, Church of Santa Cruz, the ex-ESMA), we gained on-the-ground access to some contents related to what historian Steve Stern has called a societal "memory chest," a collection of scripted "albums" that document and shape understandings of significant historical moments, such as the *Proceso* in Argentina. As the preceding chapters highlighted, people across these three research sites opened this chest to look for an "emblematic memory" that condemned the ideologies and actions of the *Proceso* and aligned strongly with the long-standing justice efforts led by groups like Las Madres. While the commemorative literacies at the UBA, Church of Santa Cruz, and ex-ESMA pointed to the different emphases these labors of justice can have—as resistance, reconciliation, and recovery—these projects came together in La Plaza on March 24, 2016, the nexus for memory mobilizations advancing calls of "Nunca mas!" The joining of these groups in the Plaza de Mayo, including ones that were forging transnational connections, framed a shared purpose to remain vigilant against any threats to hard-won justice victories of the recent past.

Of course, not all Argentines were at La Plaza on this day. Many who remained sympathetic to the policies and actions of the *Proceso* were unlikely to be among the marchers. These Argentines were more likely to retrieve and embrace a competing emblematic memory from the societal memory chest, something akin to what Stern called "memory as salvation" in which the *Proceso* would be viewed as saving the country from subversives.[2] Throughout our time in Buenos Aires, we did not engage much with this contrasting emblematic memory. In this concluding chapter, however, we consider this larger context of memory work in Argentina, one that situates the findings from the three preceding chapters in light of these competing emblematic memories. By doing so, we can see how commemorative literacies and labors of justice are not enacted in isolation, separate or above the politics of contestation and struggle; they are forged through these politics. We then turn to an example in the United States, the annual holiday that commemorates the life and legacy of Dr. Martin Luther King, Jr., to explore the potential of a commemorative literacies and labors of justice framework. We conclude with thoughts about how a commemorative ethics stance might inform the ways we map political space where the remembrance of events like the Argentine period of state terror is linked to justice struggles elsewhere.

Commemorative Literacies through Contestation and Difference in Buenos Aires

The first main assertion of this book is that **commemorative literacies mobilized memory of the past to advance present-day concerns**. Again, the Argentines across the three focal sites reclaimed an emblematic memory from the societal memory chest that was resolutely critical of the dictatorship and its putative process of national reorganization after 1976. This emblematic memory had gained traction in the preceding 12 years, from 2003 to 2015, during the presidencies of Nestor and Cristina Kirchner. In this sense, March 2016, with a new center-right President less committed to a similar human rights agenda, represented a rupture point, opening up spaces to embolden opposing emblematic memories. It is in this light that we see the intensive, intentional efforts of stakeholders across the UBA, Church of Santa Cruz, and the ex-ESMA. Substantive evidence across the three sites highlights how commemorative literacies mobilized the past to address contemporary fears and struggles. At the two UBA locations, the many signs and posters, as liturgical and testimonial texts, voiced ardent resistance to government repression and neoliberal economics, linking opposition, for example, to more recent policies to past injustices, such as security protocols or impunity for a convicted political leader. At the Church of Santa Cruz, Fr. Francisco expressed similar sentiments, describing how he and his parishioners were concerned that the election of Macri might augur a return to the time when human rights were suppressed. For that reason, he said, it was crucial for the Santa Cruz community to participate in the March 24 commemorative events, including the march to La Plaza de Mayo. At the ex-ESMA, the artist, Nico Arrue, also situated his own work within a larger narrative of resistance to any return of repression and life dominated by fears, a concern that echoed at our three focal sites and also in formal and informal interactions with other Argentines throughout the week.

These various memory engagements in relation to present-day concerns across our three sites point to our second related assertion that **commemorative literacies and memory mobilizations worked spatially to enact different labors of justice**. While these labors of justice might have coexisted in each of these sites, we discerned distinct emphases in our analysis. Again, the politically fraught moment of March 2016 seemed to bring into focus and amplify labors of justice across the three sites. At the UBA, the visual landscape in the hallways and classrooms at the UBA expressed labors of justice as resistance to present-day policies of the Macri administration, including "Security Protocols" which established new guidelines for police responses to street mobilizations. Unequivocal expressions of resistance to what were deemed to be unjust economic policies, including the calamitous impact of the U.S.-influenced International Monetary Fund (IMF) during the past few decades, also appeared in this landscape. Overall, the Filo and Ciencias Sociales sites unlocked the Argentine societal memory chest to recover materials that could thematize resistance in the present.

These materials included the albums, scripts, and lore of resistance relating to the 1976 coup; impunity for military leaders; the damaging impact of economic policies; and practices linked to long-established traditions of student protest in Argentine university spaces.

At the Church of Santa Cruz, labors of justice centered on reconciliation framed through a particular Argentine Catholic lens. This involved a reconciliation or integration of the religious and political as well as a reconciliation between Argentina and the United States, or Argentines and U.S. citizens, from the time of the dictatorship through the ongoing impact of U.S.-supported economic policies and programs led by the IMF. The spatial configuration of commemorative literacies at the Church of Santa Cruz reflected a Committed Catholic ethos through which the work of the church, as well as political martyrs in the community, centered on alleviating suffering of the poor and on broader goals of social and economic justice. We also explored the ways a prominent mural by 1980 Nobel peace laureate, Adolfo Pérez Esquivel, which was located behind the reconfigured altar at Santa Cruz, invoked notions of radical reconciliation and beloved community.

At the ex-ESMA, we identified three interwoven layers of justice work as recovery: an individual layer that centered on an artist's attempt to recover a relationship with his father who was disappeared; a societal layer that connected this type of individual account to a wider, collective narrative of human rights struggles; and a spatial layer about the reclamation, development, and evolution of the ex-ESMA as a site of memory, truth, and justice. This third spatial layer highlighted how, in connection with a two-decade-long debate, the ex-ESMA transitioned from a naval base and clandestine detention center to a memory space and headquarters for a range of human rights organizations. This manifestation of justice work as recovery was closely tied to ideas about reclamation, as people and organizations have attempted to recover and repurpose the space of the ex-ESMA to align with their own social and political goals.

Notably, these deeply intentional and exacting labors of justice across these three sites were forged in a crucible of competing memory investments. Justice as resistance at the UBA as described above contrasted sharply with an emblematic memory of justice as victory over dangerous subversives. Justice as reconciliation at the Church of Santa Cruz, because it demanded a prior acknowledgement of past wrongs (confession and penance, in the committed Catholic lexicon), diverged from the "forgive and forget" framing of reconciliation in the post-dictatorship years when, rather than fully unearth and litigate the crimes of the past, it was deemed best to acknowledge crimes had been committed (by "both sides") and to move forward anew. A similar dynamic was at play at the ex-ESMA where what we discerned to be labors of justice as recovery took place in a site President Menem wanted to demolish and turn into a public park. There were also present-day fears that the Macri administration might reduce funding for the memory and justice initiatives at the ex-ESMA.

Our third main assertion in this book is that **commemorative literacies and labors of justice as resistance, reconciliation, and recovery resonated transnationally**. These resonances were most pronounced at the University of Buenos Aires where the United States remained a principal target of justice as resistance in these two spaces. Commemorative literacies at these sites also expressed solidarity commitments with justice struggles in Syria and Palestine, for example—and in doing so invited transnational connections between the remembrance of the Argentine period of state terror and justice struggles elsewhere. At the Church of Santa Cruz, we saw the ways Fr. Francisco compared the Argentine context to the truth and reconciliation process in South Africa and also linked justice efforts in Argentina with the struggles of the Vietnamese people. And at the ex-ESMA, Alejandra's Oberti discussed the human rights networks that the ex-ESMA helped anchor across Latin America. The opening vignette also highlights transnational resonances during the March 24, 2016 march to *La Plaza de Mayo* through our exchange with demonstrators from Ayotzinapa, Mexico.

These transnational resonances also highlight ways that the societal memory chest in Argentina was and is not hermetically sealed, inaccessible to anyone but those with direct personal or familial ties to the *Proceso*. Justice struggles in other parts of the world, for example, have adopted the Madres, and the iconic image of their white kerchief as a symbol.

Again, there were different perspectives about the meanings of these transnational resonances. This was perhaps most clearly the case with views and portrayals of the United States. Sharp, unwavering criticism of the United States, and President Barack Obama, filled the UBA sites and seemed to course through the March 24 crowds at La Plaza de Mayo. At one point, in fact, a man approached several of us yelling and pointing his finger "Are you from the United States? You don't belong here! Are you from the US?!?" One of our team members replied, "No, we are from Canada," which immediately de-escalated the situation. However, many Argentines welcomed President Obama's visit to Argentina. On our many cab rides throughout the week, for example, taxi drivers[3] told us that Obama's visit was "a good thing for the country" or "this is what we need now."

With this understanding of commemorative literacies and labors of justice being enacted or forged through politics of difference, contestation, or struggle, we turn to an example in the United States to consider the potential of this framework. This begins with basic *who, what, when,* and *why* questions: Who is being commemorated? What is being commemorated? When do the commemorations take place? Why is the person, event, or time period being commemorated? We can then more fully engage with the *how* question: How is the person, event, or time period being commemorated? A number of commemorative events in the United States are potentially suitable to explore how commemorative literacies and varied labors of justice might be more directly linked to historical atrocities and ongoing injustices. Efforts to abolish and rename Columbus Day and Thanksgiving to Indigenous People's Day represent one example. We instead focus on the annual commemorative holiday to celebrate the life and legacy of Dr. Martin Luther King, Jr. This affords an opportunity to explore a commemorative literacies and labors of justice framework as well as to consider transnational resonances of this U.S. holiday in Buenos Aires at the Church of Santa Cruz.

Commemorative Literacies and Labors of Justice: An Example in the United States

The third Monday of each January is a U.S. federal holiday to commemorate the birthday, life, and legacy of civil rights leader, Dr. Martin Luther King, Jr. The holiday highlights one individual's life, in contrast to Argentina's "Day of Remembrance for Truth and Justice" with its links to a specific time period of state terrorism. The federal holiday for Dr. King was signed into law in 1983 and began officially in 1986. With these basic *who, what, when,* and *why* questions answered, we can address the *how,* asking what commemorative literacies we see enacted on and around this holiday. As Cornel West has argued, much of the media focus and coverage of this day leans toward "sanitized" or "sterilized versions of his legacy," portraying him as a "universally loved moderate" rather than a deeply radical man with a searing indictment of U.S. capitalism, racism and militarism (2018, para. 3). As a result, King's 1963 "I Have a Dream" speech at the Lincoln Memorial in Washington, DC, which pinned hope to a future of genuine equality and unity, is much more commonly known and mobilized for the holiday than, for example, his "Beyond Vietnam" speech at the Riverside Church in New York City on April 4, 1967, exactly a year before his assassination. In that second speech, King voiced widely unpopular criticism of U.S. involvement in Vietnam, citing it as evidence that the U. S. government was "the greatest purveyor of violence in the world" as he called for a "true revolution of values" to deal with racial and economic injustice.

Despite the tendency toward neutralized depictions of Dr. Martin Luther King, Jr, on this annual holiday, we can discern the ways commemorative literacies intersect with justice work in different ways. There is opposition to mass incarceration of people of color, what Michelle Alexander (2010) has called the "The New Jim Crow," with protests against police brutality and violence that disproportionately affect communities of color. In these cases, the memory of Dr. King can be mobilized to oppose and help dismantle policies and procedures steeped in white supremacy. The leadership of Reverend Dr. William J. Barber II with the "Poor People's Campaign" perhaps best exemplifies a present-day continuation of Dr. King's justice work as resistance to racial and economic repression.[4] This campaign, with its 14 policy priorities to "heal the nation," can be understood broadly as resistance to decades-long devastation wrought by neoliberal economic reforms that have intensified gross inequalities between the rich and powerful and the rest of society.

In terms of MLK day and justice as reconciliation, any commemorative literacies that address the need to reconcile differences between egalitarian and justice-centered ideals and the ongoing realities of structural racism—themes that appeared, for example, in the Esquivel mural at the Church of Santa Cruz—would align with this type of labor. Given the centrality of religion and spirituality in Dr. King's life, ideas of "radical reconciliation" merit particular attention (Boesak & DeYoung, 2012). A radical reconciliation stance "reaches to the very roots of injustice" because "injustice creates the need for reconciliation" such that "social justice and reconciliation are two sides of the same coin" (Boesak & DeYoung, 2012, pp. 18–19). While not completely distinct from justice work as resistance, with an emphasis on reconciliation, memory of Dr. King can be mobilized to help reckon with and ultimately reconcile conflicting narratives about the legacies of slavery in the United States. This involves a truth-seeking process and confronting denial which "is the heartbeat of racism" (Kendi, 2018). One of the most cogent and stirring attempts to confront this denial is the National Memorial for Peace and Justice in Montgomery, Alabama, which opened in April 2018. Led by the Equal Justice Initiative, this memorial commemorates the victims of racial terror and lynching in the United States and is part of a broader movement for restorative truth-telling and justice. This includes grappling with present-day concerns about police violence and mass incarceration as contemporary forms of racialized terror.

When it comes to MLK day commemorative literacies that advance justice work as recovery, perhaps the most compelling example is the argument for reparations for African Americans, as laid out by Ta-Nehisi Coates (2014), a case based on 250 years of slavery, 90 years of Jim Crow, 60 years of separate but equal and 35 years of racist housing policies. Reparations offer a direct approach for recovering vast amounts of wealth and reclaiming portions of it for present-day ancestors of slaves who created this wealth. In the wake of the New Jim Crow (Alexander, 2010) and widespread voter suppression in communities of color across the country (Anderson, 2018), the recovery of basic voting rights is also relevant here. In these cases, particular texts and memories of Dr. King can be mobilized to advance justice labor as recovery.

Of course, there is much overlap across justice labor as resistance, reconciliation, and recovery when it comes to commemorative literacies related to Dr. MLK, Jr day. Dr. Reverend Barber, co-chair of the Poor People's Campaign, highlighted this mutuality on MLK day in 2021 during a program called "MLK and the Fierce Urgency of Now! (WNYC & Apollo Theater, 2021). Again, with a clear example of mobilizing the past for present-day purposes, Dr. Barber prioritized continued vigilance and a "comprehensive just response to COVID" (the global pandemic), the need for ongoing resistance to ensure high quality, accessible health care, free vaccines, and rent and mortgage moratoriums, especially for poor and low wealth people disproportionately devastated by this crisis. At the same time, Dr. Barber cited Dr. King's work to unify poor people across racial backgrounds, in this sense reconciling racial animosities and divisions that have served the interests of the wealthy elite since the First Reconstruction in 1868. Citing a 1965 speech by Dr. King, Reverend Barber pointed out that it was "the fear of the aristocracy of the masses of Negroes and white people joining together to build the beloved community and create a kind of voting bloc." This type of reconciliation also dovetailed with justice labor as recovery, to recover or reclaim the possibilities of an intersectional, interracial movement. With this in mind, Reverend Barber, again drawing from Dr. King, cited the need to "create fusion coalitions of black and white and brown people building a political base to change reality."

Of course, what gets commemorated on Dr. MLK, Jr. day in the United States—the different ways memories of Dr. King are mobilized—can vary significantly. While someone like Reverend Barber might invoke Dr. King's memory to contextualize contemporary justice struggles in ways that suggest a deep alignment with King's vision and life's work, there are also gun rights advocates who have used Dr. King to support their views. In 2013, for example, Larry Ward, chairman of Gun Appreciation Day, contended that his event honored the legacy of Dr. King, saying that "if African Americans had been given the right to keep and bear arms from day one of the country's founding, perhaps slavery might not have been a chapter in our history" (Shen, 2013).

In terms of possibilities for further inquiry related to Dr. MLK, Jr. Day, our findings in this book point to the value of applying a spatial lens to investigate commemorative literacies (Massey, 2005), where space is a "product of interrelations," a "sphere in which distinct trajectories coexist" that are dynamic, indeterminate and "always under construction" (2005, p. 9). Attending to particular practices within and across distinct sites, one could, for example, document what commemorative literacies are evident on this day each year at the King Memorial in Washington, DC, the National Memorial for Peace and Justice (also known as the National Lynching Memorial) in Montgomery, Alabama, and the National Civil Rights Museum at the Lorraine Motel in Memphis, Tennessee where Dr. King was assassinated on April 4, 1968. One could also investigate the ways commemorative literacies might be similar or different to what happens on college and university campuses on this day, from major public institutions to small colleges, from historically Black colleges and universities (HBCUs) to predominantly white, private institutions. As explored above, in what ways might memory mobilizations reflect present-day concerns at and across these sites, especially with different labors of justice in mind?

Paths Ahead

> Global meaning making requires an interrogation of global and local meanings in terms of their antecedents and constitution—especially their relevance to sociopolitical considerations historically, culturally, and ecologically.

> It requires being vigilant about what is presented by whom to whom, why, when, and where—cognizant of the intentions and possible effects.
>
> (Tierney, 2018, p. 413)

Since the Holocaust, commemoration and memorialization have become especially linked to calls of "Never again!" and the cause of human rights enshrined in international covenants. The creation of archives, museums, curricula, and collective rituals of remembrance institute the refusal to forget mass atrocities. The persistence of state-sponsored violence against political enemies and vulnerable minorities deemed threats to the nation—for example, the Rohingya in Burma; Palestinians in Gaza and the West Bank; Darfurians in Sudan; Uyghurs in the People's Republic of China; and Central American immigrants and asylum seekers, Arab and Muslim minorities, indigenous Native Americans, and other marginalized groups in the United States—render memory and the demand for justice an ongoing struggle. The technological acceleration of state surveillance and violence, alongside collective responses to state repression, has globalized these struggles, connecting and implicating communities of memory, justice, and solidarity across national borders (Collins, 2011).

Nancy Fraser (2008) has offered a comprehensive understanding of justice that is responsive to rapid globalization and the expanding influence of transnational corporations and organizations as well as the rise of transnational social movements, including human rights activists and international feminists. These developments require a remapping of political space in ways that render "undivided state sovereignty [as] no longer plausible" because "a sharp division between domestic and international space" is increasingly questionable. In her remapping of political space, ideas of transnational solidarity and emancipatory border-crossing projects are central to justice. The commemorative literacies we encountered in Buenos Aires also suggest a mapping of political space that includes other places—Vietnam, South Africa, Syria, and Palestine, for example—and in doing so invites transnational connections between the remembrance of the Argentine period of state terror and justice struggles elsewhere.

Our earlier discussion on the commemorative practices and contested memory surrounding Dr. Martin Luther King, Jr. demonstrates how a highly localized investigation (in Buenos Aires in March 2016) can ground a comparative analysis of justice labors occurring elsewhere (in the United States). This movement from the local to the transnational must be taken with great care, however, since a struggle in one historical and social context does not necessarily map directly onto another seemingly similar context. This problem actually emerged for us in a different and quite direct way in Buenos Aires. During our visit to the Church of Santa Cruz, we encountered the striking inclusion of Dr. Martin Luther King, Jr. in the church's "Hall of Memory" (Salon de la memoria).

In the image (Figure 6.1), Dr. King appeared with his prison identification number and holding a scroll with words asking, "How long will justice

FIGURE 6.1 Dr. Martin Luther King, Jr.

be crucified and truth buried?," featured in a vertical display that included the images of Joan of Arc, John of the Cross (who is named not only in Spanish at the bottom of his frame but also in Arabic on the image itself inside the frame), and Archbishop Romero. Each of these images was cast in the style of a Greek Orthodox icon with stylized hand and arm positions and gold halos behind the heads (see Figure 6.2).

A Black Protestant (Baptist) preacher, Dr. King's inclusion among these Catholic saints effectively beatified him within a specifically Latin American and Argentine "committed" tradition rooted in the theology of the people (and Liberation Theology). A plaque embedded in the floor of the hall emphasized that justice, and the willingness to give one's life for it, brought these figures together within a shared sainthood as Santa Cruz understood and expressed it spatially (see Figure 6.3). Paraphrasing from the Gospel of Matthew 5-12, the plaque declared: "Blessed are those who labor for Peace—the persecuted for practicing Justice and Truth…" The date on the plaque (August 1976) is five months after the March 24 coup.[5]

Santa Cruz's inclusion of Dr. King's image in its Hall of Memory dedicated to champions of truth and justice points to the potential of transnational resonances to link highly specific local contexts within which labors of justice occur. Care is

FIGURE 6.2 Vertical row of four religious icons

needed here. We cannot presume to know immediately what the invocation of Dr. King might mean, specifically, at Santa Cruz. We have to resist reading U.S. American assumptions into his presence at the church. Adopting the methods we have embraced in this book, we might first inquire into the particular webs of significance within which Dr. King's image is integrated here. Santa Cruz's "justice as reconciliation" theme that we have discerned potentially transforms Dr. King and the Black American civil rights struggle into a metonym of the Argentine—and especially the Committed Catholic—struggle to remember the disappeared, hold accountable the perpetrators of injustice, and ensure that "never again" will any such period of terror ever occur. In this sense, Dr. King ceases to be a strictly U.S. American icon (even if he remains that, complexly, too). He is now an Argentine Catholic icon endowed with a highly localized set of particular meanings that one can investigate and understand through the methods we have employed in this book.

These same methods—and the suspension of immediate assumptions about meaning that they entail—can be applied in other contexts in which Dr. King's image might appear, transnationally. Dr. King traveled to India in February-March 1959, for example (India Trip, n.d.; Wilkerson, 2020). He slept in the Bombay residence of Mahatma Gandhi, noting his debt to this pioneer of

FIGURE 6.3 Plaque in floor paraphrasing Gospel of Matthew 5:12

strategic non-violence (*satyagraha*, or, "truth force") in the lodging's guestbook. He spoke to audiences during this trip and traveled to the southern region of the subcontinent, where he was introduced as a champion of the dalit ("untouchable") struggle for equality and justice. Much research has focused on the impact of this trip—and his assimilation to dalit status—on his understanding of race as caste as well as on his deepening commitment to nonviolence as a virtue and as a tactic in the struggle for justice. But how might Indian communities remember him? A question like this, stemming from a perception of transnational resonances, can lead into inquiries that trace the particularities of specific spaces of memory and specific labors of justice that include but likely go well beyond Dr. King. In this case, the transnational leads to the highly local and the discovery of unforeseen histories and formations of struggles for justice in those other spaces.

Beyond Method: The Commemorative Ethics of Commemorative Literacies

In our many conversations during the writing of this book, we have grappled with the necessity to focus on the specificities of space (and time). Space, as we have emphasized, is agentive: it can testify through the symbols and narratives that cohere in their making and remaking from one moment to the next. Diverse, specific histories intersect to produce particular places. These intersections constitute a meaningful context. This context is always fluid: meanings shift as participants in a space work with it (and within it), adding, moving, removing, and reinterpreting the images and narratives that create it as a meaningful context. To invoke Stern's (2004, 2006, 2010) memory chest, participants create and recreate space by retrieving images of the past as they labor to make sense of and transform the present. Through this work, they render space capable of speaking to the present. Space comes to testify, for example, in the way that the banners and procession "spoke" during Santa Cruz's commemoration of the disappeared or in the way Nico's moving (literal and figurative) installation of images invoking his lost childhood "spoke" to loss and to the will to render the disappeared "present now and always."

In order to grasp the particular agentive quality, the specific trajectories that intersect and produce space as an address to the present at particular moments in time, it is necessary to suspend immediate assumptions about meaning and instead give close attention to the who, what, when, where, and how of the specific historical and symbolic references that one encounters in a given context. At the Church of Santa Cruz, for example, we had to learn to discern the difference between the distinctly Argentine "theology of the people" and the better-known Liberation Theology that had guided left-oriented Catholic social justice movements in Latin America since the 1960s. The appearance of the image of Archbishop Oscar Romero notwithstanding, the Committed Catholicism that espoused this theology of the people responded to the particular historical exigencies of Argentina even as it eventually linked up with the Liberation Theology movement and other regional formations such as the Movement of Priests for the Third World.

Attention to difference through this close reading of context goes beyond questions of method. The agentive, testimonial force of space entails not only an epistemic demand to suspend assumptions so as to better understand a specific context of meaning; it also involves what Simon and Eppert (1997) call "commemorative ethics" in which testimonial accounts are admitted "into a contemporary moral community in ways that make an active claim on one's present and future actions in ways that do not simply reduce the terms of this admittance to projections of one's own identities and desires" (p. 178). The suspension of assumptions, in this sense, seeks to stem projection to allow for the unforeseen to emerge on its own terms as much as possible and, more to Simon and Eppert's point, in doing so to challenge us to respond to its moral and political demands. The attention to difference and specificity, in this sense, is thus critical to any notion and practice of solidarity rooted in principles of democratic inclusion, dialog and critical self-reflection, human rights, and acceptance of difference. Expressions of solidarity flowing from a facile perception of sameness risk suppressing meanings important to the very groups and individuals with whom one wishes to enter into alliance. When, instead, one attends to difference, space can emerge within which to discover understandings and practices of justice that might not have been immediately obvious.

In this book, we have attempted to model a form of inquiry that allows such space to appear. This approach grounds a transnational perspective in the particularities of a specific place and time, in this case, Buenos Aires in March 2016. We have shown, in the process, how the analysis of specific commemorative literacies in a particular time and place can lead to the discovery of forms of justice labor that then can bring justice work occurring elsewhere into comparative perspective. We have shown briefly how such comparison might occur once one has completed the labor of careful local analysis. This move to the transnational, comparative context flows from connections we draw as a result of our specific historical and cultural positions. Other researchers situated in other ways would draw other kinds of comparisons. How productive our method can be for locally grounded transnational comparisons awaits further research focusing on other contexts of justice work. We have also suggested in this concluding chapter that perceptions of transnational connection—Dr. King and Argentina, Dr. King and India—can lead to explorations of particular contexts of meaning and possibly into new understandings of the distinct forms that labors of justice can take in diverse locations, globally. The transition between the local and the transnational can move in either direction but in every case we must attend to particularity even as we trace cross-context connections.

The struggle for "Nunca Más" continues in Buenos Aires and beyond. Research inevitably trails behind, attempting to make sense of what has taken place. But the effort to understand and to respond through careful examination of the particularities of distinct spaces is critical, we think, to ongoing labors of justice. We hope our efforts, by illuminating commemorative literacies at work in Argentina, have demonstrated why this is so. Whether "Nunca Más" is possible in Argentina depends principally on the local struggles of Argentines themselves. However, "never again" is not only an Argentine demand; it is also a global one, as the transnational references at our three sites in Buenos Aires—to "Global Palestine," South Africa, Vietnam, El Salvador, and the Civil Rights struggle in the United States—attest. These spaces in Buenos Aires "testify" to these connections even as the localities in which these diverse labors of justice occur remain historically distinct. When we pause for a moment to listen, to admit these testimonies into our awareness, we allow a moral community to form that is not a mere projection but rather the consequence of careful attention to others and to the histories and meanings they bring to bear on the present moment. A shared horizon of what "never again" means, and what is entailed in laboring for it, can emerge at such a moment. In such a moment, we might discover, in echo of Fr. Francisco, that we are traveling toward the same shore even if the pasts that orient us remain distinct. As we travel, we can cast our glances laterally in the ways we have tried to do in this book to perceive those distinctions and in so doing understand better where we are headed together, commemorating the dead and disappeared, who remain, through our separate yet intersecting labors of justice and remembrance, "presente, ahora y siempre."

Notes

1 On September 26, 2014, students from a teacher training school in southern Mexico got on buses heading toward Mexico City. Forty-three of the students went missing and were presumed dead. Investigative journalist, Anabel Hernández, explores what happened in her book, *A Massacre in Mexico: The True Story Behind the Missing Forty-Three Students* (Hernández, 2018).
2 The emblematic memory as salvation applied to the Argentine context has also evolved over time. Valentina Salvi (2017), for example, notes attempts by military leaders and relatives of military officers to shift the narrative from "victors of the antisubversive war" or "saviors of the fatherland" to a narrative of "victims of terrorism" to signal the hardships, sacrifices, and lives lost of those fighting against the purported terrorism of subversives (p. 40). Noting this problematic framing, Salvi draws on Hannah Arendt's (2007) caution about situations "where everyone is a victim [and] no one is guilty" (p. 151).
3 Taxi drivers in Buenos Aires tend to be conservative and the taxi drivers' union was one of the few that openly supported Macri.
4 For more on this organization, see its website at https://www.poorpeoplescampaign.org/ See also Jones (2019).
5 We are not certain but this date might refer to the death of Bishop Angellili who was killed on August 4, 1976.

References

Alexander, M. (2010). *The new Jim Crow: Mass incarceration in the age of colorblindness.* New Press.
Anderson, C. (2018). *One person, no vote: How voter suppression is destroying our democracy.* Bloomsbury.
Arendt, H. (2007). *Responsibilidad colectiva in responsibilidad y juicio.* Paidos.
Boesak, A.A. & DeYoung, C.P. (2012). *Radical reconciliation: Beyond political pietism and Christian quietism.* Orbis Books.
Coates, T. (2014, April). The case for reparations. *The Atlantic.* https://www.theatlantic.com/magazine/archive/2014/06/the-case-for-reparations/361631/
Collins, J. (2011). *Global Palestine.* Hurst & Company.
Fraser, N. (2008). *Scales of justice: Reimagining political space in a globalizing world.* Columbia University Press.
Hernández, A. (2018). *A massacre in Mexico: The true story behind the missing forty-three students.* Verso.
India Trip. (n.d.). *King Encyclopedia. The Martin Luther King, Jr. Research and Education Institute, Stanford University.* Retrieved April 10, 2021 from https://kinginstitute.stanford.edu/encyclopedia/india-trip.
Jones, S. (2019, December 5). Rev. William Barber on the political power of poor people: 'We have to change our whole narrative'. *New York Magazine.* https://nymag.com/intelligencer/2019/12/rev-william-barber-on-the-political-power-of-poor-people.html

Kendi, I.X. (2018, January 13). The heartbeat of racism is denial. *The New York Times.* https://www.nytimes.com/2018/01/13/opinion/sunday/heartbeat-of-racism-denial.html

Massey, D.B. (2005). *For space*. SAGE.

Salvi, V. (2017). "We're all victims": Changes in the narrative of "National Reconciliation" in Argentina. In R. Villalòn (Ed.), *Memory, truth, and justice in contemporary Latin America* (pp. 31–42). Lanham: Rowman & Littlefield.

Shen, A. (2013). Pro-gun advocate: Arming Black people would have prevented slavery. *Think Progress.* https://archive.thinkprogress.org/pro-gun-advocate-arming-black-people-would-have-prevented-slavery-a46f79ad0f7c/

Simon, R.I. & Eppert, C. (1997). Remembering obligation: Pedagogy and the witnessing of testimony of historical trauma. *Canadian Journal of Education / Revue canadienne de l'éducation, 22*(2), 175–191. https://doi.org/10.2307/1585906

Stern, S.J. (2004). *Remembering Pinochet's Chile: On the eve of London, 1998.* Duke University Press.

Stern, S.J. (2006). *Battling for hearts and minds: Memory struggles in Pinochet's Chile, 1973–1988.* Duke University Press.

Stern, S.J. (2010). *Reckoning with Pinochet: The memory question in democratic Chile, 1989–2006.* Duke University Press.

Tierney, R.J. (2018). Toward a model of global meaning making. *Journal of Literacy Research, 50*(4), 397–422. https://doi.org/10.1177/1086296x18803134

West, C. (2018, April 4). Martin Luther King Jr was a radical. We must not sterilize his legacy. *The Guardian.* https://www.theguardian.com/commentisfree/2018/apr/04/martin-luther-king-cornel-west-legacy

Wilkerson, I. (2020). *Caste: The origins of our discontents*. Random House.

WNYC & Apollo Theater. (2021, January 18). *MLK and the Fierce Urgency of Now!* https://www.facebook.com/watch/live/?v=3076758895920808&ref=watch_permalink

EPILOGUE

On August 11, 2019, Argentine voters participated in the Open, Simultaneous, and Obligatory Primaries (PASO) that function as the first round of presidential campaigns. While pre-election polls showed a tight race between the center-right coalition of incumbent President Mauricio Macri and the center-left alliance of Justicialist Party candidate Alberto Fernández, the PASO surprised almost everyone. Fernández, running with former President Cristina Fernández de Kirchner as his vice-president, dominated the primaries, outpacing Macri by more than 16 points. Six weeks later, Argentines confirmed their choice, electing the Fernández-Fernández ticket with 48.2% of the vote and thereby eliminating the need for a runoff.[1] Despite being the first non-Peronist to successfully serve out the full term since Perón's first election in 1946, after four years in office, Macri had been soundly defeated.

More than a year later, a full postmortem of the 2019 campaign remains in progress.[2] What seems apparent, however, is that the primary concern for voters was neither human rights nor justice work. The Macri government's security protocols, alongside the high-profile imprisonment of social movement leaders like Milagro Salas (in 2016) and the extrajudicial killing of activists like Santiago Maldonado (in 2017), undeniably captured the country's attention and mobilized thousands against Macri. As we observed in the demonstrations at and around the Plaza de Mayo on March 24, 2016, various groups equated this repression with Argentina's authoritarian past, connecting these incidents to the most recent dictatorship. Yet by 2019, those issues—though still important for some—had faded considerably. Instead, the 2019 campaign and elections were dominated by questions about the economy and specifically the perceived failure of the Macri government to live up to its lofty promises about widespread economic growth.

DOI: 10.4324/9781003184195-8

By mid-2019, the battlelines of the election had largely been drawn. Four years earlier, the idea of Mauricio Macri, successful businessman, had helped him tap into frustration around high inflation rates and economic instability during the Kirchner administration. This, in turn, propelled him into the Casa Rosada, as he promised to fix Argentina's broken financial system. However, by 2019, some 40% of Argentina's population lived at or below the poverty line; unemployment had doubled from approximately 6% to 12%; the costs of services skyrocketed; and the national debt had grown to nearly 100% of the country's GDP (Parisí & Parisí, 2020, p. 42). In short, while fears about human rights, ongoing justice work, and a return to the Menemist policies of forgive and forget had motivated tens of thousands to take to the streets at the start of the Macri government, by the end the opposition had coalesced around another, more material, set of concerns. Although the margin of victory for Fernández's *Frente para todos* (Alliance for All) in the PASO caught many observers off-guard, in retrospect it begins to make more sense.

On taking office, Fernández made a point of welcoming human rights organizations to the Casa Rosada, publicly stating "you bring prestige to Argentina and to this House, which is yours" ("Alberto Fernández recibió," 2020). These efforts continued during the first months of his mandate, with the President declaring in a speech to Congress that "without memory, truth, and justice...the country cannot truly right itself" ("La defensa," 2020). However, the COVID-19 crisis erupted just weeks later and would eventually affect more than 2,000,000 Argentines, leaving more than 50,000 dead. The administration's focus shifted from justice work to controlling the pandemic, which continues to dominate political conversations in Argentina at the time of publication of this volume.

Given the dual economic and humanitarian crises that began in late 2019/early 2020 as the novel coronavirus pandemic spread rapidly around the world, it remains unclear how the Fernández administration will approach those questions directly related to the themes considered in this book over the long term. Looking back to previous *kirchnerista* governments, we might assume that human rights will once again assume a privileged place in the policy sphere, yet more immediate concerns are apparently claiming the lion's share of the attention. The economic contraction that has wracked much of the world resulting from the COVID-19 pandemic has amplified existing difficulties inherited by Fernández from the Macri presidency. Most telling, in 2018, Macri negotiated a series of loans from the International Monetary Fund for an amount that eventually reached $57 billion, the largest total number in history ("Argentina gets biggest loan," 2018). Many Argentines responded with anger and frustration to the IMF once again playing a key role in deciding national policy. As some analysts noted in the wake of the August 2019 primaries, the attempted reimposition of austerity measures in the wake of the IMF loan did little to rally public support (Weisbrodt, 2019). Beyond the material regression overseen by the Macri administration, the perceived loss of sovereignty likely also contributed to Alberto Fernández's performance in the 2019 elections.

Ultimately, the labors of justice as resistance, reconciliation, and recovery and their associated commemorative literacies examined in this volume will continue into the future, whether or not they are a central plank of any specific government's platform. That Argentina, and Latin America broadly, faces a generational economic challenge may disrupt some of this work. The past two domestic economic crises produced vastly different results: in 1989, hyperinflation and economic instability helped incoming President Menem enact a series of neoliberal reforms and push a policy of national reconciliation that downplayed the traumas of the *Proceso*. A decade later, those neoliberal reforms precipitated a massive financial collapse and debt default at the end of 2001, which eventually led to Néstor Kirchner's 2003 election (over Carlos Menem). Kirchner, of course, championed human rights and made the cause a central pillar of his political career, as did his wife. That Cristina now serves as Vice-President to Fernández makes the second course appear more likely than the first as Argentina faces this current crisis, but only time will tell how the country will—or will not—find new ways to continue these labors of justice.

Notes

1 Argentine election law stipulates that a runoff is necessary unless a candidate wins more than 45% of the vote or wins more than 40% with a margin of victory over 10%.
2 The novel coronavirus pandemic that exploded in March 2020 upended what might be thought of as the normal course of reflection and analysis.

References

Alberto Fernández recibió a organismos de derechos humanos. (2020, January 13). Ministerio de Justicia y de Derechos Humanos. https://www.argentina.gob.ar/noticias/alberto-fernandez-recibio-organismos-de-derechos-humanos

Argentina gets biggest loan in IMF's history at $57bn. (2018, September 26). *The Guardian*. https://www.theguardian.com/world/2018/sep/26/argentina-imf-biggest-loan

La defensa de los derechos humanos, 'columna vertebral' de la Argentina. (2020, March 1). *Télam*. https://www.telam.com.ar/notas/202003/436551-alberto-fernandez-asamblea-legislativa-derechos-humanos.html

Parisí, E.R. & Parisí, M. (2020). Argentina y su 27 de Octubre. In N. Molina Valencia (Ed.), *10-11 de 2019: Psicología Política en Latinoamérica* (pp. 39–43). ASCOFAPSI.

Weisbrodt, M. (2019, August 19). Who is to blame for Argentina's economic crisis? *The New York Times*. https://www.nytimes.com/2019/08/19/opinion/argentina-macri-elections.html

INDEX

Page numbers in *italics* refer to figures

Alexander, M. 154
Alfonsín, Raúl 50–51
Angelelli, Enrique 25, 98–100, 104, 112
anti-Peronist forces 40
anti-secularist 95
Aramburu, Pedro 39–40
Arbery, Ahmaud 7
archive and recuperation 136–137
Argentina: Catholicism 2, 95–96; economic fortunes 38; experiences 3, 35–36; March 24 public holiday 17; and United States 14–15
Argentine Anticommunist Alliance 45, 47
Argentine history: 1943 and the GOU 36–37; Alfonsín presidency 50–52; anti-Peronism 39; Aramburu presidency 40; *Cordobazo* 42–43; democratic process 40–41; *Kirchnerismo* 53–55; Liberating Revolution 39; Macri's 2015 election 55–56; Menem years 52–53; *Onganiato* 41–42; Perón as Secretary of Labor 37–38; Perón's death and Isabel government 45–46; repression and trauma 46–50; revolution 41; third Peronist government 44–45
Argentine memory chest 24
Armed Forces 43, 124
Arrúe, Nico 12, 16–17

beloved community 95, 115, 152, 156
Braden, Spruille 37–38
Buenos Aires 151–154, 162; in March 2016 7; sites 15–17; testimonios 22

Cámpora, Héctor 44
Canelo, P. 49
Castillo, Ramón 36
Catholic Church 2, 39, 114
Catholicism 94–98
Church of Santa Cruz 3, 15–16, 18, 93, 96–98, 151
Ciencias Sociales (CS) 12, 15, 61, 120, 123, 144
citizenship 37–38
Coates, T. 155
cognitive justice 4
collective memory 130
Comber, B. 21
commemorative ethics 160–163
commemorative literacies framework: historical/commemorative conjuncture 28–29; justice 26–28; literacy 20–23; space 25–26
committed Catholicism 161
community of memory 17, 26
CONADEP, *see* La Comisión Nacional sobre la Desaparición de Personas

Cordobazo 42–43
critical of Obama 78
critical of vultures 70
CS, *see* Ciencias Sociales
Cuban revolution 65

democracy 123
Día de la Memoria y Justicia 12, 14; *see also* March 24 public holiday
"dirty war," 19

EMVyJ, *see* Encuentro Memoria Verdad y Justicia
Encuentro Memoria Verdad y Justicia (EMVyJ) 70
Eppert, C. 19
Esquivel, Adolfo Pérez 61–62, 77, 88, 95, 105, 111–114
Esquivel painting 111, *111*
Evangelii Gaudium 112
ex-ESMA 16–17, 63, 99–100, 105; exhibition space 134; justice work as recovery 121–122; reclamation and control of space 141–142; recovery as reclamation 139–141

Facultad de Filosofía y Letras (Filo) 62
Father (Fr.) Francisco 12, 15–16, 93–95, 100, 104, 108–110, 113–115, 149, 153, 162
Feitlowitz, M. 18, 48
Filo, *see* Filosofía y Letras
Filosofía y Letras (Filo) 3, 12, 15, 62, 64, 74, 78, 86
Floyd, George 7
FpV, *see* Frente para la Victoria
Fraser, N. 27–28, 157
Freire, Paulo 21–23
Frente para la Victoria (FpV) 13, 53–55

Galtieri, Leopoldo 50, 109
Geertz, C. 21
Global Palestine 85, 162
Global South 4
GOU, *see* Group of United Officers
Group of United Officers (GOU) 37

Hall of Memory 157
Harvey, D. 51
Hite, K. 18
human dignity 12
human rights 14

immigrants 37
Infamous decade (1930–1943) 36–37
"institutional" Catholics 95
International Monetary Fund (IMF) 67

James, D. 3
Jelin, E. 12–13, 18, 23
Joan of Arc 158
JP, *see* Juventud Peronista
justice as reconciliation 18, 159
justice as recovery: individual layer 18; societal layer 18; spatial layer 19
justice as resistance 18
justicialismo 38, 40
Justo, Agustín Pedro 36
Juventud Peronista (JP) 44

Kirchner, Cristina Fernández de 13, 54
Kirchnerismo 53–55
Kirchner, Néstor 13, 53–54, 124, 139–140; 2004 declaration 143

labors of justice 8, 30; ex-ESMA 18–19; Santa Cruz Church 18; UBA 18
La Comisión Nacional sobre la Desaparición de Personas (CONADEP) 22, 27; commission 103–104
La lucha 85, *85*
La Plaza de Mayo 149
Las Madres 102
Lessa, F. 27
literacy: autonomous model 20; critical 21; ideological model 20; liturgy/liturgical 21, 29, 62, 87, 113, 115, 151
López Rega, José 45–46
Luke, A. 21, 27

Macri, Mauricio 13, 55–56, 74; administration 18, 61, 77; election 14; government 61, *68*; vulture funds 77
Madres de la Plaza de Mayo 11, 14, 101, *102*, 103–104
Mallimaci, Fortunato 15, 61, 95
March 23rd Vigil 105–110
March 24, 1976 *coup d'état* 11
March 24 public holiday 17
Martin Luther King Jr 154, *158*
martyrological memory 3
Marxism 1, 38, 44, 78, 96, 116
Marxist atheism 95
massacre in Gaza 86

Massey, D.B. 25
Memoria Abierta 120–121, 135–136
memory: as archive 138–139; emblematic 24; mobilized 17–18; transmission 23
"memory chest," 24, 30, 63, 87, 109, 122, 130, 140, 150–151, 161
Menem, Carlos 14, 18, 52–53, 55, 66, 71, 73, 124, 140–141, 152, 167
Miguel Cané library 65
military dictatorship 1, 17–18, 94
military regimes 13, 15
Montoneros 43–45, 96, 124
Mugica, Carlos 98, 100, 104

national reconciliation 14
"national unity," 124
National University of La Plata (UNLP) 64
neoliberalism 75–77, 80; counter-attack 76
networks of memory 137–138
networks of repression 137–138
Nico Arrúe's installation: experience 145; interview 134; photographs 126–129; *Presencias* project 16, 120, 132–133, 142, 144–145; shadow images 125–129; story 129
Nico's art installation, *see* Nico Arrúe's installation
Nico's story 129
Night of the Long Batons 66
Nora, Pierre 141
Nuestros Profetas 98–101
Nunca Más 12, 17–18, 51, 103, 150, 162

Obama, Barack 14, 61, 63, 70–72, 77–81, 86, 88
Oberti, Alejandra 121, 135–138, 142, 146, 153
Occupy Movement 6–7
Onganía, Juan Carlos 41; regime 42
Operation Condor 14–15

"Pacto Social," 45
Palestina Libre *83*
Palestinian Liberation Organization (PLO) 84
Peronism 11, 36–41, 43–45, 52, 54, 56, 65–66; and the Catholic Church 39
Peronist Party 41, 43, 51–52
Perón, Isabel 44–46, 122, 130
Perón, Juan Domingo 11, 37; anti-Peronism 39; death 45; Evita 38; Isabel government 45–46; María Estela Martínez de Perón 44; as Secretary of Labor 37–38; third Peronist government 44–45
Pinochet dictatorship 24
Plaza de Mayo 11, 15, 37
Poor People's Campaign 154
"Presencias," 16
"presente ahora y siempre," 134–135
PRN, *see* Proceso de Reorganización Nacional
Proceso de Reorganización Nacional (PRN) 3, 11–12, 24, 36, 47, 74

radicalization 122
Radical Party 40
reconciliation 2
refugees *82*
Rega, Jose López 45–46
religious icons *159*
repression and trauma: climate of terror 48–49; March 24, 1976 46; *Proceso* collapse 49–50; war against subversion 47–48
Revolución Libertadora 65
Robben, A. 27

Santa Cruz Church 63
Scollon, R. 21
Scollon, S. 21
secularism 1
security protocols 68
Simon, R.I. 19
social justice 27–28
social media platforms 6
spaces of experience 13
spatial reconciliation: Familiares/Militantes 101–104; Madres de la Plaza 101–104, *102*; Nuestras hermanas *101*, 101–104; Nuestros Profetas 98–101, *99*; reconciliation 104–105
state repression 13, 16; and impunity 67–73
Stern, S.J. 24, 133, 145
Street, B.V. 20
Syria and Palestine 80–87

Taylor, Breonna 7
Taylor, D. 131
testimony/testimonio 2, 19, 22, 29, 51, 72, 88, 113, 123, 135, 140–141, 151, 161–162
"the horror," 114

transnational resonances 2, 6–7, 63, 79, 86, 95, 113, 137, 153–154, 158, 160
"two demons theory," 19, 52

UBA, *see* University of Buenos Aires
United States: labors of justice 154–156; MLK day 156; paths ahead 156–160
Universidad de Buenos Aires (UBA) 3, 12, 18, 149; Church of Santa Cruz 15–16; economic policies 75–80; ex-ESMA 16–17; historical background 64–67; interlude 74–75; justice as resistance 67; transnational solidarity 80–87; U.S. flag 80
University of Córdoba 64
Uriburu, José Félix 36

Vasena, Adalbert Krieger 42
Videla, Jorge Rafael 45–46
villas miserias 97

Zecker, Liliana 15–16, 93, 121

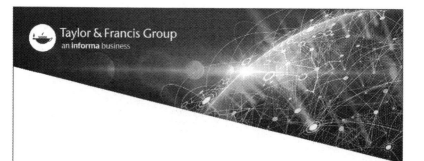